T0244726

HUNTING THE PRESIDENT

HUNTING THE PRESIDENT

Threats, Plots, and Assassination Attempts— from FDR to Obama

MEL AYTON

REGNERY
HISTORY

Copyright © 2014 by Mel Ayton
Paperback edition © 2024

All rights reserved. No part of this book may be reproduced in any manner without the express written consent of the publisher, except in the case of brief excerpts in critical reviews or articles. All inquiries should be addressed to Regnery, 307 West 36th Street, 11th Floor, New York, NY 10018.

Regnery books may be purchased in bulk at special discounts for sales promotion, corporate gifts, fund-raising, or educational purposes. Special editions can also be created to specifications. For details, contact the Special Sales Department, Regnery, 307 West 36th Street, 11th Floor, New York, NY 10018 or info@skyhorsepublishing.com.

Regnery History® is an imprint of Skyhorse Publishing, Inc.®, a Delaware corporation.

Visit our website at www.regnery.com.

Please follow our publisher Tony Lyons on Instagram @tonylyonsisuncertain.

10 9 8 7 6 5 4 3 2 1

Library of Congress Cataloging-in-Publication Data is available on file.

Cover design by Jason Sunde

Print ISBN: 978-1-5107-8310-2
eBook ISBN: 978-1-62157-234-3

Printed in the United States of America

To my wife, Sheila

ALSO BY MEL AYTON:

Questions of Controversy: The Kennedy Brothers

*A Racial Crime: James Earl Ray
and the Murder of Martin Luther King Jr.*

*The Forgotten Terrorist: Sirhan Sirhan
and the Assassination of Robert F. Kennedy*

*The JFK Assassination:
Dispelling the Myths and Challenging the Conspiracy Theorists*

*Dark Soul of the South: The Life and Crimes
of Racist Killer Joseph Paul Franklin*

*Justice Denied: Bermuda's Black Militants, the "Third Man,"
and the Assassinations of a Police Chief and Governor*

CONTENTS

PREFACE

unting the President is an account of the threats, plots, and assassination attempts made against U.S. presidents over an eighty-year period, beginning with the election of Franklin D. Roosevelt. Drawing on many previously undisclosed materials, the book presents a richly informative sequence of case studies of presidential attackers, plotters, and threateners, some of whom nearly changed the course of history. *Hunting the President* is a corrective to the numerous history books and biographies that have ignored or overlooked the many threats modern presidents have faced. It is an original work based on archived interviews with Secret Service agents, U.S. presidents and their family members; oral histories from presidential libraries; congressional reports; the published memoirs of Secret Service agents; police files; FBI files; government agency reports; newspaper archives; and court records.

During my research I discovered that there was an extraordinary array of cases that did not gain public attention even as they rang alarm bells at the highest levels of government. *Hunting the President* reveals some of these stories for the first time. Many of the Secret Service's records are closed to public scrutiny, so we cannot know how many plots have been thwarted, but there are likely more than most readers suspect.

While the Secret Service tries to limit publicity about presidential threats, former Secret Service agents have published their memoirs, given interviews to presidential libraries and the media, and even spoken about the private lives of the first families. In 1993, the Secret Service acknowledged that it would provide "technical assistance for virtually any project provided it portrays us in a positive light." That included advising Clint Eastwood during the making of the movie *In the Line of Fire*. And in 2009, Mark Sullivan, the then-director of the Secret Service, and more than one hundred of his agents broke what the *Washington Post* called "his agency's long-standing policy of absolute silence" and cooperated with bestselling author Ronald Kessler for his book, *In the President's Secret Service*. As the *Washington Post* commented, "Lest they forget, all agents have the motto [Worthy of Trust and Confidence] emblazoned on their IDs. But in light of an odd decision by the current director ... the motto should be changed to 'Have You Heard This One?'.... [H]oping for some good, ego-enhancing publicity, Sullivan ... allowed Ronald Kessler to get an earful."[1] Individual former and current agents also revealed secrets of the Secret Service to investigative journalist Seymour Hersh for his 1997 book, *The Dark Side of Camelot*.

Apart from the memoirs of agents and books delineating the work of the Secret Service, there have been a number of works that have provided psychological profiles of the perpetrators of attempted assassinations, notably James W. Clarke's *American Assassins: The Darker Side of Politics* (1982) and John Douglas's *The Anatomy of Motive*. A book published in 2010, *Killing the President* by Willard M. Oliver and Nancy E. Marion, whilst commendable for its scholarship, is limited in what it covers, ignoring many plots and threats. While understanding the necessity of being selective, as this book is as well, the reader will soon discover that historians, presidential biographers, former Secret Service agents, and the media, for all they have revealed about presidential assassination attempts, have neglected a treasure trove of material, much of it presented here for the first time.

NOTE: *Since the time of Harry Truman, commanders in chief and their families have been assigned security code names. Code names used to be used to protect the movements of the candidates. Now that the Secret Service has more secure communications, the code names are no longer secret. The military-run White House Communications Agency comes up with the names in coordination with the Secret Service.*

The White House Communications Agency does not comment on the selection process, except to say that the names are assigned by "sheer whim." But some have turned out to have obvious connections to the president—Rawhide (Reagan) and Deacon (Carter), for example. Others not so—Searchlight (Nixon), Passkey (Ford), Timberwolf (Bush 41). The first ladies are given code names beginning with the same first letter as their husband's.

CHAPTER ONE

THE BOSS

*Since you can't control these things [assassination threats]
you don't worry about them.*
—FDR

President Roosevelt, the only president elected four times, who led America during the Great Depression and through World War II, was the target of would-be assassins who threatened to bomb his train, blow up the White House, and simply shoot him. Most of these threats were the rantings of mentally ill individuals, drunks, or attention-seekers, but even they can be assassins, and some of the threats were considered extremely dangerous by FDR's protectors.

Roosevelt received an average of forty thousand letters a month at the White House. Five thousand of those were threatening. According to the chief of the White House Secret Service detail,

Michael Reilly, the greatest threat to the president came not from the foreign agents or American traitors, but from people who were just "plain nuts." Reilly singled out Los Angeles as the most dangerous city for the president, as it had "more nuts per acre than any other American city."[1]

In 1937, President Roosevelt appointed Frank J. Wilson as Secret Service chief. Wilson is sometimes called the "father of the modern Secret Service" because of the way he improved the president's security after the Japanese attack on Pearl Harbor. Wilson's security procedures remained the Secret Service standard until the 1980s.[2]

Franklin Roosevelt was popular among the agents who guarded his life. They affectionately called him "The Boss," and he returned their affection. According to Reilly, "When you did something for him that he felt was either a favor or a task well done he told you about it," Reilly wrote, "On the other hand, if you erred he let you know he was displeased. Quietly but thoroughly."[3] Reilly and his detail believed FDR was a "nice guy" but recognized the aristocratic Roosevelt would never be "one of the boys ... although he frequently made a good try." Reilly said that Roosevelt, although imbued with a pleasant manner, could be "ruthless" when he so desired.[4]

The Secret Service protective detail was often the target of FDR's practical jokes. President Roosevelt drove his own car, a Ford Phaeton that had been fitted with hand controls because of his disability. During these trips he frequently played pranks on his agents and would try to "lose" them on his drives in the country at Hyde Park or Warm Springs. On his return he would ask his head of detail, Colonel Edmund Starling, "Ed, I have lost the Secret Service boys. I can't find them anywhere. Do you know where they are?"[5] Even aside from pranks to elude his security detail, FDR was difficult to guard because, as Starling observed, the president was "utterly fearless, contemptuous of danger, and full of desire to go places and do things, preferably unorthodox places and unorthodox things—for a president."[6]

FDR had been unable to walk since contracting polio in 1921. His legs were locked in steel braces, the "painful prison" as he called them. Walking, he swung one leg in an arc, moved forward, and swung the other leg. For his first inaugural speech in March 1933, he walked thirty-seven paces in this manner to a lectern. In 1936, when he walked to the podium at Philadelphia's Franklin Field to give his acceptance speech to Democratic Party Convention delegates, he fell in the mud before an audience of a hundred thousand. Secret Service agents quickly surrounded him to shield him from photographers and the crowd.[7] In fact, FDR fell at least three times in public during his presidency, but the incidents were kept out of the press.[8]

Roosevelt conceded his paralysis to an audience only a few times throughout his presidency. When he visited a veterans hospital in Hawaii, for example, he stayed in his wheelchair as a way of bonding with the men he commanded.[9] But for the most part, the president wanted to project an image of vigor, and to that end FDR perfected what he called his "splendid deception" of his disability. Agents covertly propped him up in public and installed a metal bar in the president's touring car, which allowed him to pull himself up and stand. In 1940, FDR received as a gift from the railroads the *Ferdinand Magellan*, a 142-ton car with bedrooms, baths, a study, and a dining room. Roosevelt was carried from his train to a waiting car to his wheelchair always surrounded by agents so that no one could see or photograph the helplessness of the president.[10] Agents were also aware that unless they carried the president rapidly between his car or train to a hotel entrance or boat, he was a target for a would-be assassin. So a contingent of carpenters became part of the president's entourage. Their job was to build ramps whenever they were needed, so the president could be moved at a swifter pace. Of course, the Secret Service also made sure ramps were installed around the White House and in other public buildings.

The president's disability meant he could not easily escape a fire. In fact, the idea of being trapped by fire was always at the back of FDR's mind.[11] Michael Reilly said that the president was "completely fearless" except for fire. The Secret Service considered the White House to be the "biggest firetrap in America, bar none." If a fire struck the White House, the president's agents would carry him downstairs, avoiding the elevators, which had a habit of stalling. Agents always carried canvas fire chutes that could be dropped through a window from the president's bedroom in case the stairs were aflame.[12]

— — —

Many fringe groups made the president a hate figure, including the fascist Khaki Shirts of America, the fascist Silver Shirts, the Ku Klux Klan, and a Ku Klux Klan splinter group, the Black Legion, which was centered in Ohio and Michigan. So did a group of financiers and industrialists, who in 1934 allegedly plotted a coup d'état to prevent FDR from establishing what they feared would be a socialist state. Though the media regarded it as a tall tale, retired Marine Corps major general Smedley Butler testified before a congressional committee that the conspirators had wanted Butler to deliver an ultimatum to FDR to create a new cabinet officer, a "Secretary of General Affairs," who would run things while the president recuperated from feigned ill health. If Roosevelt refused, the conspirators had promised General Butler an army of five hundred thousand war veterans who would help drive Roosevelt from office. The so-called "Wall Street Putsch" was mocked by major newspapers. The *New York Times* said the alleged plot was a "gigantic hoax" and a "bald and unconvincing narrative."[13]

While it is true that the congressional committee's investigation led to no prosecutions, Butler's testimony was later corroborated by Veterans of Foreign Wars commander James E. Van Zandt and by testimony in the congressional hearings, which were made public in 1967. Although most historians have dismissed the alleged plot as no more than wild talk, investigative journalist Sally Denton, in her book *The Plots against the President*, provides compelling evidence that the plotters were quite serious. Denton claims historians have unjustly understated the serious nature of the plans to overthrow the Roosevelt administration.

In 1938, four years after the alleged plot to topple Roosevelt, a speaker at a Chicago meeting of the Silver Shirt Legion of America was quoted as saying America would have a dictator in less than a year, and "if no one else will volunteer to kill him [FDR], I will do it myself." The Secret Service investigated, but no arrests were made for lack of substantial evidence.[14]

According to Cornelius Vanderbilt Jr., great-great-grandson of the wealthy, famous industrialist commodore Cornelius Vanderbilt, there was a second plot among rich industrialists to depose Roosevelt—after his unprecedented third-term election in 1940. Vanderbilt wrote, "I use the word 'conspiracy.' I really am talking of a plot—serious, long-discussed plan to—shall I say—capture the president." Vanderbilt said the plan was to "impose a firm restraint for the good of the country; to hold this dictator, this madman ... while some persons set up emergency controls and saved America." Vanderbilt informed federal agencies of the plot, and they in turn let him warn "those involved in the cabal." Accordingly, the plot never took off. Vanderbilt said FDR knew about the conspiracy. The story was reported in 1959. The then-head of the Secret Service, U. E. Baughman, said he had never heard of the alleged conspiracy, and FDR's Secret Service chief Frank J. Wilson also denied any recollection of it.[15]

In late 1941, there was more talk of plots against the president when the FBI reported that Ethel Brigham, an America First committee member, said that if Roosevelt took the country to war a group called the One Gun Club would rise up and revolt. The information was pure rumor, but this did not stop the FBI from "loose surveillance" on the Brigham family. FBI agents reported that Mrs. Brigham attended a New York play where she was observed to make anti-Roosevelt remarks. Nothing more came of it.[16]

— — —

The patrician politician was used to threats against his life. During the First World War, when he was assistant secretary of the navy, he was the target of a bomb sent in the mail. It was discovered before it reached him.[17]

Roosevelt was also in harm's way when anarchists tried to bomb Attorney General A. Mitchell Palmer's home in 1919 but ended up blowing up themselves when the bomb exploded prematurely, scattering anarchist literature and leaflets. Roosevelt lived across the street from Palmer and was home when the bomb exploded, blowing out all the front windows of his residence.[18]

Another bomb threat occurred in April 1929, shortly after he had been inaugurated as governor of New York. A bomb was accidently discovered by a porter, Thomas Callegy, in the parcel room at the general post office in New York City. The parcel was addressed to "Governor Roosevelt," and the sender's address turned out to be fictitious. The bomb consisted of six ounces of dynamite packed in a six-inch-long pipe that was capped at both ends and contained a fuse with a detonating device. The bomb was embedded in a tin candy box wrapped in brown paper. The detonator was a strip of sandpaper against which four matches were held by a spring.

As Callegy swept the mail room floor, he accidently hit the parcel with his broom. It began to hiss and smoke but failed to detonate. Callegy immediately stepped on the bomb to stamp out the fuse. Police later surmised that the device was designed to scare rather than kill,[19] but also believed that the bomb might be linked to the burning of Roosevelt's son-in-law's house in Mount Pleasant. Both crimes remained unsolved.

Franklin Roosevelt was elected president in November 1932. In the three months he spent as president-elect, FDR was the target of an Italian anarchist and another deranged bomber.

On February 15, 1933, while on a fishing trip with Vincent Astor, Roosevelt gave an impromptu speech at Miami's Bayfront Park. FDR was in a green Buick convertible, the lead car of a three-car motorcade. With Roosevelt in the Buick were Secret Service agent Gus Gennerich, press aide Marvin H. McIntyre, and Miami mayor R. B. Gauthier.

FDR did not leave his car but stood addressing the crowd. He spoke less than two minutes. In the audience was Chicago mayor

Anton Cermak, who stepped over to shake Roosevelt's hand. Someone then handed Roosevelt a telegram, and as the president reached to take it, an Italian immigrant named Giuseppe Zangara stood on a chair amidst the crowd and opened fire with a nickel-plated .32 caliber double-action revolver. Although the shots missed FDR, a bullet came within two feet of his head. Mayor Cermak was hit along with four others in the crowd. Roosevelt told his Secret Service agents to put Cermak in the presidential car and held the fatally wounded mayor on the way to the hospital.[20]

Zangara pleaded guilty to four counts of assault and was sentenced to eighty years in prison. When Mayor Cermak died on March 6, Zangara was tried a second time. He again pleaded guilty and received the death sentence. During his trial Zangara said he thought he had the "right to kill him.... I see Mr. Hoover, I kill him first. Make no difference who go get that job. Run by big money ... I sorry Roosevelt still alive.... I want to shoot Roosevelt."[21] Zangara's self-proclaimed mission was to "kill kings and presidents first and next all capitalists."[22]

Zangara was electrocuted with 230 volts from Raiford Prison's "Old Sparky" surging through his body at 9:27 a.m. on March 20. His last words were "Viva Italia! Goodbye to all poor people everywhere! Pusha da button! Go ahead, pusha da button."[23]

Many were convinced Zangara had been hired by Chicago gangster Frank Nitti to kill Mayor Cermak as an act of vengeance. The famous 1930s columnist Walter Winchell, for one, believed this rumor to be true. The warden of the prison that held Zangara, however, had a different opinion. He told his guards to write down everything the assassin said, and himself questioned Zangara over a period of ten days. He concluded that the "guileless" assassin was neither insane nor a conspirator, but had acted alone.[24]

The shooting was fully investigated by federal agents, and they could find no link between Zangara and the Chicago mob. As author Blaise Picchi concluded, "The question of a government cover-up might arise, but there is no credible evidence to justify such a cover-up in 1933. The opposite seems to be true. If the Secret Service, the FBI, or the Miami police had discovered that Zangara had links to organized crime, terrorist groups, or foreign governments, it seems certain that these links would have been hotly pursued. Apparently this line of enquiry came to nothing."[25] Picchi also concluded that "If [Zangara] had been hired to kill Cermak, why would he do it in the midst of one of the largest crowds ever to gather in Miami history? Cermak had a home in Miami Beach and was vacationing there—that fact would have offered many opportunities for a mob hit."[26]

Picchi believes Zangara's likely motive was both political and personal. Zangara was in constant pain from an intestinal ailment, and an acquaintance of his testified that Zangara was suicidal over his dwindling finances and had thought about jumping off a bridge or injecting himself with poison. Picchi believes it plausible that Zangara thought he could "kill two birds with one stone: commit suicide and at the same time become famous as a champion of the downtrodden."[27]

Within a week of the Zangara shooting, the Secret Service was hot on the trail of a copycat would-be assassin who sent a package in the mail addressed to the president-elect. The package, postmarked "Watertown, New York," broke open in a Washington, D.C., post office. The bomb consisted of a shotgun shell with wiring over the cap. Postal authorities said it had a one-in-ten chance of exploding and then only after being dropped in a perpendicular position.[28] An accompanying note read: "Dear Roosevelt, I want to congratulate you for escape [*sic*] gunman Zangara. Yours, Paul Altroni." The same day a letter arrived at police headquarters, Watertown, which read, in part, "My friend Zangara missed Roosevelt. I take his place to get rid of him."

A month later Watertown postmaster George A. Huger found a second bomb that police determined was "very similar to the first." A team of Secret Service agents descended on Watertown but failed to identify the bomber. But in June 1933, on the basis of a tip, they arrested twenty-year-old Joseph Doldo. Police described the suspect as "mentally deficient," but he admitted he was the mysterious bomber and told Secret Service agents, "I, Joe Doldo, done do it! I hate Presidents."[29]

In August 1934, nine sticks of dynamite and a short fuse were discovered in a gulch below a railway trestle outside Spokane, Washington. The explosives were discovered by a Union Pacific agent who became suspicious of three men he saw depositing a package at the bottom of the sixty-foot ravine. A train carrying the president was scheduled to pass over the bridge. Although several members of a radical organization were suspected of depositing the explosives, no arrests were made.[30]

In April 1935, FDR was aboard a train that crashed into a stolen car near the town of Wilson, North Carolina. Two men were seen to leap from the car before the accident occurred. The impact was not felt by FDR who was in the rear car of the train.[31] While the Secret Service investigated the incident, it found no evidence of a plot to derail the train.

Throughout the 1930s, Roosevelt was the target of abusive letters, White House phone calls, and other threats of violence, some of which led to prosecutions. In one example, in January 1936, fifty-two-year-old Austin Phelps Palmer, a mechanical engineer, wrote two letters to President Roosevelt, blaming the president for the loss of his $1 million fortune and threatening his life. In one of the letters, he wrote, "Franklin Delano Roosevelt, Communist and destroyer of private business. I warn you, if you destroy my business I will strangle you with my own hands. May your soul be exterminated in hell." Palmer was charged with sending threatening letters to the president. He pleaded guilty, admitted to sending the letters, and on January 24, 1936, Palmer was sentenced to ninety days in prison.[32]

To the Secret Service, "approachers" were much more dangerous than letter writers. In 1936, as Roosevelt's motorcade traveled through Boston, a man slipped through police lines and ran toward the presidential limousine. Fist raised and shouting, "You dirty son-of-a-bitch," it looked like he was going to throw himself at the president. Secret Service agent Mike Reilly jumped from the running board and hit the man—"a flying body block." Roosevelt later told Reilly, "Thanks Mike, you saved me from a punch in the nose." Boston police eventually released the would-be attacker. "That guy was nuts so we let him go," a police spokesman said.[33]

Less humorous, except in retrospect, was an incident in 1936, when a dagger was thrown at Roosevelt as he was finishing a speech from the back of a train in Erie, Pennsylvania. The dagger missed the president but hit an aide standing beside him. Agents quickly surrounded Roosevelt. The dagger, however, proved to be made of rubber.[34]

In 1938, Roosevelt was once more threatened by a potential attacker when he traveled in a motorcade. As Roosevelt was driven through Oklahoma City campaigning for the midterm elections,

fifty-two-year-old Woody Hockaday broke from the ranks of spectators lining the route and ran toward FDR's car, carrying a black
shoeshine leather in his hand. A Secret Service agent on the running
board of the car leapt toward Hockaday and struck him in the face,
sending him sprawling. Firemen and National Guardsmen pinioned
Hockaday's arms then saved him from a mob of infuriated spectators. When Hockaday was searched, it was discovered he was not
armed. He simply wanted to get close to the president to "shine his
shoes" for a dime and also the shoes of fourteen other prominent
men to show how much wheat and how little bread the money would
buy. The Secret Service judged Hockaday to be a "harmless eccentric," and no charges were brought against him.[35]

– – –

While Roosevelt expressed no alarm about previous attempts on
his life, he did become more security conscious during the Second
World War. According to those close to him, he used to talk about
what a twenty-five-pound bomb could do to his house in Hyde Park,
New York.[36] Understandably, special protection was afforded Roosevelt during the Second World War to thwart any would-be Axis
assassin. The size of the presidential detail reached sixteen agents
and two supervisors by 1939. After the United States entered the
war—leading to Roosevelt attending war conferences in Canada,
North Africa, Iran, and Yalta—the detail was increased to thirty-
seven men.

Before the war, the White House grounds had been open to the
public, welcoming as many as fifteen thousand persons a day. Visitors could walk up to the front door and leave a message for the
president, drivers could pass by the North Portico, and anyone could

saunter through the north White House grounds without a pass or any challenge from the Secret Service.

After the Japanese attack on Pearl Harbor, access to the White House was severely restricted. Gates were closed, tourists were banned, and armed soldiers assisted the Secret Service in guarding the executive mansion. Invited guests to the White House and dignitaries who met the president on his tours around the country were told to keep their hands out of their pockets. FDR's food was also carefully tested in case Nazi agents tried to poison him. On one occasion a fish sent from Cuba was found to be poisoned, but the Secret Service was unable to track down the provenance of the package.[37]

There were also a number of breaches in the security around the White House. Somehow, despite the heightened security, a stranger managed to enter the executive mansion, walk to an upstairs hall where a movie was showing, and when the lights went on ask the president for his autograph.[38]

Another concern was German prisoners of war held in the United States, who were escaping at the rate of seventy-five a month. FBI director J. Edgar Hoover believed that escaped prisoners might commit sabotage and espionage, and there was an intelligence report indicating that German prisoners planned a mass escape, with one objective being to reach and kill Roosevelt.[39]

Threats that in peacetime might have been ignored or received light sentences were judged more severely during the war, even before the United States entered it. After "constitutional psychopath" Edward De Roulhac Blount told acquaintances on two occasions that he was going to kill the president, he was arrested and given a two-to-six-year prison sentence.[40] In a similar case in 1943 a known Nazi sympathizer, William Thomas Reid, was convicted of threatening the life of the president, a federal offense, for telling an associate in the oil business, "President Roosevelt is one guy I hate. If I had the money I would go to Washington and kill the president and if he ever comes south I will."[41]

More dangerous perhaps was Christopher Clarence Cull, from Tulsa, Oklahoma, a racist who believed Hitler was the "greatest man in the world."[42] Cull told friends he wanted to go to Germany, volunteer for special training in sabotage, and then return to the United States to blow up ships and aircraft factories. Shortly after the Japanese bombing of Pearl Harbor, Cull enlisted as a sailor in the U.S. Navy but deserted from the USS *Florida* when it docked at Para, Brazil. Cull made his way back to America and visited a friend, Dick Seibert, in Bellmore, Long Island. Cull told Seibert he was going to manufacture a nitroglycerine bomb and "get close to ... Roosevelt and blow him to hell and I'll go along with him."[43]

Seibert unsuccessfully tried to persuade Cull to abandon his plans, calling the idea "preposterous." According to Seibert, Cull was determined to carry out his assassination plan.[44] When Cull left Seibert's house, he traveled to New York City and registered at a hotel, carrying a case of nitroglycerine.

Seibert and his mother immediately contacted the police. Seibert said Cull had nearly enough nitroglycerine "to blow up a battleship. He's a clever mechanic and knows exactly how to make a bomb. He hates Roosevelt and our form of government. He's desperate and really intends to carry out his threat."[45] The Secret Service began a manhunt for Cull. A background investigation revealed that Cull had abandoned his wife, deserted from the U.S. Army (before deserting from the navy), been arrested for an armed robbery in Tulsa, escaped from a mental asylum in Oklahoma, and been indicted for stabbing a shipmate, but had eluded police custody.

Secret Service agents discovered Cull had taken a room (though he was out) at a New York hotel. They occupied a room directly opposite and arrested him on his return in the early hours of the next morning. Cull was armed with a sixteen-inch-long butcher's knife. In his room they found bomb-making materials. At another hotel where Cull had rented a room, they found a black suitcase containing two bottles of nitroglycerine and a bottle of nitric acid.

Cull was taken to New York City police headquarters. He first denied but then admitted that his "purpose was to kill that son-of-a-bitch Roosevelt. I want to destroy him in order that we can get a new commander-in-chief who will make peace with Germany and then go after the Japanese. I hate President Roosevelt. He was responsible for our entry into the war and the killing of a great many sailors in the North Atlantic."[46] Cull's signed confession stated that he planned to strap three nitroglycerine bombs to his waist. He would wear an army uniform to get close to Roosevelt's car as the president exited the White House and then "blow myself and the [redacted] President to bits and also kill any goddamn Secret Service agents or other people who were nearby."[47]

After Cull was sent to a psychiatric hospital, he continued to threaten to kill Roosevelt and told staff he would have no difficulty escaping from the institution. The Secret Service responded by insisting Cull be sent to a more secure hospital, the Matteawan State Hospital for the Criminally Insane in Beacon, New York.[48]

Arguably the most serious threat to President Roosevelt's life occurred shortly before the president set sail for the Tehran-Cairo war conference. The incident has been overlooked by historians for the past seventy years.

In early November 1943, an armed stalker waited for FDR for ten days in Lafayette Park across the street from the White House.

The would-be assassin was Walter Harold Best, a thirty-eight-year-old native of Nelson, Wisconsin. After arriving in Michigan in 1938, Best married and became the father of two small children. He was variously employed as a farmhand, a magazine salesman, and at a restaurant. Although he did not serve in the army during the Second World War, he had a brother who served in Italy.

On November 2, 1943, Best left his home in Pontiac, Michigan, armed with a loaded .38 caliber revolver and ten additional rounds of ammunition. He arrived in Washington, D.C., on November 3 and registered at the Congress Hotel. He wrote a letter to his wife, telling her he intended to "get rid of Roosevelt." He had learned that the president was "out of town," but he intended to await his return.[49] Best's statement that the president at that time was "out of town" was correct. The president had left the White House and traveled by train to Hyde Park on October 29 and did not return to Washington until November 4.

Best spent the period of November 3 to November 13 observing the comings and goings of White House staff. He walked around Lafayette Park across the street from the executive mansion, hoping to "get a pot-shot" at the president when FDR left the White House to attend church or carry out one of his official duties. He was also aware that Roosevelt was often driven in an open limousine and sometimes drove himself in a convertible. (The fabric tops of the convertibles were reinforced to repel grenades, but FDR often drove with the tops down.)

There were certainly numerous opportunities during this period for Best to carry out his attack. On November 6, two days after his return from Hyde Park, the president "motored" to Camp David (then called Shangri-La) and returned to the White House the following day.

On November 10 he "motored" to National Airport from the White House to meet his returning secretary of state, Cordell Hull, and returned to the White House at 4:00 p.m. At 10:40 a.m. on November 11, his Secret Service protectors drove him to Arlington National Cemetery for a wreath-laying ceremony at the Tomb of the Unknown Soldier, returning at 11:30 a.m. At 9:30 p.m. that same day, FDR left the White House to travel by motorcar to Quantico, where he boarded the USS *Potomac* for the first leg of his sea journey to the Tehran-Cairo Conference.[50]

The dangers of Roosevelt traveling in an open-top convertible were not lost on Kenneth B. Seckel, who was a captain of the White House Police Force. Seckel recalled driving one day from Hyde Park, the president's home, to FDR's mother's apartment in New York. "My God," Seckel said, "we had about 20% of the police force of New York City involved [in the president's protection] and I got out of his car and there were a thousand people all over the neighbourhood. I said to one of the Secret Service men then if anyone wanted to take a pot shot there wasn't much that could be done."[51]

In Best's letter to his wife, he told her he had infiltrated a group of soldiers who were unloading a truck at a White House gate. He said the soldiers were busy, which made it possible for him to gain access to the White House. However, as he deliberated whether or not to steal a soldier's rifle lying on the ground nearby, he was discovered, and he quickly walked away. Best's account was partially confirmed in 1966, when former Secret Service director Frank J. Wilson said an unnamed would-be assassin had stolen a rifle from White House army sentries, and "the next day it was found in [a] flower box [at the back of the State Department building]. The soldiers were severely disciplined for their serious lapse of duty."[52]

Best's wife contacted the police, who relayed her information to the Secret Service on November 13. That same day, Best was ticketed for jaywalking, was abusive to the police officer, and was arrested. At the police station, he was identified as wanted by the Secret Service.

Best was not armed when he was arrested, but Secret Service agents soon discovered the pistol and bullets in his hotel room. During his interrogation, Best admitted he had been stalking President Roosevelt. "I had electrodes running through my brain," he told agents, "and they told me to get rid of Roosevelt."[53] On November 23, 1943, ten days after his arrest, Best was judged insane and sent to Gallinger Hospital in Washington before being sent to a Michigan psychiatric hospital.[54]

On November 14, one day after Best was arrested, FDR was nearly killed when he was aboard the USS *Iowa* bound for the Tehran-Cairo Conference. Around 8:00 a.m., during an air defense drill, there was a shattering explosion close by the battleship.[55] The *Iowa*'s captain saw the wake of a torpedo and promptly heeled his ship to port, making a ninety-degree turn. The torpedo missed the ship by a mere twenty feet. Fearing that German submarines were attacking, the president's security detail prepared to take the president off the ship, in a lifeboat if necessary. But a few minutes later, an escort ship reported that a live torpedo had been fired by accident. Were it not for the alert captain's maneuver, the torpedo would have struck the *Iowa* directly below FDR's quarters.[56]

According to Soviet agents, Waffen-SS commander Otto Skorzeny, Hitler's favorite cloak-and-dagger operative, also had Roosevelt in his sights. Skorzeny allegedly had been given the mission of assassinating FDR, Winston Churchill, and Joseph Stalin when the "Big Three" met for a conference in Tehran in November 1943.

Tehran had been chosen by Stalin because it was close to the Soviet Union and the Red Army bases of Northern Iran. Tehran, however, had also been rife with German agents eager to tap into anti-British sentiment. Stalin informed Roosevelt of the plot, code-named Operation Long Jump, and persuaded FDR to stay at the Russian Embassy where it was "safer." In Tehran, U.S. general Herbert Norman Schwarzkopf and his British counterpart, Colonel Joseph Spencer, put their subordinates on alert for Skorzeny's assassins. All but six of the thirty-eight German commandos, who had parachuted into Tehran, were quickly rounded up, the remainder captured three months later. All were executed by the Russians.[57]

Roosevelt said the plot, if successful, would have been a "pretty good haul,"[58] and Churchill "was very excited, even pleased" when he heard his life had been threatened. "He looked into everyone's face with the happiest sort of suspicion."[59]

Not everyone believed the plot was real. America's ambassador to the Soviet Union, Averell Harriman, suspected the Russians had "cooked it up." Additionally, the British Joint Intelligence Committee of the War Cabinet concluded the so-called Nazi plot against the Big Three was "complete baloney."[60]

Initially, Skorzeny himself denied the existence of any such plot, and Western historians have always been skeptical. But Skorzeny eventually admitted the plot in 1966. And Russian sources continue to insist that the plot really existed. In 2007, one of the KGB operatives involved in the attempt to stop the alleged assassination plot stated flatly, "the success of our group in locating the Nazi advance party and our subsequent actions thwarted an attempt to assassinate the Big Three."[61]

British author Charles Whiting, in his book *Target Eisenhower*, provided compelling evidence for the Russian case.[62] Hans Gurgen

Isenheim, a former German paratrooper who, after the war, became a U.S. Army employee in Bonn, Germany, said he was a member of a handful of chosen German paratroopers who were ordered on a suicide mission to kill Churchill, Stalin, and Roosevelt when they met at the Yalta Conference in February 1945. The German air force base where the plot was organized was near the Russian front and was attacked before the mission could take off; the conspirators were pressed into defending the base, and half of them were killed. That effectively ended the plot.[63]

— — —

Roosevelt died not from the bullet of an assassin but from the onerous burden he had undertaken as the "War President." In April 1945, FDR went south to his Warm Springs house in Georgia, "the Little White House," to try to recover his strength. He was accompanied by his friend Elizabeth Shoumatoff, an artist who was to paint his portrait. On the morning of April 12, FDR complained to his doctor of a slight headache and stiffness to his neck. As he posed for his picture and spoke to his mistress, Lucy Rutherford, he went through his wallet and tossed his draft card in the wastebasket. He had carried it with him throughout the war. "I have a terrific headache," he said, then slumped forward. Roosevelt died two hours later in his small bedroom.

CHAPTER TWO

GENERAL

The Secret Service is the only boss the president has.
—Harry S. Truman

[The White House] is the finest prison in the world.
—Harry S. Truman

fter Harry S. Truman succeeded to the presidency on the death of President Roosevelt, the media tarnished him with the epithet "dunce." Decades later, however, historians came to challenge that view, recognizing Truman as a man who could communicate serious ideas in common words and who had been a lifetime student of history, which had prepared him well for the great challenges that faced him at the end of World War II.

Truman's character was also impressive. He was a plain-talking, unassuming, middle-class, average-looking, apparently ordinary man who never tried to be something he was not. Although the American public initially saw him as a "common man," they gradually realized he had an uncommon ability to lead. He stood for common sense and common decency, did not adopt airs, and had an abiding belief in God.

Truman's greatness as a president was defined by his unshakable conviction of the importance of "national security" during the early stages of the Cold War. It was Truman who decided to drop the atomic bomb. It was the Truman Doctrine that shattered the long-held U.S. tradition of peacetime isolation by supporting Greece and Turkey against Communist threats. And it was Truman's Marshall Plan that committed U.S. resources to the rebuilding of Europe. Later Truman defied the Soviet Union's blockade of Berlin and risked war by authorizing an airlift to support the Berliners. Two years later he laid down the gauntlet in Korea and placed the United States at the head of a United Nations force, determined to help South Korea resist North Korean aggression.

Truman had been content as a senator from Missouri. He never wanted to be president, or vice president, and dreaded the thought that anything might happen to President Roosevelt. Once, during the 1944 presidential campaign, he awoke in a cold sweat having dreamed that the president had died, and he was called upon to assume the presidency. On April 12, 1945, that dream became a reality.

Truman never liked living in the White House. He thought of it as a "prison." He yearned to return to Missouri to pursue his hobbies, play the piano, and take walks. For twelve years the Secret Service agents had gotten into the habit of standing around Roosevelt, who moved slowly and infrequently. They did the same. But Harry Truman loved to walk, and walked briskly, so briskly that the president's agents had trouble keeping pace.[1]

During his first morning at the White House, Truman caught his security detail off guard as he exited his bedroom at 6:00 a.m. and appeared downstairs in a suit and hat. The Secret Service was used to the late-rising FDR. Truman walked straight out the front door and headed up Pennsylvania Avenue at a military quick-time pace of 120 steps a minute, with only one agent accompanying him instead of the standard four. The other agents did not catch up until Truman was well over half a mile away.[2]

At first Truman was oblivious to the dangers inherent in his new job. Occasionally, particularly in areas outside Washington, D.C., he would stop for a cup of coffee at a local diner, and agents were always concerned a would-be assassin would be in the vicinity. There were additional dangers. Agents were concerned because Truman's walks in Washington were usually over the same route at the same time of day—something a would-be assassin could take advantage of. Even though U. E. Baughman, the eventual Secret Service chief, considered Truman's walks to be highly dangerous, there was little he could do to change the president's habits.[3] Truman brushed aside his security detail's fears, occasionally asking them, "Do you think they'll try to rub us out today?"[4] The Secret Service also couldn't stop him, on his frequent visits home to Independence, Missouri, from darting into crowds to shake hands and talk, or stopping his car to get out and chat with an old friend, or even inviting a friend to join him for a ride in the presidential limousine.

— — —

Truman received death threats before he became vice president. A threatening letter was sent to then-senator Truman in 1937, and the authorities considered it serious enough to station a Capitol policeman at the door of each public gallery when the Senate convened.[5]

During his eighty-two days as vice president, Truman moved around Washington seemingly unprotected, as the law at that time did not grant vice presidents Secret Service protection. However, two months before Roosevelt's death, Secret Service agents were assigned to protect Truman without his knowledge. After FDR's death he was guarded by around thirty agents on his personal detail, supported by one hundred uniformed guards. Truman told reporters, "It's going to be tough for me. I can't get used to having whole swarms of people follow me wherever I go."[6]

In time Truman came to appreciate the necessity of his protective detail and the difficulties they encountered in guarding him. When Baughman was appointed Secret Service chief in 1948, Truman told him, "You have one of the hardest jobs in Washington. And I want you to know I realize the fact."[7]

During Truman's first two years in office, the Secret Service was headed by James J. Maloney. In 1946, Jim Rowley was appointed head of the president's detail.[8] Rowley was President Truman's companion on most of the president's walks. When the president told Rowley that "... if any son-of-a-gun tried to kill me I'd take the gun away and shove it down his throat," Rowley responded by telling the president that he would never get close enough to do that but the Secret Service would.[9]

Truman's security detail found the new president to be courteous and cooperative, a man extremely "gentlemanly in his personal dealings." They "loved him," according to U. E. Baughman, because the president had "the common touch," unfailing kindness, and they realized his elevation to the White House "had not changed him a bit." Agent Rex Scouten said, "He treated us like sons. He talked nearly the whole time as we walked."[10] Agent Floyd M. Boring said Truman was an "uncle-like" figure who "knew everybody by name, all the agents by name. We'd bring new agents in and he'd talk to them. He liked to talk to young people, loved to talk to young people."[11] When the president met Boring as his driver, he asked if he could call the agent by his first name. "You couldn't do enough for a man like that," Boring said. "Imagine, President of the United States and that humble and ordinary with his temporary chauffeur. That's greatness to me."[12]

In time Truman became very attached to his agents, sometimes asking them to join him in a card game. He treated his agents as his social equals and would frequently ask them their opinion about the state of the country and the well-being of their family members. He preferred to call everyone by their first name.[13] His detail was also fond of Truman's wife and daughter. They found Bess Truman to be "the soul of cooperation and she never occasioned ... agents a moment's concern." Truman's daughter Margaret was "easy, sociable and charming."[14]

Truman's detail also admired the president for his blunt, no-nonsense approach. Newspaper columnist Drew Pearson once criticized Bess Truman for using a private train compartment when travel space was sparse. The next time the president saw Pearson, he jabbed a finger in the columnist's stomach and said, "God damn you, you call me what you want—thief, robber—but the next time you tell a falsehood about my wife I will punch you right in the nose and don't think that I wouldn't."[15]

Truman was no less blunt when he reflected on the possibility that he might be assassinated. In 1948, he gave his views on the subject to journalist Fred Blumenthal. He began by recalling that one of his heroes, Andrew Jackson, had been attacked by a deranged would-be assassin, Richard Lawrence. Truman recalled that after Lawrence's pistols misfired Jackson struck the attacker with his cane. "I'm the best protected man in the world," Truman said, "But if, through some freak accident, an assassin were to burst through that door with a gun in his hand, I know what I would do. He'd expect me to duck down and hide under this table [in the White House Cabinet Room]. But I'd throw him off base. I'd do what Andy Jackson did. I would rush him, grab the gun away from him, and shove it down his throat."[16]

By the time Truman took office, the Secret Service had "50,000 odd records" in their files of people who had written threatening or obscene letters to the president or his family or who had turned up at the White House.[17] The Secret Service refused to be drawn on details but told reporters that would-be assassins were "hustled to St. Elizabeth's mental hospital." Almost 90 percent of the people on the "threats" list were described as "crackpots." Agents said some threateners had "pocketed guns and tried to enter the White House."[18]

In the period 1949–1950, the Secret Service investigated 1,925 threats against Truman's life.[19] In the first year of the Korean War, arrests and detentions doubled, according to Baughman.[20] In the last year of the Truman administration, the president received more than three thousand threats.

According to Agent Floyd M. Boring, the Secret Service referred abusive letters to field offices. "Sometimes the guy was arrested if he made a threat," Boring said, "and of course, they actually had a copy of the letter right with them … some of these people were just voluminous writers." Boring said most of them were "psychotics." Talking to the threatener usually did the job, Boring said, and field officers would tell them, "We don't mind if you talk to the president or write to him, or disagree with him, but you can't become abusive. You can't call him a son-of-a-bitch or whatever."[21]

Most of the verbal and written threats Truman received were thought to be "non-serious," the result of drunken or inappropriate remarks spoken at the wrong time and in the wrong place. In December 1950, President Truman attended the Army-Navy football game in Philadelphia. Fans Adolph Ruszyek and Michael Pantzykouski had traveled from their homes in Lackawanna, New York. As the president's train pulled into the station, an alert police officer heard one of the men say, "If I had a gun I would have bumped him off." The men were arrested and taken to police headquarters for questioning. After an hour agents decided the men had simply made "foolish remarks" and were "just a couple of punks blowing off." Ruszyek and Pantzykouski were taken to the stadium to watch the remainder of the game. Ruszyck said he had made the remark, but he was just making a wisecrack to point out that it appeared to him the president was not well protected.[22]

Typical of the "non-serious" written threats Truman received was the case of a Kansan woman married to a tenant farmer. Forty-five-year-old Mary Lois Jones, a self-confessed "communist sympathizer," sent five letters and four postcards to Truman in 1952, using "obscene, abusive and defamatory language and making threats to inflict bodily harm on the president of the United States." A postcard dated January 14 contained the sentence, "I hope someone kills you." In a letter dated January 19, she wrote, "I just want to tell you, Harry, I'd rather be a slave of the Kremlin, than a slave of big business, big land holders and the big city racketeers." She was arrested by federal agents. When she was charged, she described them as "Truman's Gestapo."[23]

Another typical letter writer who threatened Truman was Robert T. Gaudlitz, a twenty-two-year-old student who came from Columbia, Ohio, and attended Ohio State University. He was a research fellow in chemical engineering and worked at the university's engineering experiment station. He was described by a colleague as a "quiet sort of fellow who doesn't use profanity." In April 1951, Gaudlitz sent President Truman two letters. One of the letters was addressed to "That jackass in the White House." The letter read, "You [expletive]. This stupid bungle of kicking [General Douglas] McArthur out should entitle you to the electric chair. However, if that is not done by Congress you may be sure that I will take it upon myself to see that your head is blown off with a high-powered rifle if you ever stick your nose in Columbus. How could I serve my country better?" After a post office employee noticed obscene words on the envelopes, he informed the Secret Service, and Gaudlitz was arrested and charged.[24]

President Truman was the subject of numerous threats by former military men who had received dishonorable discharges. One threatener, Dennis E. Porter, was a slightly built twenty-year-old ex–U.S. Marine with a crew cut who came from Hermon, Louisiana. He had been dishonorably discharged from the Marines when they discovered he had a criminal record. "They threw me out after telling me I wasn't much good," he said. After he was arrested and imprisoned in Franklinton, Louisiana, for "defamation of character," he wrote to President Truman and threatened his life. The letter was mailed on October 28, 1948, a week before Truman's reelection. His letter stated, "I'll write you a few lines to let you know what I think of your rotten political schemes. It is a shame and disgrace for anyone to treat the American people like you do. Even if you win the office of president you won't live to glorify in it … if God gives me the strength, you won't be president long. I'll see to that."[25]

The Secret Service traced the letter to Porter. He was charged with threatening the life of the president and examined by psychiatrists who found him to be sane. On December 1, 1948, he pleaded guilty. He was sentenced to three years in prison. After sentencing he told the court he was "angry with the entire United States" and that President Truman was "not adequate to supervise the people of the United States." He also told the judge that he had intended all along to carry out the threat, and when the judge asked him if he was serious in his intentions, he said, "If the chance comes." He allowed that if the Marines had not discharged him, "things might have been different … I don't think having a dishonorable discharge I am a citizen of the United States and after I have served my sentence I wish to be deported. The U.S. doesn't mean much to me anyhow."[26]

Some threats the Secret Service investigated were considered to be extremely dangerous. In August 1946, the agency was alarmed when a man who described himself as an "executioner" threatened to kill President Truman. The agency classified the case as "the most significant" of the year and refused to divulge further details.[27]

In 1953, the Secret Service arrested forty-year-old Albert J. Drevney, who was described by Chief Baughman as a "homicidal maniac experienced in the use of small firearms." Drevney first came to the attention of the Secret Service in 1941, when he was arrested in San Francisco for threatening the life of President Roosevelt. In the years that followed, he was in and out of half a dozen mental institutions from which he escaped or had been released. During one of his periods of freedom, he wrote a threatening letter to President Truman. He was finally arrested and again put in a mental hospital after threatening the life of the Harrisburg, Pennsylvania, postmaster and recently inaugurated president Dwight Eisenhower, which led to a nationwide manhunt.[28]

— — —

President Truman was the target of a number of terror groups, including the notorious Stern Gang, named after Abraham Stern, a Zionist militant killed by the British in 1942. According to Margaret Truman, the Stern Gang sent letter bombs to the White House in 1947. Around that same time, the gang tried unsuccessfully to use letter bombs to assassinate at least eight prominent British politicians and military figures.[29] The British warned the White House about the possibility of letter bombs, and the incident was described in a 1949 book, *Dear Mr. President: The Story of 50 Years in the White House Mail Room*, by Ira T. Smith, a White House staff mail reader. The cream-colored envelopes were addressed to the president and members of his staff and contained powdered gelignite, a pencil battery, and a detonator. They were rigged to explode when the envelope was opened. Smith said the gang claimed responsibility for the letter bombs.[30]

Stern Gang leader Nathan Yellin-More denied that his group tried to kill Truman, although he did admit to the attacks on the British leaders. Yellin-More said, "I am sure the accusation by Miss Truman has no basis. During that period we did, however, send letter bombs, but they were all directed against the British who were directly responsible for the situation [in Palestine]. We didn't do anything against other people or any other state. We had nothing against President Truman who took a favorable stand toward our mission." Yellin-More denied his members could have sent the bombs without his knowledge. "Definitely not," he said, "Nothing was done without the knowledge of the central command, including our branch in Europe."[31]

Truman was also the target of Puerto Rican nationalists. The president was staying at Blair House, across the street from the White House which was under renovation. Around 2:15 p.m., November 1, 1950, two Puerto Rican nationalists, thirty-seven-year-old Oscar Collazo and twenty-four-year-old Griselio Torresola, approached Blair House from opposite directions, determined to assassinate President Truman. Collazo was armed with a Walther P-38 and Torresola with a Luger, both 9 mm pistols. Collazo later said he and Torresola "just took a chance" that Truman would be in Blair House when they attacked. In fact, the president was upstairs taking a nap.[32]

Torresola went to the guard booth on the west side of the Blair House entrance, drew his gun, and shot White House police officer Leslie Coffelt at point-blank range three times.

Collazo, meanwhile, arrived at the east booth and attempted to walk up the steps to the front door. Seeing a police officer blocking his way, Collazo pulled out his gun, but being unfamiliar with guns, he did not realize that the safety was on. When he eventually turned it off, he sent a bullet into the leg of Officer Donald T. Birdzell.

Inside Blair House, Secret Service agent Stewart Stout snapped up a Thompson automatic submachine gun and waited for the would-be assassin. Collazo turned to run up the remaining steps to the front door of Blair House but was caught in a gunfight with White House police officer P. Davidson and Secret Service agent

Floyd Boring, who were at the east booth. Pausing only to reload, he was finally brought down by a shot from Boring that hit him in the chest.

At the other side of Blair House, Torresola shot another officer before trying to rescue Collazo. The mortally wounded Coffelt, lying on the floor of the guardhouse, aimed his gun at Torresola and fired. The bullet hit the assassin in the head, killing him instantly.[33] When agents searched Torresola's corpse, they found a letter from Puerto Rican nationalist Pedro Albizu Campos, which read: "My dear Griselio, if for any reason it should be necessary for you to assume the leadership of the [nationalist] movement in the United States, you will do so without hesitation of any kind. We are leaving to your high sense of patriotism and sane judgment everything regarding this matter. Cordially yours."[34] His compatriot Collazo survived his wounds and was arrested.

In 1961, Truman recalled what he had been doing when Collazo and Torresola attempted to kill him. "I remember it all very well," Truman said, "I was taking my afternoon nap as usual, in preparation for going to Arlington Cemetery to dedicate a monument to the late Sir John Dill. We heard sounds from Pennsylvania Avenue that sounded like backfires. I looked out and said to Mrs. Truman, 'Somebody is shooting at our guards.'... I looked out ... and saw a policeman lying badly wounded in the street. I stuck my head out the window and asked, 'Who's that?' A Secret Service man said, 'Get back, Mr. President.' Another Secret Service man, a fine shot, killed one of the assassins. The bullet went in one ear and came out the other and that disposed of his case."[35]

According to Truman, the assassins had acted prematurely, "I don't know what those damn fools were thinking of," Truman said.

"If they had waited about 10 minutes Mrs. Truman and I would have been walking down the front steps of Blair House and there's no telling what might have happened. Of course, they were both drunk. [Secret Service head of detail] Jim Rowley told me so." Truman also said he was taken to task by Rowley for "sticking my head out the window. He asked me severely, 'Mr. President, when you were in France and the air raid alarm sounded did you stick your head out?' I said, 'No, Jim, I guess I didn't.'"[36] Agent Boring, however, said Truman never appeared at the window. "They had President Truman coming to the window upstairs," he said, "and I'm supposed to have waved and told him to go back. But he never showed up there ... what happened was that [Howard G. Crim] came to the front door, and stuck his head out. I said, 'Get the hell back in there.'"[37]

At his trial Collazo claimed the "gunplay" was not an actual attempt to kill the president but a "demonstration" designed to shock Americans into giving Puerto Ricans their independence. He said the two men did not intend to kill anybody, though he also confessed that Pedro Albizu Campos—leader of the Puerto Rican Nationalist party, which had received only five thousand votes out of the hundreds of thousands cast in recent Puerto Rican elections—had ordered them to kill Truman. He said there were to be four assassins, but only he and Torresola showed up.[38]

On March 7, 1951, Collazo was found guilty and sentenced to death. He eagerly looked forward to martyrdom and was annoyed when his execution was stayed. He became enraged when in June 1952 President Truman commuted his death sentence to life in prison. Truman said he "was sentenced to die but I commuted the sentence to life imprisonment because that was the law in Puerto Rico—they didn't have capital punishment there then."[39]

Little more was heard about the imprisoned nationalist until the mid-1970s, when a group called Fuerzas Armadas Liberación Nacional or FALN began blowing up banks and office buildings in New York. Among the FALN demands was the release of their hero Collazo. In September 1979, following a human rights campaign spearheaded by Representative Robert Garcia of the Bronx, Collazo was pardoned by President Jimmy Carter over the protests of Puerto Rican governor Carlos Romero Barcelo, who insisted that the unrepentant Collazo remained a menace to society. Even Representative Garcia was shocked when he learned Collazo had publicly embraced FALN and given them his endorsement for political violence. Two months after Collazo left prison, Fidel Castro invited him to Cuba, where he received a hero's welcome. Collazo died in Puerto Rico in February 1994, aged eighty.[40]

Naturally, security around President Truman tightened after the attack. His walking routes were changed and heavily patrolled, he was accompanied by at least sixteen agents, and he was driven between Blair House and the White House. Truman never got used to the new arrangements for his security. "I ride across the street in a car the roof of which will turn a grenade, the windows and sides will turn a bullet and the floor will stop a landmine," he said, "Behind me in an open car ride six or seven men with automatics and machine guns. The uniformed police stop traffic in every direction—and I cross the street in state and wonder why anyone would want to live like that."[41]

The Secret Service purportedly had information that further attempts would be made on the president's life. In December 1950, U. E. Baughman, appearing before a House of Representatives Appropriations Committee subcommittee, said the agency had "information that there might be other attempts and, as a matter of fact, the wives of would-be assassins said to the effect...." The committee questioning Baughman cut him off in the middle of his statement, and it was not completed for the record.[42]

— — —

President Truman continued to be the target of would-be assassins after he left office. In 1957, Leroy Shadrick, a Korean War veteran whose brother was purportedly the first U.S. soldier to die in the conflict, stalked the president he held responsible for his brother's death. In March 1955, Shadrick, who had a history of mental illness, visited Truman's hometown of Independence, to "case it" and to learn about the former president's daily routine. Coincidentally, he was arrested by the FBI for income tax fraud, convicted, and served eighteen months in a federal prison in West Virginia. He was released in December 1956 and continued to plot Truman's assassination. He bought a shotgun, sawed off the barrel, and rigged a crude holster to carry the weapon in his coat. To finance his plot, he attempted to rob the Albemarle, North Carolina, Home Builders Association. He hoped to steal enough money to hide out until July 1957, the seventh anniversary of his brother's death, when he would complete his "mission." Shadrick's scheme was foiled, however, when a woman teller screamed during his hold-up attempt. Shadrick panicked, dropped his gun, and fled. An off-duty fireman picked up the gun and apprehended Shadrick, holding him until police arrived.

Shadrick pleaded guilty to the attempted robbery, and a federal judge recommended he be sent to an institution for treatment for schizophrenia and paranoia. In May 1958, he escaped from the institution with four other inmates by sawing through a window

screen. He was soon recaptured and sent to a hospital for the criminally insane.[43]

The Trumans were without Secret Service protection the moment
Dwight D. Eisenhower was inaugurated president on January 20,
1953. But on December 16, 1965, President Lyndon Johnson signed
Public Law 89-186, which extended lifetime Secret Service protection
to former presidents, their widows, and their minor children. President Truman accepted the protection in principle, but he had to be
coaxed by President Johnson into accepting agents at the Truman
Library, where he kept an office.[44]

In July 1966, after an incident with a former mental patient, Truman requested temporary Secret Service protection at his home. In
May 1967, Truman and his wife were afforded twenty-four-hour
protection, though the agents never stayed overnight inside the Truman home.

— — —

Truman died on December 26, 1972. He had personally approved
plans for an elaborate five-day state funeral. He said it would be a
"damn fine show. I just hate that I'm not going to be around to see
it." Bess Truman, however, vetoed the former president's plans in
favor of a far simpler ceremony, with the thirty-third president of
the United States laid to rest in the courtyard of the Truman Library.[45]

Asked how he wanted to be remembered, Truman said he liked
the words chiseled on a frontier grave: "Here lies Jack Williams—he
done his damndest." He wished to be remembered, he said, as the
man who "did what had to be done."[46]

CHAPTER THREE

SCORECARD

My faith in him has never wavered nor ever will.
—President Harry S. Truman, November 1951

If anybody really wanted to climb up there and shoot me [Eisenhower pointed to a fire escape outside his Denver hotel room] it would be an easy thing to do. So why worry about it.
—President Eisenhower, in a conversation with presidential aide Sherman Adams

Dwight D. Eisenhower was born in Denison, Texas, in 1890 and was brought up in Abilene, Kansas. In his early army career, after graduating from West Point, he excelled at staff assignments, serving under Generals John J. Pershing, Douglas MacArthur, and Walter Krueger. After Pearl Harbor, General George C. Marshall called him to Washington for a war plans assignment. He commanded the Allied Forces landing in North Africa in November 1942, and he was the supreme commander of the troops invading France on D-Day, June 1944.

After the war, he was named president of Columbia University, and in 1951 he became the first supreme commander of NATO.

Eisenhower turned down Republican and Democrat requests, including from President Truman, that he run for president, until 1952, when he ran and won as a Republican. He was reelected in 1956. Both times he defeated Democratic candidate Adlai Stevenson by a substantial margin.

As president, Eisenhower ended the war in Korea and at home oversaw a decade of rising prosperity. Historian Stephen Ambrose thought Eisenhower was the best president of the twentieth century. Eisenhower "thought things through," Ambrose wrote. "He had a lot of shortcomings and weaknesses, but ... he was the smartest man I've ever met and the one with the highest power of concentration. ... He was the most naturally generous man." Eisenhower, he noted, brought the American people through the "eight toughest years of the Cold War without losing a single soldier, and without giving up an inch of territory ... he got us through the decade. I don't know if anybody else could have. I know that he did."[1]

Historians and the media initially dismissed Eisenhower as a "bumbling lightweight," but behind the bland smile and apparent simplemindedness, historian Evan Thomas argues, he was a brilliant political tactician, a "master of calculated duplicity," a patient, subtle leader with quiet moral courage.[2]

— — —

Eisenhower called the Secret Service "one of the finest and most efficient organizations of men I have ever known."[3] Secret Service agents liked Eisenhower as a man and also as an assignment because he was not impetuous or unpredictable in his movements. "Protecting Ike worked like clockwork," former Secret Service agent Gerald Blaine said. The Secret Service appreciated that Eisenhower did not feel compelled to wade into crowds. On the odd occasion when he did want to stop his car and shake hands, the Secret Service always said no and Eisenhower acceded to their wishes.[4] When he took up oil painting on the South Lawn of the White House, the Secret Service warned him that he was exposing himself to an armed assassin, so he moved indoors.[5] Few presidents have been so accommodating of their armed guards.

First Lady Mamie Eisenhower was fond of her Secret Service protectors. Some of her longest-serving agents even called her "Mom."[6] She, in turn, gave nicknames to the agents, calling one of them "Twinkletoes" because he was a good dancer.[7]

The Eisenhowers did not mind having agents around because Eisenhower got used to having guards when he was in the army. He was heavily guarded in North Africa and later as supreme commander of the Allied Forces in Europe. Sometimes he even had a guard inside his office. He did, however, resent the French security police who guarded him as head of NATO because he refused to believe they were necessary. Eisenhower frequently left his French guards behind. The French feared Communist plots to assassinate him.[8]

When it came to understanding the need for presidential security, Mamie Eisenhower said, "I think Ike was almost better fitted for it than anybody else, because we had lived all over the world, we didn't have to be told these things. I wasn't unhappy because I was there, or felt that I was a prisoner; I never had that feeling at all.... We've had Secret Service for years around us. That doesn't bother me any, I'm grateful to them."[9]

During the late 1940s, the Secret Service received notification of a serious threat against Eisenhower's life, but he refused President Truman's offer of protection "point blank." Truman, an admirer of

Eisenhower's, nevertheless insisted that the Secret Service give the general covert twenty-four-hour protection.[10]

When he became president, Eisenhower was aware that his family had to be guarded too. He told Secret Service chief U. E. Baughman, "You don't have to worry about me—but don't let anything happen to my grandchildren."[11] Agents assigned to guard the four Eisenhower grandchildren called it the "diaper detail." They sat with the children all day at school. If one of the children was invited to sleep at a friend's house, an agent went along. Eisenhower's daughter-in-law, Barbara Eisenhower-Foltz, said the Secret Service "were wonderful" and "became our good friends."[12]

Although Eisenhower had immense respect for his protectors, he was not on intimate terms with them. "He was not warm and fuzzy with the agents," former agent Gerald Blaine said, "but he had confidence in his agents' ability and he understood unnecessary exposure."[13] By the end of his second term Eisenhower had "lost interest" in learning the names of the newer agents and would call out "Agent!"[14] But he did have a very friendly relationship with the head of his presidential detail, James Rowley. Rowley was a forty-six-year-old burly Irishman from the Bronx. He went to work as a bank investigator at eighteen but continued to go to school nights; nine years later, he earned his law degree from Brooklyn's St. John's University. In 1938, Rowley joined the Secret Service, went to the White House within a year, and became the agent in charge of the White House detail in 1946.[15]

Rowley had been guarding presidents since 1939, and his office during the Eisenhower years was located just inside the West Wing, only a few paces from the Oval Office. He was almost always at Eisenhower's side when the president left the White House, and he usually walked a pace behind him, always alert. When the president rode in a car, Rowley sat in the front seat.

Eisenhower did not suffer fools gladly, and incompetence at any level made him "testy." On a few occasions, the famous Eisenhower temper would explode when he became frustrated with his protectors. When the president visited army bases around the country or abroad he believed the Secret Service was overzealous when it suspected American soldiers might attempt to assassinate him. According to author Merle Miller, "Just the fact that the Secret Service failed to take into account the Army's loyalty made Ike furious...."[16]

There were also occasions early on in his administration when he would bristle at the surveillance of the Secret Service. But as he learned more about the threats, he came to have a greater respect for the Secret Service's mission. Eisenhower read Robert Donovan's *The Assassins*, an account of seven attempts on the lives of presidents. After making some inquiries, he was shocked to discover some disturbing statistics related to assassination attempts and threats, especially the fact that in the first four months of 1955, 401 threats were made against his life. The previous year eighty people had been convicted on charges of threatening the president and sent to prison or psychiatric facilities. During the same period, Eisenhower learned, 118 mentally disturbed individuals were arrested at the White House gates. Eisenhower also stopped complaining to the Secret Service about the closing of a tower near his Gettysburg farm that the Secret Service judged to be an ideal sniper's nest.[17]

— — —

Historians and biographers have tended to ignore the numerous threats and plots against President Eisenhower, though many were taken very seriously by the Secret Service. Eisenhower's press secretary, James C. Hagerty, for instance, remembered at least two assassination plots traced to the Nationalist party of Puerto Rico.[18] In 1953, Eisenhower's first year in office, there were 1,650 threats against his life that merited investigation. In 1954, the Secret Service investigated 1,400 threats and eighty-four persons were arrested as dangerous to the president. Eighty were convicted and sent to prisons or psychiatric hospitals.[19] In 1955, 1,400 threatening letters were investigated, and ninety cases warranted action.[20] Between 1957 and 1958, 17,801 letters to President Eisenhower were referred to the Secret Service. Nine hundred forty-nine case investigations were sent out to field offices manned by 209 agents, and sixty-six people were arrested for making threats. During 1957–1958, White House police arrested 130 "mentally disturbed persons" who turned up at the executive mansion.[21]

The Secret Service believed that guarding Eisenhower was a less onerous task than protecting Harry Truman—Eisenhower did not, for example, get up at 5:30 a.m. for his early morning walk. However, Eisenhower's obsession with golf did pose security problems, because golf courses with thick wooded areas afforded cover for would-be snipers. When Eisenhower went to one of his three favorite golf clubs—the Burning Tree Country Club in Bethesda, Maryland; the Augusta, Georgia, National Country Club; or the Cherry Hills Country Club in Denver, Colorado—three agents with high-powered rifles would survey the area and take positions at the highest points. Two more agents, dressed in golf clothes, would stay with the president. They carried .351 rifles with telescopic sights in their golf bags. Two agents, one in a golf buggy armed with a submachine gun, would travel behind Eisenhower. Other agents were scattered throughout the grounds frequently leaving the fairway to check on surrounding woodlands. Police and agents patrolled the roads surrounding the course and a doctor was always on hand. A contingent of agents was responsible for bags containing communications equipment whilst other agents would remain at the command center—the armored touring car known as the "Queen Mary."[22]

— — —

Long before Eisenhower became president, he had been the victim of threats against his life. As the Allied supreme commander during the Second World War, he knew he was a target, and in fact, during the Battle of the Bulge, German troops disguised as GIs hoped to get close enough to General Eisenhower to kill him. Corporal Wilheim Schmidt, who was captured and later executed, told interrogators that his task was to "kill General Eisenhower" and that his "unit included a group of engineers whose job it was to destroy headquarters and kill the headquarters' personnel."[23] Additionally, General Courtney Hodges of the U.S. First Army warned Supreme Headquarters that Otto Skorzeny of the Waffen-SS, "is on his way to Versailles to assassinate Eisenhower."[24]

Eisenhower believed the whole plot was "greatly exaggerated," though his staff told him it had "complete and positive proof,"[25] and he accepted increased security—including having a hundred soldiers accompany him to the mess hall.

Historian Timothy Naftali believes the plot to kill Eisenhower was a "false alarm" but that "by early 1945, a consensus developed among Allied intelligence officers that the liberation of Germany would unleash an unprecedented terrorist campaign," likely led by Skorzeny, and that "Nazi collaborators in liberated Europe were expected to 'cause political upheaval by assassinations, terrorism, and acts of violence at political meetings....'"[26]

Former German soldier Fritz Christ confirmed details of the plot, however, when he decided to speak out on the sixtieth anniversary of D-Day. Christ said that in October 1944 he was duped into taking part in Operation Greif. "We were accompanied by a fanatical SS officer who told us that our mission was to take Eisenhower dead or alive," Christ said. "We had detailed maps of French back roads leading to the general's headquarters at Fontainebleau."[27] In 1951, the FBI investigated an alleged plot to kill Eisenhower. According to an FBI memo dated January 12, 1951, recent rumors of a plot against Eisenhower had resulted in "several communists in France" being arrested. The FBI's files, however, do not reveal the results of the bureau's own investigation.[28]

— — —

During Eisenhower's time as president, the Secret Service investigated thousands of people who wrote the president threatening letters or made alleged attempts on his life. The FBI even took seriously information from "mediums" who warned that Eisenhower would be assassinated or die in an air crash. In 1952 the agency noted that an "Egyptian medium" had warned that the president would be assassinated shortly after his election, and in 1953 an FBI memo discussed the advice of a "medium" who said there "was danger in store for the President if he returned to the United States by air" from a trip to Bermuda.[29]

In 1954, the Secret Service estimated that "every six hours someone in the United States made a threat against the president or his family." The agency also acknowledged that it was extremely difficult for the Secret Service to discriminate between the inappropriate remarks of a drunken person, an outburst by an angered citizen, or the cold intent of a would-be assassin.[30]

Among the non-serious threats the agency investigated were a number of cases that initially caused alarm but were eventually proven to be innocuous, including an incident that occurred at Eisenhower's inauguration. A professional cowboy, Montie Montana, surprised Secret Service agents when he approached the stage and slung a lasso around the president. Montana later claimed he had the president's permission.[31]

The Secret Service was plagued by reports of threats to the president that were the result of drunken behavior. A typical threatener of this type was alcoholic James L. Winterstein, a thirty-one-year-old from Biloxi, Mississippi. He wrote to President Eisenhower when he was drinking in a Mobile, Alabama, tavern on February 20, 1956. "I'm going to kill you," Winterstein wrote, and he repeated his threat four more times. At the bottom of his letter he wrote, "I mean it." Foolishly, he added his name. Winterstein was arrested and pleaded guilty to threatening the president. He was sentenced to forty-two months in a federal prison.[32]

There were numerous bomb scares during Eisenhower's presidency. Most turned out to be hoaxes. In 1954, for example, during a routine examination of a New England college where the president was to receive an honorary degree, a Secret Service man spotted two tin cans under the stage where the president was to give his commencement address. He lifted the can out gently and raised the top. Inside was a note: "To the Guardians of the Beloved President of the United States of America—We students have decided that you, the Secret Service, have been too lax in your precautions. We are in the midst of proving that even a young college student, untrained in the methods of subterfuge and surreptitious actions, can devise a scheme which could go unobserved and thereby constitute a threat to our great leader. This can, placed under the podium on which Dwight D. Eisenhower will walk Graduation Day, could easily have been a powerful bomb." The Secret Service was unable to track down the "pranksters."[33]

Eisenhower, like presidents before him, was plagued by individuals who tried to breach the president's security to either shake his hand or give him "advice." The Secret Service had to determine if the individual had any lethal intent. In 1958, Eisenhower and his wife visited the Smithsonian in Washington, D.C., to view oil paintings by British war leader Sir Winston Churchill. As they exited the building, they were greeted by a crowd of around three hundred people. Mamie Eisenhower had just entered the presidential limousine when a Brookline, Massachusetts, woman, Edith Finch, broke ranks and rushed toward the president. Agents lunged toward her, hauling her back. She screamed, "I've got to get him." As Finch was placed in a police car, she stuck her head out the window and shouted, "A New York FBI man has done terrible things to me—extortion!" Secret Service chief Baughman said the woman had been in Washington for a week and had been spotted at the White House gates, where she told White House police officers she wanted to see someone to complain about not being able to collect her army husband's monthly allotment checks. After her arrest, she was sent to St. Elizabeth's Hospital.[34]

Particularly irksome to the Secret Service were repeat offenders who had either been incarcerated in mental institutions or had served prison sentences for making threats. In March 1956, drug addict

Laurence J. Thompson sent a letter to Eisenhower written on the stationery of a Gulfport, Mississippi, hotel. "I'm going to kill you if you run for office again," Thompson wrote. "I hope you will take this as a warning." The Secret Service investigated the threat and tracked Thompson down to his half sister's home in Meridian, Mississippi. On May 5 he was arrested. Thompson pleaded guilty to threatening the president and was sentenced to eighteen months in prison. On his release, he phoned the Secret Service office in Jackson, Mississippi, and told agents he was going to kill Eisenhower if the president did not send him $500. "I may just kill you anyway," Thompson said, "and [vice president] Nixon, too. I mean this." The threatener was once again found guilty of threatening the president, and this time he was given a three-year prison sentence.[35]

Another repeat threatener was Sam Stepp Jr., an eccentric "drifter" who wore white canvas gloves and smoked a corncob pipe. In 1953, Stepp, who had done time in jail and mental institutions, was dishonorably discharged from military service. He wanted President Eisenhower or Treasury Secretary George Humphrey to grant him an honorable discharge.

In 1956, agents were tipped off that Stepp had made threatening remarks in a Buena Vista, Colorado, bar. Stepp purportedly said, "If I ever get close to the president I'll kill him. I have a 30-30 bullet for him." He was arrested in Glenwood Springs, Colorado, on March 28, 1956, and agents discovered two bullets in his possession. At his trial he denied making the statement but admitted threatening the life of the president. Stepp was sentenced to six months' imprisonment. On September 20, 1957, he was arrested again after he set fire to a telephone booth. He had attempted to call Eisenhower and made statements that he had a gun and was going to kill the president.

Stepp was charged with disorderly conduct and spent a further short period in a mental institution. After his release on October 8, 1957, Secret Service agents kept track of his movements.[36]

One of the most serious breaches of presidential security occurred when a member of the press corps who covered the president's daily activities told a bystander in the White House he was "going upstairs to kill the president." The journalist, whose identity was kept secret beyond saying he was a "White House regular," had almost total access to Eisenhower. The journalist's comments were overheard by a Secret Service agent who had him placed in a mental hospital.[37]

In 1957, the Secret Service investigated several cases involving four young inmates at a federal prison. Each had written threatening letters to President Eisenhower and Vice President Richard Nixon. One inmate told an agent that he believed the president and all government officials were "communistic and therefore traitors." Three of the youths told agents they would have no hesitation in shooting the president. The Secret Service considered them dangerous, and on their release they were put under surveillance.[38]

Two years later agents investigated the case of a fifty-year-old man who appeared outside the Northwest Gate of the White House armed with a knife. He was disarmed after White House police overpowered him. The would-be assailant said he was convinced President Eisenhower did not exist. He threatened to stab anyone who stopped him from entering the White House to prove his point.[39]

The Secret Service believed twenty-year-old Howard Reed Liggett was "particularly dangerous." In 1959, when Liggett was in prison for auto theft, he mailed a letter to President Eisenhower threatening to kill him. He persuaded three other inmates to write similar letters. All four men repeated their threats to Secret Service agents. Liggett's friends were given additional prison sentences. Liggett was committed to a mental institution "indefinitely." Doctors told agents that Liggett was one of the worst cases they had examined. He was "a young man," they told the Secret Service, "who was obsessed by murder and mutilation."[40]

— — —

One of the most perilous assignments for the Secret Service was protecting President-elect Eisenhower when he fulfilled his campaign pledge to "go to Korea." Eisenhower insisted on visiting the front lines, in view of enemy snipers. He did not consult his security detail but simply expected them to follow him wherever he went.

According to a CIA memo, there might even have been a KGB plan to assassinate Eisenhower in Korea.

On October 19, 1954, Russian defector Peter Deryabin reported that while he was acting chief of the German branch of the KGB in 1952, he had occasion to speak to a new officer, Lieutenant Colonel Brusov. Brusov allegedly said, "We were preparing an operation to assassinate Eisenhower during his visit to Korea in order to create panic among the Americans and win the war in Korea." Deryabin knew that Brusov had been in North Korea from 1949 to 1952 and had worked for SPETSBURO #1, which was responsible for assassinations and "other executive action type projects."[41]

On March 1, 1954, four years after Puerto Rican terrorists attempted to assassinate President Truman, fanatical nationalists struck again when four terrorists fired thirty rounds from semiautomatic pistols from the Ladies' Gallery of the House of Representatives. Twenty-five-year-old Rafael Cancel-Miranda, thirty-four-year-old Lolita Lebron, twenty-nine-year-old Andres Figueroa Cordero, and twenty-eight-year-old Irving Flores Rodriguez unfurled a Puerto Rican flag before they began shooting at the 240 representatives present in the chamber. The assassins wounded five congressmen. Representative James E. Van Zandt helped disarm the assailants, wrestling a Luger pistol from one of the Puerto Rican terrorists.[42]

All four nationalists were arrested within minutes. After a trial they were found guilty and sentenced to death. Their death sentences were commuted by President Eisenhower and they were given a minimum of seventy years in prison. The Secret Service worried that Eisenhower might be the Puerto Rican terrorists' next target. The investigation into the attack on the House of Representatives revealed seventeen plotters, and Secret Service chief U. E. Baughman said Puerto Rican terrorists "might try to harm the president."[43]

One of the captured plotters, Gonzales Lebron Sotomayor said at his trial that Julio Pinto Gandia had been responsible for targeting Eisenhower. Gandia was the head of the Chicago junta of the Nationalist party. He had issued orders in November 1953 for the group to keep tabs on the movements of the president and several congressmen. During his trial, Sotomayor, who pleaded guilty to a seditious conspiracy charge and turned state's evidence, said Eisenhower was slated to be assassinated in October 1953, but Eisenhower went on a fishing trip in Colorado, foiling their plan.[44]

Once again Puerto Rican nationalists had chosen the wrong target if revenge for America's "imperialist" position in Puerto Rico was the motive. Like Truman, President Eisenhower was willing to grant Puerto Rico independence "whenever the Puerto Rican legislature asked for it." But the nationalists did not represent Puerto Rican public opinion. In January 1954, the legislature voted 42 to 12 to reject the idea of independence from the United States.[45]

Following the House of Representatives shooting, Baughman and his men became more sensitive about Eisenhower's personal security, and a special committee of Secret Service agents, FBI agents, and government intelligence agents began to assess the president's itinerary more closely. The group raised the subject of Eisenhower's golfing practice and painting on the White House lawn. When they raised the matter with him, he acceded to some of their wishes. He stopped painting but kept on practicing his golf shots.[46] Agents also spent a busy weekend in early May 1954, two months after the shooting, investigating a report they received from Fredericksburg police that Eisenhower would be assassinated when he attended a wreath-laying ceremony at the grave of George Washington's mother. The Mother's Day ceremony passed without incident and Baughman said he had been "satisfied there was nothing to it."[47] They also investigated a telephone call made by a man named "Gomez," who said he had planted two boxes of explosives at a baseball park the president attended.[48]

The House of Representatives shooting incident inspired "copycat crimes." The day after the shooting, Pedro Orosco Sanchez was arrested on a charge of "non-support of his wife." While fingerprinted by police, he reportedly said he would "kill the president." Sanchez's recent trips to New York and Detroit from his home in Connecticut raised Secret Service suspicions about a possible terrorist plot, and Sanchez was indicted by a federal grand jury.[49]

Within days of Sanchez's threat, a gardener found a hand grenade on the White House lawn and informed the Secret Service. The bomb detail discovered it was a dud. U. E. Baughman said he was "concerned some insane person had simply lobbed it over the fence," and he worried that there was little he could do to prevent such actions.[50]

The following week, on March 12, 1954, thirty-year-old Jose Rivera Colon, a Puerto Rican nationalist and itinerant spray painter who had once been committed to a mental institution, telephoned FBI agent Neil Heiner from a New York pay booth and told him he was going to kill the president "in the next couple of months." When time ran out on the call and the operator asked for another nickel, Heiner volunteered to call Colon back to save him the five cents. Colon gave Heiner the number of the public phone—situated at a 96th Street and Broadway drugstore—which saved the agent the trouble of tracing the call. Colon and Heiner were still conversing when FBI agents and police arrived at the phone booth and arrested the threatener. On April 28, 1954, Colon pleaded guilty to threatening the life of President Eisenhower and was sentenced to three years in prison.[51]

Puerto Rican nationalists were still plotting to kill Eisenhower in 1958 and 1959, according to White House press secretary James Hagerty. Two plots had been uncovered. In the spring of 1958, Secret Service agents learned an attempt would be made to throw grenades into Eisenhower's car during a trip through a "mid-west city." The second plan Hagerty referred to was reported to a Secret Service agent in the spring of 1959. The plot involved a group of nationalists who had "decided to kill the president."[52]

Puerto Rican nationalists continued plotting to kill an American president for years to come. House of Representatives shooter Rafael Cancel-Miranda said after serving twenty years of his sentence, "When I get out of here [Marion Prison, Illinois], I will go to a store, buy a gun, go to the White House and start shooting." Cancel-Miranda turned down clemency because he would not apologize for his crime. President Carter set the forty-nine-year-old free in 1977. On his release he told a reporter, "If you want war, you're gonna get it."[53]

— — —

Although Eisenhower said he felt hemmed in by his security, he had come to rely on his agents and missed them when he left the presidency. But he missed them for other reasons than his personal security. As an army general he was used to a retinue of aides. As president, Secret Service agents had always taken care of his golf clubs, his hat and gloves, and other personal items. And they kept him on schedule. When Eisenhower returned to his Gettysburg farm, he was at a loss. He had not driven a car for years and was not used to making telephone calls by himself. He found the new technology frustrating.[54]

After Eisenhower left office, he continued to receive threats on his life. In 1961, for example, Secret Service agents arrested a man who traveled to Gettysburg, bought a gun, and announced that he intended to use it on Eisenhower. The Secret Service determined the threat was not serious.[55] More serious in the end was the condition of Eisenhower's heart. He had suffered a heart attack while president and suffered several more in the 1960s, before dying of heart failure in 1969.

CHAPTER FOUR

LANCER

If anyone wants to do it, no amount of protection is enough.
All a man needs is a willingness to trade his life for mine.
—President Kennedy, speaking to author Jim Bishop

I guess there is always the possibility [of assassination] but
that is what the Secret Service is for. I guess that is one of
the less desirable aspects of [the presidency].
—President Kennedy

I counted ... 50 coincidences caused the assassination.
If just one of them had happened the other way....
—Secret Service chief James Rowley, in
a conversation with author Jim Bishop

John F. Kennedy was curious about the way assassination could affect a president's legacy. Kennedy asked Princeton historian David Donald if Lincoln would have been rated as such a great president if he had not been killed. Donald replied that it was unlikely, "since Lincoln's reputation would ultimately have suffered while tackling the problem of post–Civil War reconstruction."[1]

In 1960, following his election as president of the United States, John F. Kennedy told one of his aides that Secret Service protection was "excessive," and he was not at risk. "They're making me uncomfortable," Kennedy insisted to his aide Kenneth O'Donnell. "Nobody is going to shoot me, so tell them to relax." He also joked about being assassinated, according to his wife, Jacqueline Kennedy. She said she remembered JFK saying after the Cuban Missile Crisis, "Well, if anyone's ever going to shoot me, this would be the day they should do it."[2] He also joked about assassination with his Secret Service detail. Once when he left a church, JFK crouched lower and lower as he said to his agents, "If there is anybody up in that choir loft trying to get me, they're going to have to get you first."[3]

On two other occasions President Kennedy predicted that he might become a target for would-be assassins. On the morning of November 22, 1963, Kennedy told Kenneth O'Donnell, "if anybody really wanted to shoot the President of the United States, it was not a very difficult job—all one had to do was get a high building some-day with a telescopic rifle, and there was nothing anybody could do to defend against such an attempt."[4] That same morning, he said to his wife, "We're heading into nut country today [Dallas]. … You know, last night would have been a hell of a night to assassinate a President … I mean it. There was the rain, and the night, and we were all getting jostled. Suppose a man had a pistol in a briefcase. Then he could have dropped the gun and the briefcase and melted away in the crowd."[5]

The night before JFK's trip to Dallas, Senator Hubert H. Humphrey, who Lyndon Johnson would select as his 1964 vice-presidential running mate, gave a speech in which he spoke of threats and assassination and warned that "the act of an emotionally unstable person or irresponsible citizen can strike down a great leader."[6]

— — —

In August 1961, James Rowley succeeded U. E. Baughman as Secret Service chief, and Gerald A. Behn was appointed head of JFK's

Secret Service detail. Behn joined the Secret Service in 1939 and was assigned to the White House in 1941. In 1946, he was promoted to the leadership of one of the three shifts that guarded the president. At the time of their appointments, the agency had 536 permanent positions, including office workers and other non-agents. Most of them were scattered across the nation in the agency's sixty field offices. In 1963, the White House detail consisted of thirty-six special agents. In addition, there were six special agent drivers, eight special agents assigned to the Kennedy family, and five special officers detailed to the Kennedy home in Hyannis Port, Massachusetts. On the fated trip to Dallas, Texas, there were twenty-eight special agents in the presidential entourage. And while the number of Secret Service agents increased during JFK's tenure in the White House, training them was not, apparently, a priority. Former agent Larry Newman remembered that "On my second day on the job as an agent, they put me in the rear seat of the president's limousine. A supervisor on the detail placed a Thompson submachine gun on my lap. I had never seen a Thompson, much less used one."[7]

In the first six weeks of the Kennedy presidency, the threatening mail increased by 300 percent. During Kennedy's first year in office, the Secret Service investigated 870 threatening letters and White House police turned away 643 callers seeking to see the president about grievances. The figures were 50 percent higher than the final years of Eisenhower's presidency.[8] The agency viewed the increase in threats as "alarming."

— — —

The Secret Service was worried about the Kennedy family's active lifestyle. After he was elected president, Kennedy was briefed by Secret Service chief Baughman, who told him not to leave his protectors behind at any point.[9] According to Secret Service agent Gerald Blaine, JFK was a challenge to protect, especially in a motorcade. Kennedy liked to stand up in an open-top car, wave to the crowds, and get out and shake hands. Kennedy often plunged into crowds with little warning.[10]

Technically, Secret Service chief James J. Rowley had the authority to forbid JFK from taking a walk, tell him where to go fishing and where to take a vacation, and veto a visit to a foreign country. But as the Secret Service served at the pleasure of the president, such authority was practically useless, and agents had to accommodate themselves to the president's wishes.

Nevertheless, his agents were shocked at the way Kennedy put his life in danger during his assignations with women.[11] The president once escaped his detail during a visit to New York's Carlyle Hotel. He returned around midnight and asked his agents, "Is there anything you'd like to talk about?" They were not amused.[12]

In the late 1990s, Seymour Hersh interviewed Secret Service men who were members of the president's protective detail. One of the agents, Larry Newman, was appalled at Kennedy's affairs with numerous women. He was also embarrassed when high-priced prostitutes were brought to JFK's hotel suite in Seattle in November 1961. Newman tried to stop them, but presidential aide Dave Powers intervened to usher the women right in. One of the local police officers asked Newman, "Does this go on all the time?'" Newman replied, "Well, we travel during the day. This only happens at night."[13] Newman said, "It was highly frustrating, because we thought so much of the guy.... We didn't know if these women were carrying listening devices, if they had syringes that carried some type of poison, or if they had Pentax cameras that would photograph the president for blackmail." Newman blamed JFK aide David Powers for the lax security.[14]

Former agent Marty Venker was also disillusioned at the way JFK conducted himself. He said agents were expected to set up JFK with "dates." If an agent "was new to the job," Venker said, "and wasn't aware of this fact, Kennedy would let him know pretty quickly. He'd say something to the effect of, 'You've been here two weeks already and still don't have any broads lined up for me? You guys get all the broads you want. How about doing something for your Commander-in-Chief?'" When New York call girl Leslie Devereaux visited JFK at the White House, an agent took her to the Lincoln Bedroom. When she expressed concern that she had to lie down on Lincoln's bed, the agent told her, "Lady, it's the best we've got."[15]

– – –

There were a number of "scares" during the Kennedy years that turned out to be innocuous but nevertheless made Secret Service agents nervous. On November 4, when Kennedy was campaigning in Chicago, police arrested two men, twenty-three-year-old Puerto Rican Jaime Cruz Alejandro and sixty-one-year-old African American minister Israel Dabney, who separately approached the Democratic presidential candidate armed with pistols. Both men were arrested and charged with a misdemeanor for carrying a concealed weapon. Both men denied having any intent to harm Kennedy.[16] Typical of the non-serious "threats" was the case of taxi driver Stanley Berman, who received a ticket to attend the president's inaugural ball from one of his fares. Berman rented a tuxedo, hopped on a bus to Washington, and strolled into the Armory. Someone mistook him for a member of the Kennedy family and showed him to a seat in the presidential box. On his left was the president's father, Joseph P. Kennedy. Berman was there long enough to have his photo taken with Kennedy Sr. before someone realized the error. "I was sitting there," Berman said, "when three Secret Service agents surrounded me. One looked at his wrist watch and told me quietly, 'There's been some mistake. You have one minute to get out of this building and off the grounds.'"[17]

The first real threat to President Kennedy's life occurred when he was president-elect. On Sunday morning December 11, 1960, seventy-three-year-old Richard Pavlick, a former postal worker from Belmont, New Hampshire, parked his Buick directly in front of Kennedy's sprawling Mediterranean-type mansion in Palm Beach, Florida. Pavlick, dressed in a dark blue suit coat, had packed himself with dynamite that could be exploded by flicking a switch wired to a small dry-cell battery in his trouser pocket. Pavlick's intention was to smash his car into the Kennedy limousine, press the dynamite switch, and kill everyone, including himself. The dynamite was sufficient, the Secret Service later said, to "have blown up a small mountain."[18]

Pavlick carried a note that said he intended to kill Kennedy because he believed he had "bought the Presidency." He also carried a note apologizing for any bystanders killed or hurt by his assassination attempt and said that if Kennedy had not been elected president, he would instead have targeted Jimmy Hoffa, president of the Teamsters union.[19]

Richard Pavlick was known as a bitter and angry man, with no family, who lived in a three-room bungalow and had once disputed a water bill with the water company with a gun in his hand. The day after JFK's election, Pavlick confided to friends that life had lost all meaning to him. He talked of "destroying" himself and "taking others with him." At one time he disappeared for a few days. "When he came back," postmaster Thomas Murphy said, "he told me he had been to Hyannis Port. He told me the Secret Service agents were stupid. At the time, I was busy and didn't pay attention. Later, I got to wondering why a man who was so opposed to Kennedy would make a trip to Hyannis Port to see him."[20]

In the middle of November 1960, Pavlick had turned over the proceeds from his property, $2,000, to the Spaulding Youth Center in Northfield, New Hampshire. He placed his belongings in his Buick then vanished. Frequently, postcards from Pavlick addressed to various townspeople would arrive at Belmont's local post office. The cards told of how the town's residents would soon hear about Pavlick "in a big way." The cards indicated, according to the Secret Service investigation, that Pavlick was following Kennedy's travels. "So if Mr. Kennedy was in St. Louis giving a speech," postmaster Murphy said, "someone would get a post card from Pavlick there. And then if the president was in San Diego, the card would come from there."[21]

According to the Secret Service, Pavlick had also visited Hyannis Port and come within ten to twenty feet of Senator Kennedy. Pavlick had photographed Kennedy's home in Hyannis Port, noted his security arrangements, and later, in Palm Beach, taken photos of the church the Kennedys attended. He had also studied the layout of the church, attending at least once when JFK was there.[22]

In early December 1960, Thomas Murphy became highly suspicious. He called the local police and characterized Pavlick as "probably insane." Belmont police passed on the information to the Secret Service, which received the report on December 9, two days before Pavlick turned up at the Palm Beach Kennedy mansion. Agents arrived in Belmont and interviewed locals but did not issue an all-points alert for him.

As Pavlick waited outside Kennedy's Palm Beach mansion, he saw the president-elect emerge from the house with his wife and young children. Kennedy got into the car, while his wife and children waited for him to drive away. Pavlick hesitated. He later said that he decided not to throw the switch on the bomb because he "did not wish to harm her [Jacqueline] or the children." Pavlick decided to "get him at the church or someplace later."

When the president left his house on his way to St. Edward's Church, Pavlick followed. As JFK took a pew, Pavlick walked toward him. Agent Gerald Blaine followed the would-be assassin, took his arm by the elbow, and gently pulled him back. Blaine led him to the church entrance, and after a few minutes Pavlick walked out and got in his car. Blaine noted the car registration number then notified Palm Beach police.[23]

As Kennedy left the church, the congregation cut around the president-elect and his guards and lined up along the path to the limousine. Pavlick found himself surrounded by men, women, and children. Rather than risk harming a child, Pavlick abandoned his attempt. Kennedy left Palm Beach December 12 but was scheduled to return on December 16 and remain there through Christmas. While Kennedy was away, the Secret Service began tracking Pavlick.

When Pavlick visited the local post office to collect any forwarded mail, two Secret Service agents were behind the counter. Pavlick was arrested on a "technical" charge of crossing a white center strip. Pavlick was taken into custody and made no effort to deny that he intended to kill President Kennedy. He was found incompetent to stand trial and incarcerated in a federal mental institution and later to a New Hampshire hospital, from which he was released on December 13, 1966, having never stood trial. Pavlick died in 1972.

JFK received hundreds of threatening letters during his presidency, including more than a few from men serving time in prison psychiatric wards.

JFK was also subject to the attentions of "repeat offenders." An "Italian born man" was arrested in 1962 after he had written a letter to the president that read, in part, "I wish to advise that if the President of the United States resists my commands, I will bash his brains in alive." He had previously been sentenced for sending a threatening letter and obscene telegram to President Truman in 1946. The patient said he was only trying to indicate to the president that if he "had the power to remove the President's brain, he would give him a different brain so he could understand how it feels when people do not have enough money to clothe and feed themselves properly."[24]

Like all presidents, Kennedy was targeted by groups and individuals who were angered at his foreign and domestic policies. In early April 1961, a few weeks before the Bay of Pigs fiasco, the Secret Service investigated a murder and kidnapping case by a pro-Castro Cuban group in the United States. Agents received reports that the group had been plotting to either kidnap or kill Kennedy, his wife Jacqueline, and their two children, John-John and Caroline. The agency tracked down four suspects in the Palm Beach area, JFK's winter home, and kept the group under surveillance. No arrests were made, however, perhaps because publicity over the case scared off the plotters.

Six months before President Kennedy was assassinated in Dallas, Texas, he came very close to being shot in Nashville, Tennessee.

According to the *Nashville Banner*, during a visit to a local high school in May 1963, the president was approached by a man with a gun underneath a sack. The man was tackled by agents and led away. The newspaper's source alleged that the incident was hushed up because the Secret Service feared "copycat" attacks.[25]

Foreign travel did not offer Kennedy reprieve from assassination threats. Ahead of a June 1963 trip to Ireland, police were alerted to two telephone messages alleging the president would be assassinated during his trip. The threats turned out to be bogus, but extra security precautions were taken. Secret Service agents were allowed to carry sidearms, even though it was against the law for foreign security personnel to be armed.[26]

It has been alleged that plotters arranged Kennedy's assassination during a presidential visit to Chicago four weeks before his death in Dallas and that the presidential visit was canceled because of the "plot." In the late 1970s, a former Chicago Secret Service agent, Abraham Bolden, told the House Select Committee on Assassinations (HSCA) that the FBI sent a message to the Chicago Secret Service office, stating that there would be an attempt on Kennedy's life in Chicago on November 2 by a four-man hit team using high-powered rifles.[27] When Kennedy's Chicago trip was canceled, Bolden claimed, the assassination plans were then adapted to Dallas and Oswald became the designated assassin.

The HSCA looked into Bolden's allegations and concluded that his story was of "questionable authenticity." The HSCA also investigated the alleged Chicago plot, but it "was unable to document the existence of the alleged assassination team. Specifically, no agent who had been assigned to Chicago confirmed any aspect of Bolden's version." The HSCA said that "One agent did state there had been a threat in Chicago during that period … but he was unable to recall details."[28] Former Secret Service agent Gerald Blaine also debunked Bolden's allegations by checking Secret Service files and discovering "pages and pages of information that refuted all the claims [Bolden] was making."[29] He also confirmed the president's trip had not been canceled because of an alleged "plot." The trip was canceled, Blaine said, because of a coup in Vietnam when the Diem Brothers were assassinated.[30]

There was a threat originating in Chicago, but it was far removed from Bolden's invented scenarios. On October 30, two days before the president was due to visit Chicago, the Secret Service learned that Thomas Arthur Vallee had allegedly become a threat to the president. Vallee was a sixty-two-year-old Marine Corps veteran and John Birch Society member with a history of mental illness who lived in Chicago and was outspokenly opposed to JFK's foreign policy. He also claimed to be an expert marksman.

Vallee's landlady had found a collage of the president and local politicians made from newspaper clippings that was taped to the wall of his room. Threatening remarks accompanied the photos. She tipped off the local police, who forwarded the information to the Chicago office of the Secret Service. Agents went to Vallee's apartment while he was at work. The next day the landlady phoned the Secret Service and told agents Vallee was planning to take a day off work—the same day Kennedy was due in Chicago. The next day Vallee was stopped by police for a minor traffic violation, and when officers searched his car, they arrested him for carrying a concealed weapon, an illegal hunting knife. When they searched his apartment, they found an M1 rifle and 2,500 rounds of ammunition. Vallee was arrested but released from custody on November 2.[31]

Three threats were made against the president ahead of his five-hour visit to Tampa, Florida, on November 18, 1963. The first threatener was Wayne Gainey, who was under "psychiatric care" in Tampa, Florida, as an outpatient. In October 1963, the Secret Service discovered he had claimed the Ku Klux Klan had authorized him to kill the president. Agents interviewed his parents, and they gave assurances that their son would be in their care during the president's visit to Tampa. As an extra precaution, an agent kept the house under surveillance.[32]

The second threatener was John William Warrington, a fifty-three-year-old Tampa man who said he would be "lying in ambush" when the president visited Florida. He wanted to kill Kennedy because of the president's association with Martin Luther King Jr. Warrington had been diagnosed as paranoid schizophrenic and had been in and out of mental hospitals for the previous fifteen years. He had a long history of writing threatening letters and making verbal threats to the president and had written threatening letters to President Kennedy postmarked October 15, 16, and 17 in Tampa. He was arrested on October 18 and was held in the city jail.[33]

The third threatener was Joseph Milteer, a right-wing activist who lived in Quitman, Georgia. He told a police informant that Kennedy was going to be assassinated. Nothing came of the threats.

One day before JFK's Dallas trip, the Secret Service investigated a threat made by a twenty-one-year-old Dallas man, Russell McLarry. McLarry worked at a firm located three blocks from the Dallas Trade Mart, where President Kennedy was due to give a speech following his motorcade through downtown Dallas the next day. McLarry told two women that he would be waiting with a gun to shoot JFK when the president reached the Trade Mart. Described by his father as a "nice kid who shoots his mouth off too much sometimes," McLarry was arrested after Kennedy was assassinated. Secret Service agents reported him as saying he was "proud—no, glad" that Kennedy had died.[34] Appearing in court, McLarry insisted his comment was a joke. A federal grand jury believed him, and jurors refused to indict McLarry on a charge of threatening the president.[35]

President Kennedy was assassinated during his Dallas trip when Lee Harvey Oswald fired three shots from a sixth-floor window of the Texas School Book Depository. John David Ready had been part of Kennedy's Secret Service detail that day and was assigned to the right front running board of the presidential follow-up car. Ready, whose job was to observe the crowds and buildings, said, "I heard what appeared to be fire crackers going off from my position."[36] The vast majority of ear-witnesses heard three shots; many of them believed they were firecrackers.

Following Kennedy's assassination, the Secret Service came under severe criticism for its failure to protect the president. The HSCA determined that the Secret Service was "deficient in the performance of its duties" and that it "possessed information that was not properly analyzed, investigated or used by the Secret Service in connection with the President's trip to Dallas." The report further found that the "Secret Service agents in the motorcade were inadequately prepared to protect the President from a sniper."[37]

Although the HSCA believed that the agents' conduct was "without firm direction and evidenced a lack of preparedness," they did conclude that many agents "reacted in a positive, protective manner." The Committee praised Agent Clint Hill, who was in the presidential follow-up car, for having "reacted almost instantaneously" when the shots rang out in Dealey Plaza. It also singled out Agent Lem Johns, who left Vice President Johnson's follow-up car in an effort to reach the vice president's limousine, for praise. The committee also noted that "other agents were beginning to react approximately 1.6 seconds after the first shot."[38] But if agents had been standing on the right rear step, they would have blocked Oswald's sight on Kennedy.

Arguably, blame for the poor protection afforded the president can be shared. According to author Ronald Kessler, who interviewed a number of agents who had been on Kennedy's detail, JFK's recklessness eventually contributed to his death. "Despite warnings of violence in Dallas," Kessler wrote, "he refused to let Secret Service agents ride on the rear running board of his limousine in the motorcade on November 22, 1963. Since the 'kill shot' to the president's head came 4.9 seconds after the first shot that hit him, Secret Service agents would have had a chance to protect him." Kessler cited Secret Service director Lewis Merletti, who confirmed the theory. "An analysis of the ensuing assassination," Merletti said, "including the trajectory of the bullets which struck the president, indicates that it might have been thwarted had agents been stationed on the car's running boards."[39]

Other government agencies were also culpable. The FBI failed in its duty to keep Oswald under observation during the presidential visit, even though the bureau had a file on Oswald that traced his movements back to time he spent in the Soviet Union. Two weeks before the assassination, Oswald marched into the local FBI office in Dallas and created a scene, complaining about the harassment his wife was receiving from its agents, who were trying to keep track of the ex-Marine Russian defector.

Kennedy's assassination had a terrible impact on agents and their families. Agent Clint Hill, who famously rescued Jacqueline Kennedy as she climbed on the trunk of the limousine after her husband was shot, sunk into a downward spiral of depression and alcoholism. In 1990, when he tried to make sense of his role in the assassination, he visited Dealey Plaza again. "I walked in Dealey Plaza for a long time," he said, "looking back and forth and up and down, at every angle, for everything possible that I could think of. How could this have been avoided? What could we have done differently? Where did we go wrong? Why did it happen?" Hill finally came to the conclusion that "because of everything that happened that day [including the weather, the configuration of the streets and the position of the shooter] that every advantage had gone to [Oswald] that day. And we had none. So I realized that based on all those conditions, there was nothing that I could have done. And finally I accepted the fact that what had happened was something that I could not avoid. And so that was a great deal of relief to me."[40]

Years later, however, the eighty-year-old Hill said, "I wasn't thinking of my own safety. I thought 'I have to shield them'…. In the same instant, blood, brain matter and bone fragments exploded from the back of the President's head … and splattered all over me—on my face, my clothes, in my hair…. The impact was like the sound of something hard hitting a melon shattering into cement. I completely failed in my responsibilities. The President was killed on my duty."[41]

Theories abound over Oswald's motivation for assassinating Kennedy. In the 1980s, Jean Davison's *Oswald's Game* gave readers a logical explanation: the assassin was a wannabe revolutionary who worshipped Cuba's Marxist dictator Fidel Castro. According to Davison, Oswald likely acted out of a distorted sense of political idealism.

In recent years Vincent Bugliosi's *Reclaiming History* examined every theory and every conspiracy claim. The former Los Angeles lawyer, who became famous for his prosecution of hippie killer Charles Manson, took the debate about conspiracy allegations a step further by providing a devastating no-nonsense approach to the ridiculous assassination scenarios constructed by conspiracy authors, all of whom, as his book ably demonstrates, deliberately skewered the evidence in the case. His book was a masterwork that decisively marginalized JFK conspiracists.

Fifty years after Kennedy's assassination, there has not been any credible evidence showing that JFK's assassination was the result of a conspiracy. Sophisticated reenactments of the assassination using state of the art technology (computer models and laser-assisted weaponry) have shown that three shots were fired, all from behind and from the direction of the sixth floor of the Texas School Book Depository, where eyewitness Howard Brennan placed Oswald at the time of the shooting. The rifle and the pistol were traced directly to Oswald. Spectrographic analysis of photographs purporting to show gunmen on a "grassy knoll" reveal only light and shadows. Neutron-activation analyses of bullet fragments support the single-bullet theory, which was central to the single-assassin conclusion. A computer-enhanced version of the Zapruder film has confirmed that Oswald could have fired the three shots in the time sequence required. Ballistics experts have testified that Oswald's rifle was more than adequate for the job. Forensic pathologists and physicists have proven that the backward snap of Kennedy's head is consistent with a shot from the rear.

Incontrovertible evidence links Oswald with the murder weapon. And credible eyewitness testimony and circumstantial evidence established that Lee Harvey Oswald fired the shots that killed President Kennedy.

CHAPTER FIVE

VOLUNTEER

[It] was as brave an act as I have ever seen anyone perform.
When a man, without a moment's thought or hesitation,
places himself between you and a possible assassin's bullet
you know you have seen courage. And you never forget it.
—President Johnson, speaking about
Secret Service agent Rufus Youngblood

Lyndon Baines Johnson, who had been seated in his car traveling behind JFK's limousine in Dallas, Texas, was the only president in American history who witnessed his predecessor's murder.

At age thirteen Johnson boasted to his school friends that he was going to be president someday. Johnson went on to become a Texas congressman, U.S. Senate majority leader, and vice president after losing his bid for the Democratic nomination for president in 1960 to John F. Kennedy.

When he was Senate leader, Johnson told colleagues he was destined for the presidency. But, frightened of failure, Johnson waited too long to announce his candidacy for the 1960 Democratic Party presidential nomination, which gave JFK a head start. When LBJ accepted the vice-presidential nomination, he told friends that one in four presidents had died in office and that he had a good chance of becoming president someday.

Johnson spent his three years as vice president sulking and complaining that he had nothing to do. The vice presidency fueled his extreme inferiority complex. Many of Kennedy's White House staff held Johnson in contempt, which added to Johnson's feelings of inferiority. Behind his back, Kennedy aides poked fun at Johnson for his clumsy, unsophisticated ways. JFK's brother Bobby was especially contemptuous of Johnson, whom he saw as mean, vicious, and bitter.

JFK marginalized Johnson, meeting with him very rarely. The evidence suggests Kennedy was ready to drop Johnson in the coming 1964 presidential election. Johnson was also being investigated for making a fortune from selling political favors.

As Johnson rode through Dallas behind the president's Secret Service follow-up car on November 22, 1963, he appeared to be staring into the political abyss. When the shots rang out in Dallas, however, everything changed.

— — —

As vice president, Johnson was difficult for many Secret Service agents to deal with. According to aircraft steward Jack M. Woodward, when Johnson was vice president, "He did not like the Secret Service and he would try and sneak away from them ... I made the round the world tour with Mr. Johnson, and I did the same things for him that I would do for the president—laid out his clothing and so forth. He was a difficult man." Woodward said he "didn't cotton to Johnson because of his bull-in-the-china-cabinet type of carrying-ons. [Johnson] wanted everybody to know who he was, and what he was ... he would be getting into conferences with his staff, and so forth, and if someone disagreed with him, the first thing to come off was his shoe, and he would pound the table with the heel."[1]

On the day of Kennedy's assassination, as Oswald opened fire, Agent Rufus Youngblood bolted over the front seat of the vice president's car and threw his body on top of Johnson.

Johnson said Youngblood's quick reaction "was as brave an act as I have ever seen anyone perform. When a man, without a moment's thought or hesitation places himself between you and a possible assassin's bullet you know you have seen courage. And you never forget it."[2] Youngblood received the Treasury Department's "exceptional service" award for his bravery, and Johnson had him appointed deputy director under Secret Service chief James Rowley.

Five years later, Johnson said he would never forget "that day in Dallas when a great big husky roughneck from Georgia threw 185 pounds of human weight on me and said 'down.' And there wasn't any place to go but down, because he was on top of me. His life was being offered to protect mine."[3]

Despite Johnson's admiration for Rufus Youngblood, he turned to Jackie Kennedy's senior agent for advice about his security arrangements. Johnson frequently phoned Agent Clint Hill, telling him he had been having premonitions that he would be assassinated.[4] In a series of late-night conversations, Hill reassured Johnson that he would be there when he was needed.

After Kennedy's assassination, his Secret Service presidential detail was integrated with Johnson's. Gerald Blaine said the effect was "not in any way seamless ... the cohesiveness of the Kennedy

Detail unraveled like a slow death." Blaine said the "joking and the camaraderie between the agents disappeared instantly...."[5] Part of the problem, he said, was that LBJ's agents were conscious of the fact JFK's detail had "lost" a president, and they began to triple and quadruple check the new president's security arrangements.[6]

The director of the White House Military Office, Bill Gulley, said the Secret Service "kept Johnson scared to death ... [they] never missed an opportunity to frighten the president. Before he went anywhere they'd tell him all about the possible assailants that were last known to be in the area, or that could be coming to the area, or that they had lost sight of but might possible turn up in the area."[7]

Gulley said that Johnson did not respect his agents. "Look at those bastards back there," LBJ once said, "They're supposed to be Secret Service but they look like a bunch of goddamn Mexican Generals...."[8] Dennis McCarthy, who served on the White House detail during the last two years of Johnson's presidency, said the president treated agents who accompanied him on visits to his Texas ranch as though they were "hired help."[9] The president often ordered them to carry out menial jobs including washing his car. Agents acceeded to LBJ's wish for the pool to be cleaned at his ranch but drew the line at washing the car.[10]

Most of Johnson's detail disliked him, some to the point that they looked for ways to "get even" with him. When the president ordered one of his agents to walk his dog during a rainy stay at his Texas ranch, the agent took the muddy dog to the president's bedroom and left it there. The next morning, LBJ ordered that his dogs be cleaned up before they were returned to him.[11]

Agents who had been on LBJ's vice presidential detail advised their peers "to stand up to [LBJ] or he would bowl you over."[12] One agent took that advice. Once when he was seated in the front seat of the presidential limousine, he was struck by a newspaper-wielding Johnson. When the agent asked the president to stop hitting him, LBJ ignored him. The agent ordered the driver to stop the car, opened the back door, and punched the president in the eye.[13]

Johnson did not know the names of any of his agents except for three or four of the most senior members of the detail. He would usually simply shout, "Secret Service!" followed by some type of demand.[14] Johnson sometimes got violent with the agents, pushing them and, according to former agent Tony Sherman, on one occasion even knocking an agent off a motorcycle.[15] Johnson, who had a quick temper, would frequently swear at his protectors. "You never knew what kind of mood he would be in and what might suddenly set him off in a tirade," Gerald Blaine said.[16] McCarthy said Johnson was "generally a royal pain to deal with."[17]

Rufus Youngblood took a more balanced view of Johnson, saying, "[LBJ] ... had a streak of impetuosity ... [he] could chew you out in a way that would have been the envy of a seasoned Marine drill instructor, yet, when the mood was on him, he could be the most sentimental of men, sometimes almost to the point of being maudlin. If you could not adjust to this pendulum action, it could be unusually difficult working with him."[18]

Johnson was not altogether insensitive about the demands he made on his protective detail. In 1966, he invited twelve agents and their wives to a pre-Christmas barbecue on his ranch. The group had a tour of his ranch, and each wife received a gift of an oak tree picture autographed by the president.[19] Shortly before he left the presidency, during a ceremony on the White House lawn to honor James Rowley for his distinguished service, Johnson acknowledged that he had been less than civil with some of his agents. "A lot of things you have had to live with through me," he said. "If I could rewrite them, I would change a lot of them. I have spent more time telling you what you did wrong than what you have done right. But Luci, Lynda and Mrs. Johnson remind me every day of how blessed you have been to them."[20]

— — —

Strangely, one of the most serious threats to Johnson's life came not from a would-be assassin but one of his own agents. The night after the Kennedy assassination, Gerald Blaine was assigned to protect Johnson's two-story house in Washington when he heard the sound of someone approaching, prompting him to pick up a Thompson submachine gun. He expected the footsteps to retreat with the loud sound of the gun activating, but they kept coming closer. Blaine's heart was pounding as he placed his finger firmly on the trigger. The next instant he saw the new president of the United States. Johnson had just rounded the corner, and Blaine had the gun pointed directly at his chest. "Johnson's face went completely white," Blaine later said. The agent said that a split second later he would have pulled the trigger. Just hours after JFK was assassinated, America came close to losing his successor.[21]

Lyndon Johnson was a difficult president to protect because he was a "chance-taker" and had an impulsive personality, according to White House journalist Merriman Smith. Smith said Johnson would frequently give his agents a hard time about their presence in "friendly crowds." According to Vice President Hubert Humphrey, LBJ plunged into crowds because "it is good politics" and "most important, it makes you feel very good."[22] Johnson told his agents in plain terms that he did not want them interfering by getting between him and the crowds at airports or political rallies. Accordingly, agents had to work behind him or at his side. His agents were annoyed at the way Johnson would become angry if an agent stepped in front of him to hold crowds back.[23] According to *Time* magazine, Johnson's agents "tended to be tenser and more belligerent, sometimes silencing hecklers with flying tackles."[24]

Former president Truman voiced his disapproval of President Johnson's impetuousness. Truman was aware that the president had recently rode in an open car in Pittsburgh for the first time since JFK's assassination and had been surrounded by crowds on a visit to a poverty-stricken area in Appalachia. "The Secret Service used to give me hell for taking chances," Truman told reporters.[25] During the presidential election campaign six months later, the Secret Service acknowledged that the president's life could not be adequately protected if Johnson failed to obey Secret Service rules designed to protect him.[26]

It was not only Johnson's campaigning technique that concerned agents, but also the way he would be oblivious to the risks he took in open areas. When campaigning in El Paso, Texas, in the summer of 1964, Johnson left his bulletproof car ten times to shake hands with crowds in the streets. In Providence, Rhode Island, in September 1964, he stood on top of his car to address a large crowd. And during the Democratic National Convention in Atlantic City, he frequently left himself open to an assassin's bullet, especially during his birthday celebration, when he stood on a balcony in the convention hall in bright lights while a firework display complicated security issues.[27]

Johnson's behavior on his Texas ranch also created difficulties for his detail. Johnson took every opportunity to leave his agents behind as he jumped in his car and sped off around the ranch. When in December 1963 he made his first visit to the ranch as president, Johnson left his airplane and jumped in his car with a friend, A. W. Moursand, to go deer hunting. The men eluded the Secret Service as agents rushed to their vehicles in hasty pursuit. As time passed, agents became accustomed to Johnson's routine of taking off with visitors at speeds of 90 mph.[28] On one occasion, LBJ told his agents he was going to shoot out a tire if agents got too close to his car.[29]

There was little the Secret Service could do to prevent the president from trying to elude agents. "There is no discussion more futile than the public dialogue that invariably follows threats to the life of a president," Johnson's press secretary, George Reedy, once observed. "It really doesn't matter what anyone says. There is only one man who can do anything about presidential assassination and that is the president himself."[30]

— — —

JFK's assassination prompted the Secret Service to double the number of agents to around 650 and install computers. Most importantly, the agency began to receive on a systematic basis thousands of reports from the Defense Intelligence Agency, the FBI, the Department of State, the Post Office, the Immigration and Naturalization Service, and state and local police departments. By doing so, the number of pieces of information the Service received increased from eight hundred a year to twenty thousand.

In November 1964, the special agent in charge of the Protective Research Section of the Secret Service, Robert I. Bouck, revealed that four hundred persons were regarded by the Secret Service as "definite risks to any president." He said that in the two-year period prior to the Kennedy assassination, the Secret Service had investigated 1,372 cases, with 167 resulting in arrests or convictions and 91 designated "unsolved."[31]

In 1966, a special committee of government experts found that threats against the president had more than doubled following the assassination of President Kennedy. The number of "dangerous persons" grew from 1,400 to 1,800 in two years. Individuals on the "dangerous persons" list were the biggest security problem. The list had been increasing year by year at the rate of ten a month and included more than one hundred United States "defectors" who disappeared in Communist countries. More than one hundred telephone calls had been intercepted in a single night, and in the period from 1965 to 1966, nearly a dozen intruders had been apprehended on the White House grounds. Most alarming was the discovery that people had been found carrying arms near the White House or in crowds Johnson had been preparing to pass through.

By 1968, the number of Secret Service agents had increased to around 760, a consequence of the stark increase in threats to the president's life.

Like other presidents, Johnson was the victim of "copycat" threats. Many of Johnson's threateners made associations between him and his predecessor. In December 1963, a month after the Kennedy assassination, James Francis Burns, an unemployed kitchen worker, visited the office of William Johnston, a staff assistant in the contact division of the Veterans Administration. Burns told Johnston that "if he didn't get satisfaction on his claim for a revision of his undesirable discharge, he would go to Washington and pull an Oswald and get satisfaction one way or another." He was arrested and charged with threatening the president.[32]

During the same month, the Secret Service arrested nineteen-year-old Cuban immigrant Omar Padilla in New York City for threatening to assassinate the president. Johnson was planning to visit the city for the funeral of former New York governor and U.S. senator Herbert H. Lehman. Padilla had told coworkers at a Manhattan graving plant that President Kennedy had been "asking for it" when he was assassinated and that Oswald's act was successful because of the "lack of security." He then told his coworkers he was "going to shoot LBJ."

But the Secret Service was taking no chances following the criticisms they received after JFK was killed. During his two-and-a-half-hour trip to New York to attend the funeral, Johnson was guarded by five thousand officers. The contingent of protectors included Secret Service agents, FBI personnel, uniformed police, and plainclothes police officers. Policemen were posted on roof tops within a mile radius of the venue. Despite the heavy security, a spokesman for the New York Police Department told reporters that "If someone had wanted to get the president he could have done it. There is no way to stop a determined assassin. It was the other means of assassination we were worried about. Someone could have tossed a hand grenade under the car. There is just too much to watch."[33]

On December 7, 1963, acting on a tip-off, police visited Padilla's place of work and found a makeshift target range in an eighth-floor stockroom. There were nineteen holes in a plywood and copper-plated target. Police and Secret Service agents arrested Padilla later that day at his home and found a .22 caliber rifle in his bedroom, along with fifty shells. Padilla, who insisted his remark to his coworkers was "only a joke," was charged with firing a firearm in a public place and breaking a law that made it illegal for an alien to own a rifle without a permit.[34]

The following year, the Secret Service investigated other possible sniper plots with links to Kennedy's assassination. In October 1964, LBJ was campaigning in Buffalo, New York, when agents received a tip-off about a man who had made assassination plans. When agents arrived at his workplace, they observed a rifle lying on the ledge of a window overlooking the street below, which was on the presidential motorcade route. When agents searched him, they found a single cartridge in his pocket. He told the agents that he was a brigadier general in the Minutemen and that he needed only "one bullet to do the job." He was arrested and committed to a mental hospital.[35]

The Secret Service took as equally serious the threat made by twenty-nine-year-old former mental patient Michael Vaughn Cramer. Cramer, who had a Bad Conduct Discharge from the Marine Corps, had threatened to kill President Johnson at the Democratic National Convention in Atlantic City in August 1964. He sent letters to President Johnson from New Orleans and Philadelphia. In one letter he claimed he was with Lee Harvey Oswald in Dallas when President Kennedy was assassinated. (Agents checked and found out he was in Washington, D.C., at the time.)

On March 12, 1964, Cramer wrote to FBI director J. Edgar Hoover. "I warn you. For in August, in Atlantic City, Lyndon B. Johnson will follow Kennedy to the grave," he wrote. "I'll kill him and there ain't a thing you or the Secret Service can do about it." The letter was traced to Cramer after another threatening letter he wrote in the San Francisco City Jail was intercepted by guards on April 1. Cramer had been arrested on March 20 for burglary and forgery and given a six-month sentence. On April 22 Cramer was visited in the San Francisco jail by Secret Service agents. He told them that if he had not been in jail he "would have gone to Atlantic City in August to kill President Johnson."[36] After undergoing psychiatric treatment at the U.S. Medical Center for Federal Prisoners in Springfield, Missouri, Cramer was held to be sane and sentenced to five years in prison.[37]

Many threateners actually accused the president of being behind JFK's assassination. Fifty-eight-year-old Everett DeHarpote sent a letter to the White House in 1965, in which he stated, "Johnson killed John Fitzgerald Kennedy…. Have made arrangements to keep my mother away from radio and television because I'm going to kill that dirty skunk."[38] Thirty-six-year-old ex-convict Walter Daniel Hendrickson had been paroled from Sing Sing Prison in New York in 1956 and had subsequently been convicted for burglary, grand larceny, and assault, serving prison sentences in Columbus, Ohio, Elmira, New York, and California. He had become obsessed with the JFK assassination and mailed a letter in April 1965, threatening President Johnson's life. His letter stated: "This is to inform you that your turn will come. I will do a better job than Oswald and will succeed in escaping."[39]

The Secret Service issued an all-points bulletin for Hendrickson's arrest and described him as "armed and dangerous." In July 1965, Hendrickson's name was seen by Amarillo police, which had him in custody for stealing a rental car in New York. LBJ had been in New York at the time the car was stolen. They contacted the Secret Service, which interviewed then arrested the would-be assassin. Hendrickson pleaded guilty and was given a three-year prison sentence for threatening President Johnson.[40]

The following year, two further JFK assassination "copycat threats" were investigated by the Secret Service. On November 14, 1965, thirty-one-year-old Billy Ray Pursley of Summersville, Georgia, was charged with threatening President Johnson. Pursley told the store clerk who sold him a rifle, which was the same type used in the Kennedy assassination, "Do you know why I want this … to kill LBJ?" The clerk called the FBI, and Pursley was arrested. He was found guilty, given an eighteen-month suspended prison sentence, and placed on probation for three years.[41]

In March 1966, twenty-seven-year-old Air Force veteran Oswald S. Pick called the FBI and said he was going to kill President Johnson and that "two Cubans had put him up to it." He also challenged the FBI to find him before he carried out his threat. FBI agents thought Pick's first and last name may in some bizarre way have connected the would-be assassin to JFK's killer. (Pick was the surname of Lee Harvey Oswald's half brother.) Pick was tracked down and arrested as he was about to board a Washington, D.C.–bound train. Pick pleaded guilty in a federal court and was given a five-year prison term.[42]

— — —

According to James Rowley, LBJ faced a greater threat than those directed against former presidents. "The Secret Service," Rowley said, "has become concerned about the rising crescendo of national militancy and confrontation and instances of the preachment of assassination and violent revolution … in my view, the militancy of the dissident groups in our midst will increase in fervor. The questioning of all authority and the frequency of attempts at the disruption of our society will continue. This activity could generate a greater propensity for attacks upon our leaders."[43]

President Johnson's efforts to pass the 1964 Civil Rights Act and 1965 Voting Rights Act attracted threats from race-hate groups. But he also faced threats from black militants.

One such threat was made by black militant Robert Watts. Watts had participated in a discussion group dealing with police brutality at a DuBois Clubs meeting. Watts allegedly made a statement that he would refuse induction into the armed forces, and "if they ever make me carry a rifle the first person I want (or would want or would like to have) in my sights is LBJ." The following day he was arrested by Secret Service agents for threatening the life of the president. Watts was found guilty, but the U.S. Supreme Court reversed Watts's conviction. The court ruled that only "true" threats were outside the First Amendment and that Watts's statement was "a kind of very crude offensive method of stating a political opposition to the President."[44]

— — —

The risk of assassination faced by Johnson diminished in his final two years as president. As opposition to the Vietnam War increased, the president eschewed public appearances apart from events at military bases and other "secure" areas. In 1968, when Johnson decided he would not run for a second elected term in office, the Secret Service breathed a collective sigh of relief that one of the most difficult presidents to guard was leaving office. However, they did not know that an assassin who went on to murder Senator Robert F. Kennedy first had Johnson in his sights. Sirhan Sirhan wrote in his diary of his "hatred" for Johnson and his desire to kill him. "Must begin work on … solving the problems and difficulties of assassinating the 36th president of the glorious United States … the so-called president of the United States must be advised of their punishments for their treasonable crimes against the state more over we believe that the glorious United States of America will eventually be felled by a blow of an assassin's bullet...."[45]

After leaving office, Johnson, like all former presidents, continued to be at risk of assassination. In April 1970, the staff of Johnson's office in the Austin, Texas, federal building was evacuated when an anonymous caller warned that a bomb was set to go off. Police searched the building but found nothing.[46] The Secret Service also continued to monitor letters threatening Johnson's life, many of them angry missives about the former president's handling of the Vietnam War.

In January 1973, four years after he left the presidency, agents were present when Johnson died. Two days before Richard M. Nixon took the oath of office for his second term as president, Johnson was in his bedroom for his regular afternoon nap when he was struck with severe chest pains. He called the ranch switchboard and asked for Mike Howard, head of his Secret Service detail, but he was not available. The switchboard operator contacted Agents Ed Nowland and Harry Harris, who raced to the bedroom with a portable oxygen unit and found Johnson lying beside his bed. They noticed that he had already turned dark blue and appeared to be dead. Nevertheless, they began trying to revive him. Nowland administered mouth-to-mouth resuscitation. Two doctors were telephoned. When Howard returned to the ranch, he ran to LBJ's bedroom and tried unsuccessfully to resuscitate him. Agents made arrangements to fly Johnson to a hospital in San Antonio. When the plane arrived, doctors pronounced the former president dead of a heart attack. He was sixty-four years old.[47]

CHAPTER SIX

SEARCHLIGHT

Does the world remember if Sirhan's tie was on straight?
That night Nixon went to a concert in his honor
at the performing arts center. To wear white tie and tails
and get Nixon—boy, Wow!
—Nixon stalker Arthur Bremer

I remember us watching [Jack Ruby shooting
Lee Harvey Oswald] on TV together. Art was impressed with it.
Could that have anything to do with what happened?
—William Bremer, father of Arthur Bremer

Following the assassination of Senator Robert F. Kennedy in June 1968, the Secret Service was burdened with additional protective duties. The U.S. Congress passed legislation charging the agency with protecting all major candidates for the presidency and vice presidency.

The extra work took its toll on the agents. One agent died of a heart attack while making advance arrangements for a candidate; others were attacked by anti-war demonstrators. In October 1968, a doctor who had been assigned to accompany George Wallace's vice-presidential candidate, Curtis LeMay, to Vietnam described some agents of LeMay's detail as suffering from "combat fatigue."[1]

The Secret Service was on heightened alert when Richard Nixon took the oath of office on January 20, 1969. During the inaugural parade, rocks were thrown at Nixon's limousine, and the police made numerous arrests as his detail struggled to keep anti-Vietnam demonstrators from disrupting the ceremonies. Throughout Nixon's presidency, the Secret Service feared that radical groups would try to harm the president.

Nixon was no stranger to the Secret Service, having been given protection by the agency when he served as Eisenhower's vice president. During his eight years in that office, he had received numerous threats and on one occasion came within seconds of losing his life.

The close call occurred when Nixon went on a goodwill tour to South America in April 1958. Secret Service chief U. E. Baughman had tried but failed to dissuade Nixon from making the trip. "It was like talking into a barrel," he said.[2] Baughman's fears originated with a tip he had received that "communist agents" had hired a student demonstrator to take a shot at Nixon in Caracas, Venezuela. But the Secret Service was unable to find any concrete proof.[3]

Nixon's last leg of the South American journey was Caracas. Throughout his tour, the vice president had been confronted by protestors inspired by the rhetoric of anti-American Communists. In Lima, Peru, a heckler had thrown a rock that grazed Nixon's throat and hit Agent Jack Sherwood in the face, breaking a tooth.[4] In Caracas, the danger escalated as protesters gathered along Nixon's motorcade route. The crowd was angry because the United States had given visas to deposed dictator Marcos Perez Jimenez and his security chief, Pedro Estrada. The U.S. government had also imposed quotas on oil, Venezuela's chief export.

Vice President Nixon and his wife, Patricia, were in separate limousines during the drive from the airport to the center of the capital, where they were confronted by protesters whom local law enforcement officers were unable or unwilling to control. Violent demonstrators surrounded the presidential limousine. According to General Robert E. Cushman, an executive assistant to Nixon, "When we got up into town ... a truck was driven out of a side street right in front of the convoy with the vice president in it and stopped. I think the driver ran away. And then out of the side streets came pouring this mob with bricks, guns, clubs, and they went to war on the automobiles with the people in them ... they were going to kill them."[5]

A steady stream of rocks, human spittle, and bottles rained down on the cars. But Secret Service agents prevented the crowd from reaching into the cars and pulling the Nixons out. Nixon's car was stalled for twelve minutes as agents fought to protect him. Agents Sherwood and Rodham pulled their pistols out as the windscreen of the car began to crack. Demonstrators rocked the car from side to side as they attempted to overturn it. As one agent said, "If you had been inside that car with us and heard that crowd and saw their faces you would have no doubts [they] meant to get their hands on Nixon and tear him to pieces."[6]

The Nixon party was finally saved by a contingent of Venezuelan soldiers who ploughed a path through the crowd, allowing the motorcade to continue its journey. Instead of heading to the National Pantheon, where he was due to lay a wreath at the tomb of Simon Bolivar, Nixon was taken to the American Embassy. Troops in Puerto Rico were put on alert in case the vice president needed to be evacuated.

Nixon cut short his visit after lunching with Venezuela's junta and President Larrazabal. His motorcade crossed the heart of Caracas along the same route where the mobs staged their attacks the previous day. It was protected by soldiers and police equipped with machine guns and automatic rifles packed into trucks and cars along the route. Hundreds of soldiers surrounded the airport.

The United States blamed Russia for inciting the riots. Government officials determined that Radio Moscow broadcasts not only incited violence against the United States, but also instructed Soviet agents in South America to induce riotous demonstrations against Nixon.[7]

U. E. Baughman said Nixon had been "very nearly killed" that day.[8] For his part Nixon said he had been saved from assassination only because of twelve Secret Service agents who used their bare hands to protect him from the mob. In July 1958, eight of the agents received the Treasury Department's exceptional civilian service award. The other four agents received gold medals at simultaneous ceremonies in the cities where they were assigned. "I can only say ... that had it not been for them, there's a very good chance Mrs. Nixon and I would not be able to be with you on this occasion," Nixon said. "These men ... demonstrated exceptional qualities in an emergency. They met it with the greatest skill, the greatest judgment and the greatest courage."[9]

The second major threat to Vice President Nixon's life occurred when he visited Moscow in 1959. According to two Secret Service agents, Nixon was exposed to intense levels of radiation at the U.S. ambassador's mansion, where he slept during his visit. "[The dosimeter] showed a reading of 18 and was climbing rapidly," one of the agents later reported. "I couldn't believe my eyes or the dosimeter.... When I tested the ambassador's bedroom it went off the scale." The radiation disappeared after the agents' concerns were made known to the Russians.[10]

The Soviets dreaded the possibility that Nixon would defeat his rival John F. Kennedy for the presidency, according to Anatol Golytsyn, a high-ranking KGB major who defected to the West. In fact, they had a "contingency plan" to kill him, to be carried out if he had been elected.[11]

Another known serious threat to Nixon before he became president occurred in early 1963, one day before the former vice president was due to visit Dallas, Texas. The threat came from the man who would assassinate President Kennedy. According to Marina Oswald, her husband hero-worshipped Cuban dictator Fidel Castro, and he had been angry at Nixon when the former vice president gave a speech on April 20, 1963, in which he called for the toppling of Castro and the ouster of the Russians from Cuba. After reading accounts of the speech the next day, Oswald put a pistol in his pocket and said, "Nixon is coming to town. I am going to have a look."[12]

Taking that as a threat, Marina Oswald asked her husband to follow her into a bedroom, then ran out and braced the door closed to lock him inside. She warned him that if he did not agree to stay home she would tell police about an assassination attempt he made ten days earlier against right-wing extremist and former army major general Edwin A. Walker. Oswald's shot had missed, and Walker was unharmed. After Oswald agreed not to stalk Nixon, she made him give her the pistol and all his clothes except his underwear. She tucked the pistol under a mattress.

— — —

By the end of the 1960s, the Secret Service had doubled in size to a force of 760 agents. The uniformed branch of the Secret Service had expanded from 250 to 850 officers and was given a new responsibility of guarding more than 130 foreign embassies in Washington, D.C. Secret Service chief James Rowley also brought in measures to improve the training of agents and an intelligence system that included computerized lists of potential attackers. The list increased to 100,000 names, adding one hundred new ones each week.[13]

As vice president, Nixon was "scrupulously polite" to his agents and "very appreciative of everything [the Secret Service] did," U. E. Baughman said.[14] As president, he was "courteous" and "at times even friendly, asking about our families or expressing concern if he heard about some problem," said former agent Dennis McCarthy.[15] Former agent Marty Venker said Nixon treated his agents "like ... human being[s]" and always "asked about your mother, and when somebody in your family was sick," Nixon was the first to send flowers, Venker said.[16]

Nixon's treatment of officers contrasted with that of his predecessor. On one occasion, McCarthy remembered, an agent accidentally blew the horn of the limousine when it was parked outside Nixon's lodge at Camp David. Nixon opened the door and said, "Okay boys, I'll be out in just a minute." McCarthy and the other agents present all thought the incident contrasted sharply with the way Johnson used to make agents wait "anywhere from ten minutes to ten hours."[17]

Nixon was a "very private man," according to his agents.[18] He believed his protectors were "great guys" who did a "fine job." But the president kept them at "arm's length." Nixon admitted he never got "familiar with the Secret Service. They've got a job to do. I've got a job. The minute you start getting familiar with people, they start taking advantage."[19] It would appear Nixon's detail was a mirror image of their boss. *Time* magazine described them as "characteristically aloof and well-organized."[20]

There was a consensus among agents that Nixon was reckless about his own safety during his eight years as vice president and six years as president. U. E. Baughman said Nixon showed "utter disregard" for his own safety and had "delusions of personal safety" and thus was "an assassin's dreamboat." Baughman said that Nixon came near to being killed on "several occasions," and when he took office in January 1953, the vice president told Baughman that he would accept Secret Service protection only when he was traveling outside Washington, D.C. Nixon wanted only a small guard. Later, however, he changed his views and allowed the Secret Service to assign him two men in Washington and more when he traveled.[21]

Despite the fears Baughman had for the way Nixon ignored risks to his personal safety, he did allow that the vice president was "incorrigibly brave."[22] When Nixon became president, Rufus Youngblood said that Nixon "seemed oblivious to personal danger."[23] On more than one occasion he would "grandstand" by standing on the door guard or roof of his limousine and taunt anti-war protestors with the V sign. "That's what they hate to see," Nixon told an aide.[24] On May 8, 1970, following the killings of four Kent State University students, anti-war demonstrators surrounded the White House. The Secret Service believed it was too dangerous for the staff to leave. But Nixon and his valet and one agent left in the middle of the night and went to the Lincoln Memorial to talk to students. The head of the detail quickly organized an impromptu team of agents who caught up with the president.[25]

In August 1973, Nixon tried to cut his detail in half, believing he was "overprotected." "I frankly think that one man is probably as good against a threat as a hundred," he said.[26] Like other presidents, he sometimes tried to elude his agents. On one occasion his valet drove him out of his home in San Clemente, California, the "Western White House," without informing his Secret Service detail. Nixon was in the back seat covered in a blanket; he had simply wanted to go to a local restaurant without his bodyguards. But reporters spotted him and informed the Secret Service, which soon caught up with the president.[27]

When Nixon took office, the permanent presidential detail consisted of forty men headed by Robert H. Taylor. Taylor joined the Secret Service in 1950 and was promoted to agent in charge of the presidential detail in 1968. Early in 1957, Taylor had accompanied Nixon on a trip to Africa and was one of Nixon's guards during the ill-fated 1958 Caracas trip.

Although Taylor had a good working relationship with Nixon, the chief agent frequently clashed with Nixon's staff, culminating in an incident that would lead to Taylor's firing. At a 1972 Nixon campaign rally, Taylor had to deal with Nixon's chief of staff, H. R. Haldeman, who former agent Dennis McCarthy said was a "power-hungry egotist who would do everything in his power to turn the Secret Service into his own private police force."[28] Haldeman wanted to drop ropes holding back the crowd at the Providence, Rhode Island, airport. When the president's airplane landed, Haldeman planned for supporters to rush across the tarmac for a "spontaneous" demonstration. Taylor refused to allow it and even threatened to arrest Haldeman if the chief of staff went ahead with the plan. Haldeman later took his revenge by having Taylor removed from his position as head of Nixon's detail.[29]

— — —

More than a hundred people each year were detained by agents and uniformed officers at the White House during the Nixon years.

Most were released without charge. But many were sent to St. Elizabeth's Hospital.

The Secret Service ruled that the detainees had to be "mentally ill and dangerous—to others or to themselves" to be sent to St. Elizabeth's. But staff there did not always agree with the Secret Service's decisions. One detainee, for example, believed one of Nixon's daughters loved him and went to the White House with flowers in hand. He was sent to St. Elizabeth's, but the director of central admissions said he was not "dangerous" and therefore should not have been detained. The hospital's director of central admissions, who challenged the Secret Service's decisions, was supported by the hospital's psychiatrists, who agreed that many alleged "threateners" should not have been arrested.[30]

But the Secret Service cited numerous individuals who needed to be hospitalized because they had repeatedly returned to the White House after a warning, sometimes reacting violently when confronted by agents or members of the uniformed branch. "We feel there are just some people you can't turn back on to the street," one Secret Service official said in 1971. "We don't feel they mean to kill the president but they just shouldn't be wandering around the streets."[31]

The Secret Service was sometimes accused of "over-reacting" when investigating threats. But ascertaining the level of seriousness of cases involving idle threats was difficult, because agents always needed to consider the rights of citizens who, in a moment of crude humor or innocent rhetoric, uttered words that comprised the vocabulary of a threat but did not intend to carry it out.

In 1969, the Supreme Court ruled that proof of a "true" threat to the president was required to sustain a conviction and that statements made in jest or as "political hyperbole" or "idle talk" were permissive free speech. Soon after the ruling, the U.S. Court of Appeals reversed the conviction of forty-nine-year-old Eugene F. Alexander, an alcoholic who telephoned the White House one evening from a phone booth in downtown Washington. He spoke to Secret Service agents in an hour-long conversation and uttered numerous threats to the president involving the use of "artillery." At the agents' request, he provided his name, address, and telephone number. He was arrested while still talking on the phone and convicted a few months later.[32]

Like presidents before him, Nixon was targeted by threateners who were either "repeat offenders," like twenty-year-old Harry Thomas Smith from Raleigh, North Carolina, or "mentally-ill threateners," like Eugene M. Hart of Denver, Colorado. Smith had been sentenced to two years in prison in 1967 for threatening President Johnson. He was subsequently released, and in 1971 he was sentenced to four years in prison for making similar threats against President Nixon. He was also convicted of threatening a federal judge. In 1981, the incorrigible Smith returned to his old ways and was arrested for threatening President Reagan.[33]

In 1969, former mental patient Carlos Valle was found guilty of making telephone calls threatening to kill President Nixon.[34] In 1968, the week after the assassination of Senator Robert F. Kennedy, he had stalked New York mayor John Lindsay. When Lindsay appeared on the steps of city hall for an outdoor ceremony, a police officer noticed Valle had a knife protruding from his belt. The officer pulled the knife out and arrested Valle. Valle was sent to a mental institution, and no charges were made against him. Nine months later he called the local offices of the FBI and Secret Service and threatened to kill Nixon.[35]

On March 24, 1970, a man with a mental illness telephoned the FBI office in Denver, Colorado, and gave his name as "Charles Hart."

He reported that "his brother," Eugene Hart, was en route to Washington, D.C., to kill President Nixon. The caller also phoned Paul Rundle, Secret Service special agent in charge of the Denver office.

Secret Service agent Gerald W. O'Rourke went to the Brown Palace in Denver and found Eugene Hart in the lobby. "I am going to kill the President," Hart told O'Rourke. The presidential threatener was taken to the Secret Service office and questioned by Rundle in the presence of O'Rourke. Hart's plan was to obtain a gun from a friend in California, fly to Washington, D.C., and then join a congressional tour of the White House. During the tour he would stay in the back of the group until he had the opportunity to hide. He told O'Rourke where security officers were stationed in the executive mansion. When President Nixon came down a stairway to work the following morning, Hart said, he was going to shoot him.

The Secret Service would later discover that Hart's description of the positions of security stations in the White House and the stairway used by the president were accurate. Hart was found guilty of threatening the president. He appealed the verdict, but his case was rejected by the appeals court, which stated, "We hold that Hart uttered a true threat against the President of the United States when he said he intended to kill him. It was not necessary for the prosecution to prove that Hart actually intended to carry out the threat. In the context of and under the circumstances reflected by this record, Hart's threatening language could not have been reasonably considered to have been uttered in jest or in the nature of a hyperbole."[36]

— — —

The Secret Service investigated numerous alleged "assassination plots" by left-wing groups during the Nixon years, nearly all of which came to naught. As David Greenburg acknowledged, "The prevalent fear of assassination confounded clear-eyed distinctions between genuine and rhetorical threats. Radicals exploited the uncertainty to nettle authorities while authorities used it to harass radicals."[37]

The Secret Service also feared that plots were being hatched by black radical groups, including alleged plots by Black Panthers and the allegations that a disgraced former New Orleans police officer, Edwin Gaudet, had threatened to kill Nixon on his August 1973 visit to the city, which led to a nationwide manhunt.[38]

The Secret Service used the "threatening the president" statute frequently, especially against Black Panthers who uttered threats to kill American judges and political leaders on numerous occasions. J. Edgar Hoover characterized the organization as "the greatest threat to the internal security of the United States."[39]

One alleged plot the Secret Service took very seriously came only six months after a Palestinian Arab, Sirhan Sirhan, assassinated presidential candidate Robert Kennedy. Kennedy's assassination caused law enforcement officers and Secret Service agents to fear that other Arab fanatics were planning to assassinate American leaders. In December 1968, when Nixon was president-elect, New York police received a tip-off of a plot to kill him. However, following a trial in which prosecutors used information provided by an unreliable informant, three Yemeni Arabs were found not guilty.[40]

In 1969, the Secret Service discovered an alleged plot by Cuban terrorists to blow up Nixon's Key Biscayne, Florida, home. A Cuban agent, Lazaro Eddy Espinosa Bonet, who was acting undercover as a Cuban diplomat, tried to recruit a Cuban-American servant inside the Nixon compound in Key Biscayne to draw up blueprints of the security arrangements. The agent threatened to harm the servant's family, who lived in Cuba, if he did not comply. The servant was told he would be provided with microtransmitters, which he should plant throughout the Nixon home. The transmitters would be monitored by Cuban agents in Miami or aboard fishing boats offshore. Allegedly, the blueprints were to be used to plan an attack on the compound by Cuban commandos. The attack group was to first blow up the communications complex inside the compound then strike the Nixon home. The plot was ultimately foiled when the servant told Secret Service agents about Bonet.

The U.S. State Department was convinced that the plot was serious, and they expelled the Cuban diplomat.[41]

— — —

In October 1969, the National Commission on the Causes and Prevention of Violence, which had been established by President Johnson after Robert Kennedy's assassination, issued a report that listed characteristics shared by most would-be presidential assassins. A disproportionate share of threateners, the report found, came from broken homes, had absent fathers, had withdrawn personalities, were unmarried or had failed at marriage, had an inability to hold down a job, and expressed a zealotry for a political cause. The report also said that most had some form of mental illness.[42]

In the years following the publication of the report, Richard Nixon would be targeted by six would-be assassins whose lives fit the report's "profile" in nearly every respect. All the cases were considered to be "extremely serious" by the Secret Service and very nearly resulted in Nixon's death.

In June 1971, the Secret Service discovered a plot to kill President Nixon while he addressed a convention of retired people in

Chicago. Before Nixon's arrival, forty-seven-year-old James E. Beavers, who lived in Squire, West Virginia, traveled there "with the definite intention of attempting to do some kind of bodily harm to the president," according to Chicago Police assistant superintendent Howard Pierson.[43]

Beavers, a World War II veteran, was a former mental patient who was known to be violent and "always talked about guns and killing people," his sister said. In 1950, he was found guilty of murdering his sister's husband and committed to a West Virginia mental hospital. Beavers, who owned two .32 caliber revolvers, had told relatives in the weeks before he arrived in Chicago that he was angry with the president's conduct in the Vietnam War. He had also recently been arrested on a weapons charge.

Shortly before Nixon's arrival, a woman noticed Beavers setting a revolver down on a salt box in Grant Park, which was near the hotel where Nixon was scheduled to address the convention. She notified the police, and after officers rushed to the scene, they surrounded the armed man and demanded he hand over his gun. Beavers refused and challenged officers to take it away from him. As he began to walk away, he turned suddenly and shot a police officer in the thumb. The other police officers opened fire, fatally wounding Beavers.[44]

Nine months later Nixon was stalked by Arthur Bremer. Bremer wanted to do "something bold and dramatic, forceful and dynamic. A statement of my manhood for the world to see." In fact, statements at the time of his trial indicated that he simply wanted to be a "celebrity."

Bremer decided around March 1, 1972, to assassinate either the president or Alabama governor George Wallace, who had been campaigning around the country in the Democratic Party's presidential primaries. Bremer wrote in his diary:

"Life has been only an enemy to me. I shall destroy my enemy when I destroy myself. But I want to take a part of this society that made me with me. I choose to take Richard M. Nixon.... Now I start my diary of my personal plot to kill by pistol either Richard Nixon or George Wallace. I intend to shoot one or the other while he attends a champagne [*sic*] rally for the Wisconsin presidential primary.... I am one sick assassin.... I have to be within spitting distance of Nixon before I can hit him ... got to think up something cute to shout out after I kill him, like Booth did—Nixon's the One! And how! Ha! Ha! Ha!"[45]

Bremer learned that President Nixon was scheduled to meet with Pierre Trudeau, the Canadian prime minister, in Ottawa on April 13, 1972. He hastily flew back to his hometown of Milwaukee, Wisconsin, to collect his two pistols and ammunition and then began to make his way to Ottawa.

When he arrived in Ottawa, Bremer discovered through newspaper reports the motorcade route into town and "drove up and down it to get familiar with it."

Bremer attempted to get into Uplands Air Force Base, the military airport where Nixon was scheduled to arrive. "From the very beginning of this plan," Bremer wrote, "I planned to get him at the airport as he was addressing a happy Canadian crowd." Bremer dressed in his conservative business suit and wore a "Vote Republican" badge. He placed one of his guns in his pocket and "felt added confidence with a suit, short hair and shaved." But at the airport, Bremer was told there were no facilities for the public.

Bremer left the airport and found a vacant service station along Nixon's motorcade route. He waited in a chilly drizzle for forty minutes to an hour. "My fingers got numb," he wrote, "and I thought that wouldn't do." Bremer sat in his car to warm up then drove up and down Nixon's motorcade route for two hours, surprised that police did not stop him in his easily identifiable dented blue Rambler car with yellow Wisconsin license plates. When he found a spot to park, he stood waiting with a gun in his pocket, fantasizing about killing Nixon by shooting over the shoulder of one of the police officers who lined the motorcade route into the city. Bremer was uncertain that the bullets from his revolver would go through the glass of Nixon's limousine, "I didn't want to get killed or imprisoned in an unsuccessful attempt. Couldn't afford that," he wrote.[46]

But when Nixon's limousine appeared, it flashed by too quickly for him to get off a shot. "I had a good view as he went past me," he wrote, "and still alive.... He went before I knew it ... like the snap of the finger."[47] He walked back to his car believing "the best day to make the attempt was over.... You can't kill Nixie boy if you can't get close to him."

Bremer made a second attempt to get near Nixon during the president's visit to Ottawa's Parliament Hill on April 14. Bremer had been captured on a Royal Canadian Mounted Police video standing near Ottawa's Eternal Flame. As Nixon was preparing to leave Canada's legislative building after addressing the House of Commons, Bremer saw what he thought to be the president's car and went immediately to his hotel to collect his gun. He confessed he had "stupidly took time" to brush his teeth and change his suit. "When I arrived back," Bremer wrote, "the car was gone."[48]

Bremer would later learn that Nixon's security was especially tight that day due to the fear of anti-war demonstrations. Bremer cursed the demonstrators for foiling his assassination attempt. After three days of foiled plans, Bremer gave up and returned to Milwaukee. After considering shooting presidential contender George

McGovern, he decided to assassinate George Wallace. "I've decided Wallace will have the honor," he wrote. Bremer shot Wallace during a campaign rally for the presidential candidate in Laurel, Maryland, in May 1972. When police searched his car, they discovered two books about Robert Kennedy's assassin, Sirhan Sirhan. Bremer spent thirty-five years in prison and was released on parole in Maryland in 2007.

Three months after Bremer shot Wallace, the Secret Service investigated an "assassin-for-hire" case in New York City. Andrew B. Topping was a twenty-seven-year-old "well-off" investment banker and right-wing radical whose wife had recently committed suicide. When police came to his apartment to investigate the suicide, they noticed Topping had "several guns," including a .45 Webley, the same kind Topping's wife used to kill herself. Topping was arrested and charged with firearms violations but released on his own recognizance pending his trial.

A week before his arrest on the guns charges, Topping, who blamed "pro rightist forces beyond his control" for his wife's death, had made a request for an appointment to see President Nixon, which prompted Secret Service agents to interview him and carry out a background check. A short while later, one of Topping's acquaintances arrived at Secret Service offices in New York and told agents that Topping had asked him for assistance in finding an assassin who would kill the president. The Secret Service arranged for one of their undercover agents, Stewart J. Henry, to pose as an assassin for hire.

On August 10, Agent Henry and the unnamed acquaintance met with Topping at the Central Park Boat Basin in New York City. After negotiations, Topping handed over $1,000 and made it clear the money was "to kill Nixon." The "assassination" was planned for

the following week. Topping was immediately arrested and taken to
a local police station. He was charged with "threatening and attempting to kill the president of the United States." During his court
appearance he was ordered to undergo "mental tests."[49] Topping
was sent to prison for his crime and returned to New York City on
his release. He died in 2006.

Later the same month, the Secret Service began a manhunt for
Ralph DeStafano, an Atlantic City resident who had written to
Nixon threatening his life. DeStafano had previously been arrested
for threatening President Johnson. Part of DeStafano's plan, which
he had outlined in his letter to the president, was to drive to Key
Biscayne, Florida, where he believed Nixon was vacationing. (In fact
Nixon was staying at his San Clemente, California, residence.) Break-
ing during his journey south, DeStafano checked into a motel near
Savannah, Georgia.

A Chatham County police officer was checking car registrations
in the motel's car park and discovered DeStafano's car, which had
been the subject of a police all-points bulletin. When the FBI arrived
at the motel, they arrested DeStefano. Agents found a .32 caliber
pistol and forty-one rounds of ammunition in his motel room.[50]

In 1973, a man described by former agent Marty Venker as an
"Illinois man" sent a letter accompanied by drawings, in which he
showed how easy it would be to kill President Nixon at a rally. The
"Illinois man" lived about thirty miles from Peoria, Illinois. He was
put on the "watch list," and when Nixon planned a visit to Pekin,
Illinois, via Great Peoria Airport, the Secret Service asked local police
to watch him at all times until the president left the region.

On June 15, 1973, the "Illinois man" drove to the airport shortly
before Nixon's plane landed. When he parked his car, a police officer

noticed a high-powered loaded rifle in the back seat and arrested him. According to Marty Venker, "[The Illinois man] said he had been heading out on a hunting trip and he got lost." Venker did not believe him, but as the Secret Service did not have any real grounds to hold him, he was released. Venker believes that a real threat of assassination had been foiled that day. Unfortunately the "Illinois man" sued Venker and was awarded an out-of-court settlement.[51]

Samuel Byck was one of those rare would-be assassins who make direct threats against the president before putting their assassination plans into effect. He was a failed businessman who blamed Nixon for all his failures. Byck was also fascinated by Mark "Jimmy" Essex, who used a high-powered sniper rifle to kill six people before he was gunned down by New Orleans police. Essex's slogan on his apartment wall, "Kill pig Nixon," had great meaning for Byck, according to Professor James W. Clarke.[52]

Byck had been investigated by the Secret Service in 1972 for threatening the president. No charges were brought against him. On Christmas Eve 1973, he picketed the White House as Santa Claus, carrying a sign that read, "Santa Sez: All I Want For Christmas is my constitutional rights to peaceably petition my government for redress of grievances."

In 1974, less than a week after Robert Preston was shot by police after landing a helicopter on the White House lawn, the forty-four-year-old Byck carried out a plan he called "Operation Pandora's Box," which called for him to hijack a commercial airliner and crash it into the White House. Early on February 22, 1974, Byck sent newspaper columnist Jack Anderson a tape describing his plan to kill the president. Listening to the tape, Anderson heard Byck say, "I will try to get the plane aloft and fly it toward the target area, which will be Washington, D.C. I will shoot the pilot and then in the last few minutes try to steer the plane into the target, which is the White House."

Later that day, Byck went to Baltimore-Washington International Airport carrying a pistol and a gasoline bomb. He forced his way onto a Delta flight destined for Atlanta by shooting a guard at the security checkpoint. Entering the cockpit he ordered the crew to take off. But after they informed him it was impossible to depart without removing the wheel blocks, he shot the pilot twice and the copilot three times. The copilot died instantly. Police outside the airplane shot into the cockpit and hit Byck twice. After falling to the floor, he put the revolver to his head and killed himself.[53]

— — —

In August 1974, the House of Representatives ruled that impeachment proceedings should go ahead against President Nixon after it was discovered he had lied about his role in the Watergate cover-up. Nixon resigned as president on August 8, 1974.

Threats to Nixon's life continued after he left office, including a kidnapping plot organized by al Qaeda in 1993 aimed at winning the release of Muslims being held in federal custody in connection with the World Trade Center bombing. The plot was revealed when an informant, Emad Salem, taped a plotter who admitted he planned the kidnap plot at the suggestion of terrorist El Sayyid Nosair, who had been convicted and imprisoned for terrorist acts. Nixon and former Secretary of State Henry Kissinger were to be exchanged for the release of Nosair. In 1995, Ali pleaded guilty to conspiracy to wage a war of urban terrorism. Sheik Omar Abdel-Rahman, the leader of Siddig Ali's terror group, and ten others were found guilty of the World Trade Center bombings and other acts of terrorism.[54]

— — —

Despite the thirty-seventh president's many accomplishments, the Watergate scandal will forever tarnish Nixon's presidency. Though entitled to lifetime Secret Service protection, Nixon gave it up in 1985. He died in 1994.

CHAPTER SEVEN

PASSKEY

Secret Service agents found Gerald Ford to be a decent man who was always respectful and polite to agents and regarded their work as important.
—Author Ronald Kessler

I went out and looked at this crowd on the other side of the street [from the St. Francis Hotel, San Francisco] and I got a bad feeling ... this sense of dread really.
—David Hume Kennerly, White House photographer

G erald R. Ford was the only politician who served as vice president and president but was never elected to either office. And of the nine vice presidents who filled a vacant presidency, Ford was the only one who was not elected. He was appointed and confirmed as vice president in October 1973, when Spiro T. Agnew resigned after pleading no contest to a charge of income tax evasion. He became president after Nixon resigned nearly a year later, taking the oath of office on August 9, 1974.

Ford was as open and straightforward as Nixon was tightly controlled and conspiratorial. *Newsweek* reporter Thomas DeFrank, who knew Ford for thirty years, said he was the "most remarkably guileless political figure" he had ever known. DeFrank said Ford had "the impulse, hardwired into his DNA like nothing else, to be a nice guy."[1]

Describing himself as a "Ford, not a Lincoln," the new president told an uneasy nation that "our long national nightmare is over." He will forever be remembered for the way he restored public confidence in the White House and in the executive branch of government after the damage Watergate had inflicted. During his brief 895 days as president, Ford had to deal with inflation, a recession, high unemployment, and an energy crisis that caused long lines at gas pumps around the country. He also addressed numerous foreign policy crises and oversaw the conclusion of the Vietnam War, which ended in defeat with the fall of Saigon in April 1975.

— — —

According to former agent Joseph Petro, Ford's Secret Service agents were surprised at how affable the new president was and considered him to be a "truly nice man."[2] Dennis McCarthy said Ford was "very popular with the White House Detail" and a man who was exactly as he appeared to be, "a nice guy trying his best to do one of the most difficult jobs in the world, which in his case hadn't been sought."[3]

Former agent Marty Venker said Ford was "well-liked" by agents. They considered the president to be "singularly good-humored ... a real agent's man...." Ford had a generous nature, Venker said. "When agents were shivering outside at Camp David," he wrote, "Ford would sneak them an egg sandwich when the boss wasn't looking. He'd wink and say, 'Boy, it's cold out here. I'll get you a cup of coffee.'" Ford also saw the humor in having a security head who looked very much like himself. According to Marty Venker, whenever Dick Kaiser exited Air Force One ahead of the president, the crowds would applaud.[4]

On the night of the Nixon resignation speech, Ford met Agent Joseph Petro and realized the agent was new to his detail. Ford shook Petro's hand and said, "I'm Jerry Ford." Petro thought to himself, "This man is two hours away from becoming the president of the United States and he has the presence of mind to introduce himself to me."[5] When Ford moved into the White House, the first reception he organized was for his vice presidential protection detail and their wives. Afterward he took them on a tour of the White House.[6]

Perhaps the only criticism agents had of Ford was that he was "cheap." Agents told author Ronald Kessler that Ford never even had pocket change for a newspaper, and at his country club in Rancho Mirage, California, he would tip caddies a single dollar when the going rate was $25.

Ford's public image was that of a "bumbler" who bumped his head on the door of the presidential helicopter Marine One, stumbled down Air Force One's steps, and managed to hit spectators when he played golf. But his Secret Service detail saw a different side of him. Agents said the president was "an expert skier who taunted agents who could not keep up with him." In a lighthearted act of revenge, his detail found an agent who was an expert skier. The agent would ski backward and wave as the president tried to keep up with him.[7]

On October 14, 1975, Ford was traveling in his presidential limousine after giving a speech in Hartford, Connecticut. As Ford's motorcade drove through the city, local motorcycle police officers blocked side streets by leap-frogging as they passed each intersection.

At one intersection, however, the motorcyclists leapt ahead too early, and a car driven by nineteen-year-old James Salamites came through on a green light and smashed into the president's car. Agent Andrew Hatch, the president's driver, swerved sharply and avoided excessive damage to both vehicles. Republican state chairman Frederick K. Biebel's hand was injured in the accident. Ford was thrown to the floor of the car by the impact, but he was unhurt. Agents, fearing an assault on the president, ran to surround the limousine as Salamites, who appeared to be in shock, was arrested and questioned. He was released a few hours later when Hartford police recognized he was not to blame for the accident.[8]

— — —

Ford was the target of "repeat offenders" such as Thomas D. Elbert, who had spent five years in prison for threatening the life of President Nixon. Shortly after being released for that crime, Elbert telephoned the Secret Service office in Sacramento and said, "I'm going to kill your boss, Ford." Elbert was arrested on August 17 after people at a gospel mission said Elbert had been bragging about his threats. He was sentenced to another five-year prison term.[9]

In 1974, President Ford became the target of a Muslim fanatic, Marshall Hill Fields. Fields turned to Islam after his father's death from cancer. He planned a "disruptive action" against the U.S. government for Christmas Day 1974. The agency had received a letter in which Fields explained his conversion from Christianity to Islam, declaring, "If it is God's will I will denounce my citizenship to this country on December 25th 1974 … and if it is God's will, I will be out of this country to seek political asylum in one of the countries now known to be a member of the 'Third World.'" Fields said he wanted to deliver a copy of the Koran to President Ford. The agency placed Fields under investigation.[10]

Around 6:00 a.m. on Christmas Day, Fields drove west in his two-door brown Chevrolet Impala and started to make what White House guards said was a U-turn. Instead, he rammed the car through the wrought iron Northwest Gate and drove up to within twenty feet of the front door of the executive mansion. Fields gunned the engine then stepped out of his car before threatening to set off sticks of dynamite taped to his body. He told Secret Service agents he was the "Messiah."

Agents with high-powered weapons hiding in nearby bushes and behind pillars of the portico withheld their fire. A standoff ensued, during which Fields said he wanted to talk to Sahabzada Yaqub Kahn, the Pakistan ambassador to the United States. When White House staff called the ambassador, they were told he had never heard of Fields. The confrontation continued for another hour before Fields asked that his demand to see the ambassador be broadcast on the Howard University radio station. The demand was met, and after he heard the broadcast on his car radio, he surrendered. Agents searched Fields and discovered his "bomb" was made of highway flares. Later a Secret Service official said they would probably have shot Fields if the Fords had been in the White House. Fields was taken to St. Elizabeth's Hospital for psychiatric examination.[11] He was sentenced to eighteen months in jail for destruction of federal property after a jury deadlocked on the question of his sanity.

One week later, a copycat threatener tried to drive into the White House grounds. He was arrested after a scuffle, and the Secret Service sent him to join Fields at St. Elizabeth's.[12]

Although President Ford was not in the White House during the incidents (he had been skiing in Vail, Colorado), they highlighted the extreme danger the president faced by "non-mentals" or "mentally ill" attackers, as the agency described them, who were determined to breach the president's security.

Between 1974 and 1976, there were many White House "intrusions" that were taken very seriously by the Secret Service although they involved no direct threat to the president's life. On Thanksgiving night 1975, Gerald B. Gainous Jr. scaled the White House wall, hid undetected for two hours, and got within reach of the president's daughter, Susan Ford, as she was unloading camera equipment from her car. Ten days later, Gainous again climbed the fence. He said he wanted to ask President Ford to pardon his father, a convicted heroin smuggler.

The following year, White House uniformed police officer Charles Garland fatally shot Chester Plummer, a thirty-year-old intruder whom Garland had told three times to put down a three-foot metal pipe that he was holding in "a threatening manner." Officers thought it was a bomb.[13] In December 1976, Steven B. Williams rammed the White House Northwest Gate on Pennsylvania Avenue with a pickup truck. He suffered cuts and bruises and was arrested and charged with destruction of government property. Williams shouted at reporters as he was led away, "Trying to wake him up before he kills us all."[14]

— — —

In 1975, President Ford was the target of a plot organized by thirty-two-year-old Gary Steven DeSure and twenty-four-year-old Preston "Mike" Mayo. DeSure was a violent, mentally deranged escapee from a Montana mental hospital who had sent threatening letters to President Ford in 1974. He had made plans to rob an armory to steal guns and dynamite to be used in the assassination plans.

After his escape, DeSure was picked up hitchhiking by Mike Mayo, an ex-convict from Virginia.

Mayo and DeSure wanted to kill Ford because he was "for the rich and they were for the poor." Their plan involved robbing a San Francisco armory to get dynamite, guns, and a sniper telescope. DeSure would create a diversion by bombing a sewer near the state capitol building. Mayo would then fire a shot at Ford.[15]

But on August 19, the two men were stopped by the California Highway Patrol at Burbank. When an officer approached their car, they took off at high speed. The officer followed but was unable to stop the fugitives before they dumped their car at the Hollywood-Burbank airport near Los Angeles. Foolishly, they left written details of their plot in the car, which police later found.

DeSure and Mayo arrived in Santa Barbara on August 24 and booked into a motel. They planned to drive to San Francisco to rob the armory but were arrested on August 26 when Santa Barbara police detective Robert Zapata was called to the motel to investigate the theft of a color television set, for which they later pleaded guilty and were given ninety days in the county jail.

The plot unraveled the day after their arrest when DeSure confessed the plot to Detective Zapata, who had been informed of the written assassination plans the would-be assassins had left behind in their car. On March 6, 1976, in the Los Angeles U.S. District Court, the two men were found guilty of planning to assassinate President Ford.

The day of the planned DeSure/Mayo plot to kill President Ford, Lynette "Squeaky" Fromme, a "disciple" of hippie leader

Charles Manson, left her apartment in Sacramento concealing a pistol under her red dress. Her mission was to assassinate President Ford.

Charles Manson was a cult leader who had masterminded two brutal Hollywood home invasions that left seven people dead. Fromme had met Charles Manson on the boardwalk in Venice Beach in 1967, the year she graduated from high school. Estranged from her family, Fromme was invited to join Manson's growing "family" of young women who were devoted to him and saw him as a charismatic "messiah-like" figure. He affectionately called Fromme "Squeaky" for her high-pitched voice.

When Manson was sent to San Quentin Prison after being found guilty of murder, Fromme made veiled threats against the judge's children and blamed political leaders for Manson's guilty verdict. The "Family" was especially angered at President Nixon, who proclaimed Manson "guilty" even before the trial ended.

Fromme said Manson had told his followers that he was mad at Nixon. Ford was just another Nixon, she insisted.[16]

Fromme had a long criminal record but had been convicted only on minor charges. On the morning of Ford's visit, Fromme decided she would kill him. "Maybe I'll take the gun," she said to herself, "I have to do this. This is the time."[17]

Around 10:00 a.m. on the morning of September 5, 1975, Fromme joined a group of spectators lining the route that President Ford would take from his Sacramento hotel to the state capitol building. He was due to meet Governor Jerry Brown then give a speech on crime and gun control to a joint session of the California legislature. Ford's motorcade was waiting, but as it was a beautiful day, he decided to walk to the capitol. After recognizing the cheers of a small crowd outside the hotel, he headed into the park area and began shaking hands with people lining the walkway.

These types of impromptu interactions by the president always create "a lot of tension in the agents," Agent Larry Buendorff said, "because we're not going into an environment that is not controlled. We don't like to do that. Yet the media, they're running with their cameras. They're trying to watch the president, watch the crowd. People start shaking hands and, you know, sometimes they hold on too long and so you're very busy trying to keep the crowd away. There's so much going on."[18]

As Ford walked through the park, he "noticed a lady in a very vivid red dress sort of walking with me as I was walking towards the capitol and all of a sudden I went to shake hands...." It was Squeaky Fromme, and she was about to reach for her .45 caliber automatic gun. Fromme said the president "had his hands out and was waving ... and [he] looked like cardboard to me." As she pointed the gun at Ford's stomach, she said, "The country is in a mess. This man is not your president."[19] Ford recoiled, put his hand up, and hunched over. He looked "alarmed, frightened," a bystander said.[20]

When twenty-seven-year-old Linda Worlow saw the pistol in Fromme's hand, she "fell to the ground,"[21] which alerted Ford's agents. Agent Larry Buendorff saw a "hand coming up with a gun." He stepped in front of the president as Fromme was "pulling back on the slide [of the gun]." He hit the gun and "stopped the slide" then pulled the gun away up to his chest. Buendorff managed to get his thumb between the hammer of the .45 and the firing pin. "She's screaming. I've got the gun and I've got her and I'm not letting go so I just pushed her away from the president," he said. "The president's going in one direction, I'm going the other direction and she tries to run and I pulled her back. She goes down on the ground and I pull out my cuffs. I cuffed her and yelled out to [an] agent. The agents covered her and they were gone." As Fromme was led away by agents, she shouted, "Easy guys, don't batter me. The gun didn't go off … it didn't go off … can you believe it? It didn't go off."

Fromme tried to kill Ford because, she told reporters after her arrest, "If Nixon's reality wearing a new Ford face continues to run the country against the law our homes will be bloodier than the Tate-LaBianca houses and My Lai put together. [Manson] wrote to us and said he was mad at Nixon and we should explain why. The Manson family has been locked up for five years for Nixon's conspiracy. The whole country was and still is dying in Nixon's thoughts. He walks loose after he dealt people's blood, lied and ruined the economy and sold us out."[22]

When Manson prosecutor Vincent Bugliosi heard about the assassination attempt, he wasn't surprised. Fromme's actions, he said, were "completely within [the Family's] life-style—to kill or attempt to kill people and in such a way as to shock the world. I'm not surprised. Not surprised at all."[23]

At her trial, Fromme's claim that she had no intention of killing Ford but simply wanted to publicize Manson's plight was rejected by the jury, which found her guilty of attempted murder. When Fromme heard the verdict, she threw herself on the floor and shouted, "You animals!" Fromme was sentenced to life in prison.

Fromme said it never occurred to her that she could wind up in prison, and when asked whether she had any regrets about the assassination attempt, Fromme said, "No. No, I don't. I feel it was fate."[24]

Seventeen days after the Fromme near-miss, Ford came face to face with another deranged woman, Sara Jane Moore.

Moore was a forty-five-year-old West Virginian who had five broken marriages behind her and four children, three of whom had been adopted by her parents.

After moving to San Francisco, Moore became friendly with radicals. And on September 22, 1975, when Ford emerged from the St. Francis Hotel in San Francisco, Moore was waiting in a crowd across the street. As she took aim at Ford and began to fire, a bystander, disabled former Marine Oliver Sipple, grabbed her gun, deflecting the shot. The bullet missed Ford by several feet, bounced off a wall, and hit a nearby cabdriver, who was slightly injured. As the shot was fired, Ford winced. He was bundled into his limousine by agents, and the car sped off at high speed. The agents were lying on top of Ford as they drove off to the airport. "I'm going to be crushed to death," Ford told them. "It's an armor-plated car. Get off of me."[25]

Following her arrest, Moore said, "If I had had my .44 with me I would have caught him."[26] The FBI case agent, Richard Vitamanti, determined that if Moore had used her other .44 gun, or if the sight of the .38 had not been faulty, she would have killed Ford. "She would have had at least a head shot," Vitamanti said, "maybe even better, because she had been practicing ... [her] shot was off about six inches."[27]

Sara Jane Moore pleaded guilty to the attempted assassination of President Ford and was sentenced to life in prison. At her sentencing hearing, Moore said: "Am I sorry I tried? Yes and no. Yes, because it accomplished little except to throw away the rest of my life. And, no, I'm not sorry I tried ... because at the time it seemed a correct expression of my anger."[28] Moore was paroled in 2007 after serving thirty-two years behind bars. In 2009, she told NBC's *Today* television program, "It was a time that people don't remember. You know we had a war ... the Vietnam War, you became, I became, immersed in it. We were saying the country needed to change. The only way it was going to change was a violent revolution. I genuinely thought that [shooting Ford] might trigger that new revolution in this country."[29]

Commentators were shocked not only by the Ford assassination attempts, but also by the realization that American democracy would have been in a parlous state had the guns aimed at Ford hit their target. Nelson Rockefeller—appointed vice president by a man appointed vice president by a president later discredited—would have been president of the United States with congressional assent but not a shred of public sanction.

Ford was "angered" by the two attempts on his life, but he insisted he should remain accessible to the public. "The American people are a good people," Ford said, "and under no circumstances will I—and I hope no others—capitulate to those who want to undercut what's good for America." He said that if a president could not appear in public and interact with the American people, "something has gone wrong in our society."[30]

In the following weeks, the Secret Service was extremely sensitive to any action at Ford appearances that might suggest an attack. During a speech at the University of Michigan, a balloon popped and Ford immediately ducked behind his podium. Agents rushed toward him and reached for their weapons.[31] Former agent Marty Venker related another incident that caused great alarm among Ford's protective detail. "One night a bunch of us were walking down a hall with Ford when a fold-up table fell on the floor. Bam! We all thought it was another gunshot. We pushed him down and piled on top of him."[32]

In the 1976 presidential election campaign, Ford became less cautious in his movements, clearly determined to show the American people that threats could not cower him. He frequently took rides in open-top limousines on preannounced routes and plunged into crowds to "press the flesh," as Lyndon Johnson described it. But he did accede to the wishes of the Secret Service and wore a bulletproof vest. Ford's first vest was bulky and made him sweat. It was replaced by a vest that was almost like an undershirt. Bulletproof linings were sewn into the vests of his three-piece suits.[33]

The Secret Service feared that Fromme's assassination attempt might encourage copycat crimes, and its fears were confirmed on September 12, one week after the Fromme attack. Ford spoke at the National Baptist Convention at Kiel Auditorium in St. Louis. On the day Ford was to give his speech, police received several bomb threats. Thirty minutes before Ford arrived, police officers spotted a man wearing a white shirt and black wig on a catwalk above the stage, armed with a .45 automatic pistol. Police gave chase, causing a stampede as mounted police galloped into the crowd. But the would-be assassin eluded police.

On September 22, 1975, seventeen days after the Fromme attack, the Secret Service arrested Benedict Silcio, a twenty-seven-year-old stevedore, in Union Square Park, San Francisco, for threatening Ford. Four hours before Sara Jane Moore fired her gun at Ford, Silcio handed a note to a cashier in the St. Francis Hotel that read, "The mission: To gun down President Ford. Need to have a room for three people." Then he ran into the park.[34]

In the months to follow, the Secret Service investigated many "copy-cat" threats they considered to be very serious. On September 30, 1975, a week after the Moore attack, a Senate committee investigating the quality of Secret Service protection was told that threats to the president's life had "tripled."[35]

A month after the Moore assassination attempt, twenty-six-year-old Michael Johnson threatened to kill the president. Johnson had been serving a prison sentence in Florida State Prison for passing a worthless check, but he escaped. He was later arrested by Hillsborough, Florida, sheriff's deputies and returned to jail. On October 24, 1975, Johnson wrote to the sheriff's office from his jail cell and confessed to plotting to kill President Johnson in 1966. The sheriff's office contacted local Secret Service agents, who interviewed Johnson. During the interview, Johnson "blurted out" his plans to "exterminate" President Ford using either an M14 rifle with a sniper scope or an elephant gun with a sniper scope. He also told an agent, "The present administration is a joke. I have no use for the president and vice president and will exterminate them." Johnson was charged with threatening the life of the president.[36]

In November 1975, the Secret Service investigated a threat from Michael Lance Carvin, an admirer of Squeaky Fromme. On November 10, Carvin phoned the Secret Service's office in Denver from the Light House Point public telephone and threatened to harm President Ford, California governor Ronald Reagan, and Vice President Nelson Rockefeller unless Squeaky Fromme was freed. He also threatened to kill Ford in a letter he sent to a Miami television station.

The same month that Carvin threatened to kill President Ford, California governor Ronald Reagan announced his intentions to challenge the president for the Republican presidential nomination. Shortly after his announcement, Reagan gave an outdoor speech in Miami to supporters gathered in front of a Ramada Inn near Miami International Airport. At the conclusion of his speech, Reagan stepped off the podium and moved along a security rope set up to keep crowds away. As Reagan shook hands, agents dived into the crowd and grabbed Carvin as he pointed a fake gun at the candidate. The California governor later said he had "gone over to that side of the audience to see an old friend. I just thought someone had fallen down and I was persuaded by the Secret Service to leave."[37]

Carvin was charged with intimidating a presidential candidate and assaulting a federal officer. Two court-appointed psychiatrists found Carvin sane and competent to stand trial. In April 1976, he was found guilty of threatening the lives of President Ford, Vice President Rockefeller, and former governor Reagan. He was also found guilty of intimidating Reagan. Carvin was sentenced to ten years in prison.

— — —

Perhaps the most dangerous threatener during the Ford years was not Fromme, Moore, DeSure, or Mayo but twenty-eight-year-old Yugoslavian immigrant Muharem Kurbegovic. The Secret Service had received information about Kurbegovic's threats to kill Ford using home-made nerve gas from the CIA. Kurbegovic, who claimed to be "The Messiah," was one of the most dangerous individuals ever to threaten a president.[38]

After immigrating to the United States in 1967, Kurbegovic moved between various engineering jobs and was considered very bright, an excellent engineer, and a personable coworker. He also had numerous conversations with coworkers about bomb construction and related matters, including one in which he asked about undertaking an extortion scheme that involved setting off a bomb, then demanding $10 million in exchange for not setting off a second.

On August 6, 1974, Kurbegovic set off a bomb in a locker in the overseas lobby at Los Angeles International Airport. More than three hundred people were packed into the lobby, many of them in the check-in line for a 9:00 a.m. flight to Hawaii. Three people were killed instantly, and thirty-six people were wounded, fourteen of them seriously. One victim had his right leg blown off.

Kurbegovic left a tape-recorded message directing police to an even larger bomb hidden in a locker in the Greyhound bus station. The depot was evacuated, and police removed one of the largest bombs in the history of Los Angeles. Kurbegovic was named "the Alphabet Bomber" because of his scheme to explode bombs at locations alphabetically to spell out Aliens of America, his imaginary terrorist group, "until our name has been written on the face of this nation with blood." The bomber had chosen the Greyhound depot because the letter "L" in the word "locker" was the second letter in "Aliens of America." The first bomb was placed at the airport because the letter "A" in the word "airport" was the first letter in "Aliens of America."[39]

Kurbegovic was simultaneously making phone calls and planting tape-recorded messages that claimed credit for other crimes and demanded changes in U.S. immigration laws. Referring to himself as "Rasim," Kurbegovic called himself a "field commander in the Symbionese Liberation Army (SLA)." The SLA was the group that kidnapped heiress Patty Hearst earlier that year. One of the tapes Kurbegovic sent claimed that deadly nerve gas concealed under postage stamps had been mailed to each U.S. Supreme Court justice.

Various witnesses tied Kurbegivic to both bombings, and by August 20, 1974, he was a suspect. Kurbegovic was arrested, and police found books on arson, explosives, and germ and chemical warfare, as well as other evidence in his apartment linking him to the bombings.

Police also discovered that Kurbegovic had assembled most of the materials for a Serin nerve gas bomb. "He was that close," Los Angeles detective Arleigh McCree, head of the Los Angeles Police Department bomb squad, said.[40]

Weapons experts Neil C. Livingstone and Joseph D. Douglas said in December 1983 that law enforcement officers with assistance from the CIA aborted Kurbegovic's plan to kill Ford.[41]

Although the Secret Service denied the agency had a record of Kurbegovic having threatened Ford, a 1987 Board of Prison Terms hearing for Kurbegovic was informed he had a history of "making threats against several public officials," and two Secret Service agents watched the proceedings.[42]

Additionally, senior LAPD detective Arleigh McCree, who led the Los Angeles police's bomb squad and headed the investigation of the "alphabet bombings," said the Secret Service told him at the time that Kurbegovic had made a threat on the president.[43]

Although he was never charged with threatening the president (prosecutors believed they had a stronger case against him on the other charges), Kurbegovic was convicted in 1980 on twenty-five counts of murder, arson, illegal use of explosives, and related charges and sentenced to life in prison.[44] From prison, Kurbegovic continued to threaten American presidents.

— — —

In the 1976 election, Ford survived an intraparty challenge from Ronald Reagan only to lose to Democrat Jimmy Carter. Gerald Ford died on September 26, 2006, at his home in Rancho Mirage, about 130 miles east of Los Angeles. He was the longest-living president.

CHAPTER EIGHT

DEACON

*It's a part of public life that gets to be routine. You always
have in the back of your mind some thought about possible injury,
but it's no different from the thoughts that I had when
I was a submarine officer. It's part of the duty and I think
the Secret Service does an outstanding job.*
—Former president Jimmy Carter, March 1981

James Earl (Jimmy) Carter's legacy as president can be described, at best, as mixed. During his four years in office, the economy deteriorated and interest rates and oil prices rose. He failed to secure the release of American hostages in Iran after sanctioning a botched rescue attempt.[1]

But Carter also balanced the budget, kept the country out of war, brought lasting peace between Israel and Egypt, reconciled China's relations with the United States, and instituted a "human rights" dimension to American foreign policy. Some historians even identify him as the real "architect" of the end of the Cold War.

— — —

Carter's relationship with his Secret Service detail was fraught with problems from the beginning. Agents, White House workers, and White House uniformed police were informed they must never speak to him unless spoken to. Carter also ordered agents to "stay discreetly" away from him.[2] "[Carter] didn't want the [White House] police officers and agents looking at him or speaking to him," White House usher Nelson Pierce said. "He didn't want them paying attention to him by going by. I never could understand why."[3] Robert Gates, who would became secretary of defense to two presidents, said Carter was "not an outgoing, friendly person ... I've always thought one of the things Presidents Carter and Nixon had in common was a not very well developed sense of humor."[4]

Carter made it clear that he wanted no regal displays of presidential power, including police sirens during his motorcades, and he wanted to replace the limousines with smaller town cars. He was also cold and dismissive of agents.[5] Former White House aide Paul Costello said Carter saw the Secret Service as "body watchers, pure and simple."[6] Agents responded in kind. During the final months of Carter's presidency, some agents even boasted that they had voted for Ronald Reagan and were unconcerned that their views might reach the president.[7]

— — —

In 1978, a year after Jimmy Carter became president, the Secret Service processed more than 14,000 cases, made 406 arrests, and obtained 311 convictions or commitments to mental hospitals. Before JFK's assassination, the Secret Service's "watch list" had one hundred names on it. By the end of the 1970s, the list came to around four hundred. Presidential threateners were interviewed four times a year. Those who resided in the city of a prospective presidential visit were watched closely. Many of the people on the list were "walking free," but most were incarcerated in prisons or mental hospitals. When they were due for release, the Secret Service was contacted.[8]

Carter's inaugural proved to be the Secret Service's first challenge. As he proceeded down Pennsylvania Avenue following his swearing-in ceremony at the Capitol, Carter suddenly got out of his limousine with his wife and walked the mile and a half to the White House, stopping on the way to shake hands with spectators. Agents quickly covered the president and Mrs. Carter and breathed a sigh of relief when their forty-minute walk ended.

Like presidents before him, Carter was the subject of numerous non-serious threateners, people whom agents believed weren't serious in their spoken intentions to harm the president.

Carter was also a victim of "repeat offenders." Perhaps the most bizarre was Louis Franklin Flowers, a thirty-seven-year-old Tampa, Florida, man who in 1978 sent a postcard to Carter, in which he wrote, "Mr. President, I am going to kill you because you are a traitor to the South." Flowers had been arrested twice before for threatening presidents and for the same reason—he wanted to be sent to a federal prison. His lawyer could give no explanation why his client wanted to be sent there, but he insisted Flowers had no intention of carrying out his threats. Flowers was found guilty of threatening the president.[9]

In April 1979, Carter received a threatening letter from fifty-eight-year-old Charles Joseph Breton. Comparing it to letters kept on file, Secret Service agents found that there were "certain similarities in writing and phraseology between the subject letter and a letter written to President Johnson on November 1, 1968, which Charles Breton had admitted writing." Breton was arrested at his Manchester, New Hampshire, home and charged with threatening the president's life.[10]

In 1977, twenty-four-year-old Edward Falvey was convicted of threatening President Carter and received probation. Twenty-six years later, while he was serving time in a New Jersey federal prison, Falvey wrote to a prison psychologist that he wanted to "spice up" his life by shooting a famous person. He suggested then-senator Hillary Clinton as a possible target. Falvey added a "hit list" to his letter, naming not only Clinton but also her husband, former president Clinton, and a number of federal judges. When Falvey was interviewed by Secret Service agents, he said he felt like "a movie star." In late December 2004, Falvey appeared in court and pleaded guilty to threatening to kill an immediate family member of a former president, earning another eighteen months in prison.[11]

Carter's Secret Service investigated many intoxicated threateners. A typical "drunk" offender was thirty-five-year-old Thomas D. Lake, who in February 1978 was arrested in a railroad yard in Duval City, Florida. When he was taken to the Duval County Jail, he told one of his jailers that he planned to hop a train to Washington and kill President Carter. Lake complained that "JFK messed up" his naval career and that he had held a grudge against presidents ever since. Lake pleaded guilty to threatening the president's life, blaming alcohol for his trouble. He was given three years' probation.[12]

Some Carter threateners were considered by the Secret Service to be "serious" but "not dangerous," including thirty-seven-year-old Fred Anthony Frederickson, a drifter who kept all his worldly possessions in an old pickup truck. On October 25, 1978, he drove to

Cedar Rapids, Iowa, to visit his sister. After the brief visit, he left to find a park where he could camp for the night. That evening he approached the gate of a corn-processing plant near Cedar Rapids, where Detective Kenneth Millsap of the Cedar Rapids Police Department served as a part-time security guard.

Frederickson talked to Millsap about where he might camp out for the night. Millsap, who was dressed in blue jeans and a sweatshirt, did not at first identify himself to Frederickson as a police officer. He described Frederickson as "anti-establishment," and Frederickson's conversation was "violent almost in its entirety." Frederickson also told Millsap that he was on his way to Washington to "kill" the president. Millsap believed the would-be assassin was serious, identified himself as a police officer, and placed Frederickson under arrest. At the police station Frederickson said, "Well, as soon as my toys get here I will eliminate all the pigs from the president on down.... I am going to blow them all up.... I start with the President and go down."

At his trial Frederickson denied having any intention to physically harm President Carter. He did admit, however, to using the threatening words. He also admitted that he had been in Washington, D.C., "ten or fifteen times," that he had been "in the White House twice," and that he had climbed over the White House fence during a civil disobedience demonstration a few years previously. Frederickson was sentenced to ten years in prison.[13]

In April 1980, Kenneth Harold Smith was serving time at the Kansas State Mental Hospital when he wrote to the president. "My name is Kenneth Harold Smith Sr. # 31600, I'm at the Kansas State Penitentiary doing a 3 to 10 yrs. for Felonious Assault with a Deadly Weapon and Criminal Damages to State Property," he wrote. "I get out on my Correctional Release Jan. 9th 1981. But if Director Robert Atkins refuses to let me out on the above date mentioned I'm going to kill you Mr. Carter when I do get out July 9th 1985, that's the end of my maximum sentence."[14]

In an interview with a Secret Service agent, Smith acknowledged writing the letter, repeated its contents as best he remembered them, and declared his intention to kill President Carter. Smith stood trial in April 1981, was found guilty, and was sentenced to serve three years in federal prison for threatening President Carter.[15]

The list of threateners during the Carter years included many individuals who were clearly mentally ill. One example was Anthony Henry, a thirty-five-year-old from Ohio who had become obsessed with the alleged "blasphemy" of placing the words "In God We Trust" on United States currency. In 1978, he decided that he must see President Carter to discuss the matter. Wearing the classical karate fighter's garb of baggy white pantaloons and blouse and barefoot, Henry scaled the White House wrought iron fence along Pennsylvania Avenue shortly before 1:00 p.m. on the afternoon of October 1, 1978. He was carrying a knife concealed inside a Bible. A short distance away, President Carter was having lunch with his wife.

As a crowd of two hundred people began to assemble to watch Henry, he charged toward the North Portico. Police officers cut him off near the front fountain, forming a ring around him. Henry kept spinning around into defensive karate stances, holding the knife and shouting anti-government slogans as officers tried to cajole him into surrendering. After around fifteen minutes, reinforcements, including dog-handling teams, were moved into back-up positions. Officers jabbed at Henry with their clubs, but during the confrontation he slashed one officer's face and another's arm. He was finally distracted enough to be thrown off balance, pulled to the ground, and hand-cuffed. Henry was taken to a guard post for questioning before being put into a police paddy wagon. As he was driven away, he shouted, "I don't know why they put 'In God We Trust' on that money." He was charged with two counts of assault and one count of unlawful entry.[16]

The following year, Carter was threatened by thirty-four-year-old Michael D. Lurie, who tried to hire someone to kill the president. According to a special agent in charge of the Cleveland, Ohio, Secret Service office, Lurie had approached a Chicago organized crime figure, John Clemente, at a party in Cleveland in May 1979 and asked him to hire hit men to kill Carter. Lurie claimed to be the Anti-Christ and head of a satanic cult called the Committee Against Physical Prejudice. He planned to establish a world government in Jerusalem. Lurie told agents his committee wanted a law to bar discrimination against people who were short, fat, disfigured, or considered ugly. He was angry about Carter's politics and said that U.S. senators were working against the Satanic Church. He had picketed the White House the previous April, attempting to interest passersby in his organization's policies, and he also appeared on a Cleveland television show to talk about bigotry against unattractive people. In June 1979, Lurie's lawyer, Bernard Berkman, said his client was a "very sick man" and that arrangements were already underway to get him institutionalized.[17]

— — —

In 1979, Carter addressed a Hispanic crowd in Los Angeles's Civic Center Mall celebrating Cinco de Mayo. Ten minutes before the president arrived, Secret Service agents noticed thirty-five-year-old Raymond Lee Harvey, an unemployed drifter from Ohio, "looking nervous" as he stood fifty feet away from the president. They detained and searched him, finding a .22 caliber eight-shot starter pistol and seventy rounds of blank ammunition.

Harvey eventually told agents he was part of a four-man plot in which he was supposed to fire the blanks into the ground, causing a diversion that would give the real assassins an opening to kill Carter. Two Mexican hit men were to assassinate the president with high-powered rifles.

A short time later, Harvey implicated a second man, twenty-one-year-old Osvaldo Espinosa Ortiz, who had been standing about ten feet away from Harvey. Ortiz was also taken into custody. The oddity of their names ("Osvaldo" is the Spanish equivalent for "Oswald") prompted references to Lee Harvey Oswald and the assassination of President John F. Kennedy.

Ortiz at first denied knowing Harvey but finally admitted that the pair had gone to the roof of the hotel the night before Carter's visit and "fired seven blanks from the pistol to see how much noise it would make."[18]

Ortiz and Harvey were eventually released for lack of sufficient evidence to charge them. FBI agent Tom Shields said, "We conducted an investigation and have satisfied ourselves that such [a plot] did not occur."[19] Secret Service spokesman Jack Warner said, "At this point we don't believe his story. Our investigation shows no evidence of a conspiracy. It sounds like the type of thing we get all the time."[20]

Some presidential threateners target presidents to become famous; others are prompted to attempt assassination in retaliation for specific policies or actions by a president. In April 1978, the Secret Service conducted a nationwide manhunt for a "37 year old, Humble, Texas man" who was considered to be "extremely dangerous." The "Texas man" was angry about Carter's Panama Canal Treaty. He stole a car in Pecos, Texas, and, on his way to Washington, D.C., picked up a hitchhiker in Flagstaff, Arizona, and two more in Albuquerque, New Mexico. He told the hitchhikers he had a gun and was on his way to the capital to kill President Carter. When the hitchhikers arrived in Henryetta, Oklahoma, they contacted the police, who in turn notified the Secret Service.

The agency discovered the "Texas man" had "[previously] indicated an interest" in President Ford. A nationwide alert was sent to all police agencies. At Springfield, Missouri, the would-be assassin developed car trouble and called a tow truck. After the car was hitched up, the Texan pulled a gun, showed a note "indicating he was insane," and told the tow truck driver that he was going to Washington to discuss the Panama Treaty with Carter. The truck driver, Bruce Fetters, complied.

The Missouri Highway Patrol and the FBI learned of the hostage situation when a motorist heard the Texan trying to contact the FBI on the truck's CB radio. Some thirty cars followed the truck across southern Missouri on Interstate 44. During the journey Fetters tried to calm the situation by faking sympathy for the Texan's anti-treaty stand. Fetters told him he would likely appear on television news and denounce the treaties if he were released. Fetters's ruse worked, and the Texan agreed to the FBI's offer to exchange Fetters for an FBI hostage. Moments after Fetters was exchanged, the FBI agent overpowered the Texan and took him to the Greene County Jail in Missouri.[21]

— — —

The Secret Service investigated at least two domestic political groups considered to be threats to President Carter's life.

In March 1977, Carter was scheduled to give a "town hall" talk in Clinton, Massachusetts, a mill town thirty miles to the west of Boston. Shortly before his scheduled visit, a factory in a nearby town was bombed by the Sam Melville–Jonathan Jackson Unit, a radical leftist group with only a few members.

The group, named after two black radicals, was formed in the early 1970s by Thomas Manning and Raymond Levasseur, two Vietnam veterans who met in a Massachusetts prison. The group was responsible for at least nineteen bombings and ten bank robberies and the murder of a New Jersey state trooper. During Carter's presidency, the Sam Melville–Jonathan Jackson Unit undertook eight bomb attacks.

The March 1977 factory bombing in Marlboro was a protest against the president's upcoming scheduled visit. "While the president wines and dines," a letter left at the scene of the bombing stated, "[we] remember our people who were brutalized in prison." The bombers also phoned the Boston FBI office and told Agent Richard Bates that "there would be more bombings." In addition to prison conditions and Carter's visit, the group's letter demanded the release of imprisoned Puerto Rican nationalist Oscar Collazo, who had been convicted of killing a White House police officer during the 1950 attempt on Truman's life, and the four Puerto Rican nationalists who had shot and wounded five congressmen in the House of Representatives in 1954.[22]

Levasseur was arrested on November 3, 1984. He was convicted and sentenced to forty-five years in prison. Manning got life for the murder of a New Jersey state trooper and fifty-three years for the New York City area bombings.

Three months after the Marlboro bombing, the Secret Service joined in the hunt for one of the most dangerous men ever to threaten a president—fifty-two-year-old Ervil LeBaron, the leader of a fanatic religious organization called the Church of the Lamb of God. LeBaron was an imposing six-foot-four-inch polygamist who had thirteen wives and at least twenty-five children. LeBaron had induced several of his forty-odd disciples to murder between thirteen and twenty people who failed to abide by what he decreed to be the "constitutional law of the Kingdom of God."[23] Lebaron had also put President Carter on his "execution list."

LeBaron's followers wandered around the deserts of the American southwest and northern Mexico. His desert camps were built like small fortresses. The cult stockpiled weapons, and LeBaron sent his followers to Mexican villages to recruit peasants for his religious army. Every child was taught how to use firearms from an early age, and he used former soldiers to teach the sect military tactics. LeBaron intended to kill every political and religious leader who stood in his way.

Ervil came to the attention of the Secret Service while serving time in a Mexican prison for murder. In the fall of 1976, an organization called the Society of American Patriots began sending letters to presidential candidate Jimmy Carter, threatening him with death if he did not intercede to free LeBaron. The Secret Service traced the letters back to two of Ervil's wives, who had rented a post office box in Pasadena in the society's name. Evidence was mounting that LeBaron was responsible for a spate of murders, and arrest warrants were issued. On June 1, 1979, the Mexican police finally captured him in the mountains south of Mexico City. Mexican police took him across the international bridge at Laredo and handed him over to waiting FBI agents.[24]

Ervil was eventually convicted of masterminding the murder of a leader of a rival polygamous cult and sentenced to life in prison. He died in prison on August 16, 1981, of an apparent heart attack.

— — —

Two "dangerous" men became threats to Carter in his final two years in office. Thirty-one-year-old former mental patient Joseph Hugh Ryan had a history of making threats against presidents, including Nixon, Ford, and Carter. According to Denver police captain Robert Shaughnessy, Ryan had "made irrational statements that [former president] Nixon had threatened him and that he had lost every job he had because the federal government was harassing him."[25]

In 1979, Ryan was committed to St. Elizabeth's Hospital for attempting to force his way into the White House. He was immediately apprehended by uniformed Secret Service officers but continued to make threats against the president. The Secret Service continued to keep tabs on Ryan following his release from St. Elizabeth's, making frequent visits to his Denver, Colorado, home to question him. On one occasion they confiscated a .357 Magnum handgun.[26]

On January 14, 1980, Ryan walked into the Denver Secret Service office and told employees in the reception area that he was armed and wanted to file a complaint about "harassment." He was confronted by Secret Service agent Stewart Watkins, and the two men began arguing. Ryan told Watkins that his problem was with former presidents and President Carter in particular. According to Glen Weaver, who was in charge of the Denver office, "I was reading a memo from our assistant director that brought to the attention of all agents the number of increased assaults on all federal agents. I was on the second paragraph when the ... shooting started."[27]

Ryan pulled out a .45 automatic from under his coat and shot Watkins in the chest and stomach. Another agent, Andrew Gruler, quickly pulled out his weapon and fired five shots at Ryan, killing him instantly. Watkins was rushed to the Denver General Hospital, where he died four and a half hours later.[28]

Arguably the most dangerous threat President Carter faced came from the man who would eventually set his sights on President Reagan.

John Hinckley was a lonely college dropout whose life was dominated by two things: the teenage actress Jodie Foster and the movie *Taxi Driver*, in which the central character, played by Robert De Niro, plans to impress a woman by assassinating a politician. Hinckley saw the movie fifteen times. Desperate to act on his obsession with the Hollywood actress (who also starred in the film), Hinckley sent her letters and stalked her at Yale, where the young star was a freshman in 1980. After Foster rejected Hinckley's advances, he became more determined than ever to prove himself worthy of her. Hinckley decided that shooting the president would do the job.

By late September 1980, Hinckley began his presidential stalking by tracking the movements of President Carter, who was campaigning across the country for his second term in office. Hinckley traveled to Dallas, Texas, to buy two revolvers and then flew to Washington, D.C., staying at a hotel only three blocks from the White House. During his stay he sent a postcard to his sister describing the White House as "Carter's Fortress." Hinckley scoured the newspapers for Carter's itinerary. He discovered that the president would be in Dayton, Ohio, for a campaign rally on October 2.[29]

In Dayton, Hinckley left his guns in his luggage at a bus station. He was standing in a crowd of supporters when the president arrived. Carter plunged into the crowd of well-wishers, smiling and waving as Hinckley looked on only a handshake distance from the president. Hinckley later said he was unarmed and did not intend to shoot

Carter but simply wanted to find out if he could get close enough to assassinate him. On that day, he became convinced he could.[30]

Following his "test run," Hinckley took a plane to another scheduled campaign rally, this time in Nashville, Tennessee. Carter was due to appear at a "town hall" meeting at the Grand Ole Opry on October 9. After arriving in Nashville, Hinckley suddenly changed his mind about shooting Carter and returned to the airport and checked in his baggage. When it went through the airport's X-ray machine, a security officer spotted his handguns, and Hinckley was arrested by Nashville police. The guns were confiscated, and Hinckley was fined $62.50.

Hinckley said he "had not been able to psyche himself up to [shooting Carter]," according to the would-be assassin's psychiatrist, Dr. William T. Carpenter. Carpenter said that after the election, Hinckley "lost interest in Carter and [devoted] his activities and thinking" to Reagan.[31]

Agent Marty Venker said Hinckley changed his mind about shooting Carter after agents guarding the president looked Hinckley in the eye and he "wilted."[32] James W. Clarke maintains that Hinckley changed his mind around the middle of October, when the media began reporting a likely Reagan victory in the presidential election. Hinckley had persuaded himself that killing a candidate who was about to lose an election would rob him of the notoriety he craved.[33]

Hinckley was not put on the "watch list" after his arrest in Nashville, because handgun arrests happened "all the time," according to Agent Marty Venker, "and without any reason to link Hinckley with Carter the FBI had no cause to alert the Secret Service."[34] FBI director William H. Webster defended the FBI's decision not to tell the Secret Service of Hinckley's arrest at the Nashville airport. Testifying before the House Judiciary subcommittee on April 8, 1981, Webster said, "We don't want to barrage the Secret Service with excessive information."[35]

After the election, Hinckley turned his attention to the new president-elect. He flew to Washington, D.C., where he was photographed outside the White House. He also visited Ford's Theatre, the scene of Abraham Lincoln's assassination, and Blair House, where the Reagans were staying during the pre-inaugural period. Armed with one of his revolvers, Hinckley observed Reagan entering and leaving Blair House but made no attempt to shoot him. The following March, Hinckley shot Reagan. A short time later, Carter told reporters that the attempt on Reagan's life "should not force prominent officials to withdraw from public view.... We have always faced prospects of deranged people making attempts on the lives of public figures. It's part of your duty and you always have Secret Service protection."[36]

— — —

Carter was the first president since Herbert Hoover to be denied a second term after having won a first. Hoover had been undone by the Great Depression. The "Great Inflation" was Carter's undoing—inflation reached double digits during the late 1970s. He was also criticized for a failed military rescue attempt of American hostages in Iran and the collapse of negotiations for their release in mid-October 1980.

Potential assassins have threatened the life of Jimmy Carter multiple times since he left the White House in 1981, making him the most threatened former president in history, according to author Larry J. Sabato. Sabato interviewed Carter for his book *The Kennedy*

Half-Century: The Presidency, Assassination, and Lasting Legacy of John F. Kennedy. Carter told Sabato that he has faced at least three home-grown assassination attempts since he left the presidency and is constantly warned by the U.S. Secret Service of personal threats during his frequent overseas travel. "I have had two or three threats to my life after I came home from the White House ... When I go on an overseas trip almost invariably, I get a report from the Secret Service that where I'm going is very dangerous," Carter said.[37]

In 2007, government authorities reported that Khalid Sheikh Mohammed, who was charged with masterminding the 9/11 attacks, planned to assassinate the former president. In June 2009, the Palestinian organization Hamas foiled a plot to kill Carter by al Qaeda–linked terrorists.

After leaving office, Carter's relationship with his security detail became much friendlier; in fact, protecting the former president became a choice job for many in the agency, especially when they were given permission to hunt and fish on his Plains, Georgia, farm.[38] Carter and his wife, Rosalynn, became close to some of the agents. "It is often a sorrowful occasion when their career advancement requires that they be transferred to other posts," Carter wrote in his diary.[39]

CHAPTER NINE

RAWHIDE

*You never think [an assassination attempt] is going to happen
to you, and when it does it's a shock that stays with you.*
—Nancy Reagan

*Here you have a delicate balance between protection and politics.
[Reagan is] a politician. He likes to be with people, he was elected
by people. Now, to prevent that man from getting close
to people ... is wrong, so we're going to have to balance that off.*
—President Reagan's Treasury secretary, Donald Regan

onald Reagan, America's fortieth president, hastened the end
of the Cold War and led a conservative revolution that revitalized the Republican Party.

His second term was marred by the Iran-Contra Affair, in which
Reagan's subordinates sold arms to Iran as ransom for hostages and
diverted profits from the sales to rebels fighting the Marxist Sandinistas then governing Nicaragua. What became known as "Irangate" invited comparisons to Watergate, undermined Reagan's
credibility, and severely weakened his powers of persuasion with
Congress. Despite the affair, Reagan achieved a nuclear arms agreement with the Soviet Union that reduced the nuclear arsenals of both

countries for the first time, setting the stage for a new relationship with the Soviets under the leadership of Mikhail S. Gorbachev. When Reagan left office, many historians lauded him as one of America's greatest presidents.

— — —

The White House Secret Service detail made no secret of the fact they were pleased when Reagan defeated Jimmy Carter in the 1980 presidential election. Reagan's agents found the new president charming, affable, and down to earth.

Reagan said he had "loved" the Secret Service ever since an agent told him in 1976 that they did not use the "crouch" position when firing their pistols because "when you are firing we're standing between you and the assassin."[1] He often joked with them, remembered their names and the names of their spouses, and always had a kind word in appreciation for the difficult jobs they had. They were also delighted that Reagan treated them as equals, something Carter seemed to find difficult to do. Former agent Joseph Petro said Reagan was "always telling stories and always happy to see the people around him laugh ... the graciousness that the Reagans always showed the agents was returned in kind ... he referred to us as 'the fellas.'"[2]

Agent Patrick Sullivan said Reagan was "just a sincere ... gentleman."[3] Air Force One flight engineer James A. Buzzelli said, "Reagan never got on or off [Air Force One] without sticking his head in the cockpit and saying 'Thanks fellas' or 'Have a nice day.' He was just as personable in person as he came across to the public."[4] Other agents drew sharp distinctions between the personalities of Reagan and his wife, Nancy. "Reagan was such a down-to-earth individual, easy to talk to," one agent said. "He was the great communicator. He wanted to be on friendly terms. He accepted people for what they were. His wife was just the opposite. If she saw that he was having a conversation with the agents and it looked like they were good ole boys, and he was laughing, she would call him away and remind him. She called the shots."[5] Former agent William J. Bell said, "Nancy was not liked by many of us."[6]

Reagan also respected the professionalism of his protective detail. He did not challenge the advice his agents gave him about what was best for his protection. Although Reagan did not like wearing the protective, but uncomfortable, four-pound Kevlar bulletproof vest, there were times his agents insisted upon it and he complied.[7]

— — —

Reagan faced the greatest threat to his life shortly after his inauguration. In November 1980, after abandoning his plans to shoot President Carter, John W. Hinckley stalked the president-elect. Although Hinckley had stalked Carter and had been arrested on weapons charges at an airport the president visited, he was not on the Secret Service's "watch list," as he had never made an overt threat. But had the airport authorities searched Hinckley's suitcase, they would have discovered his diary, which detailed his plans to kill Carter.

In February 1980, Hinckley changed his target once more, but only momentarily. He decided he wanted to be the third Kennedy assassin and kill Senator Edward M. Kennedy, the last of the Kennedy brothers. He arrived in Washington, D.C., and visited Kennedy's Senate office. He waited in the corridor for the senator to appear. Frustrated when Kennedy didn't walk by, Hinckley made his way to the Capitol, thinking he could attack the senator there. But he backed off when he saw the metal detector at the entrance to the building. Instead, he headed for the White House and joined a tour of the executive mansion.[8]

On March 29, 1981, Hinckley checked into the Park Century Hotel on 18th Street, two blocks west of the White House and directly across the street from Secret Service headquarters. His luggage contained two .22 caliber pistols and a .38 of the type used by John Lennon's killer, Mark Chapman, the previous December.

The next day, Hinckley wrote a five-page letter to Jodie Foster. "Dear Jodie, There is a definite possibility that I will be killed in my attempt to get Reagan," he wrote. "This letter is being written an hour before I leave for the Hilton Hotel. Jodie, I'm asking you to please look into your heart and at least give me the chance with this historical deed to gain your respect and love. I love you forever." Shortly afterward, he left for the Washington Hilton. He left a newspaper cutting about President Reagan's schedule on his bed. The schedule disclosed that President Reagan would leave the White House at 1:45 p.m. to address a session of the AFL-CIO's building and construction trades department at the Washington Hilton Hotel.

Hinckley shot Reagan as the president left the Hilton. The chambers of his pistol contained six devastator bullets designed to explode on impact. He shot twice, paused, then fired off four more rounds—all within two seconds. Agent Dennis McCarthy said he heard a "pop, no louder than a firecracker." It was the moment he had been training for but "dreaded." McCarthy knew he "had to get to that gun" as Hinckley continued firing. After the third shot, McCarthy saw the gun protruding between television cameras about eight feet away. He dove for the gun and landed on Hinckley's back just as the sixth shot was fired. The assassin offered no resistance and dropped the gun to the ground. As McCarthy pulled him to his feet, he saw two hands grab Hinckley's throat, and it entered his mind that his role had now changed—he was no longer protecting the president but his would-be assassin.[9] Press Secretary James Brady, Secret Service agent Timothy McCarthy, and Washington, D.C., police officer Thomas Delahanty were also shot and seriously wounded.

As he heard the sound of shots, Secret Service agent Jerry Parr shoved Reagan into his limousine, and then, after noticing the president had been wounded, directed the car to the George Washington University Hospital. The president had been hit under his left arm by a bullet that ricocheted off his limousine. It had missed his heart by a mere inch. Although not believed to be serious at the time, Reagan's wounds were in fact life-threatening.

"There's a couple of times where truth and training converge, where history and destiny converge," Parr observed years later. "I thought about that for a long time. It's that moment—either you do it or you don't, either you save him or you don't."[10] Reagan underwent surgery to remove the bullet and repair a collapsed lung.

Dennis McCarthy blamed himself for "not acting fast enough" after Hinckley began shooting. "I began to think that I might have acted like a coward outside the Hilton," McCarthy said. He and fellow agents reviewed the television footage of the shooting, and his colleagues pointed out McCarthy had reacted as fast as humanly possible. Nevertheless, McCarthy became depressed about his role in the shooting.[11]

An internal Treasury Department review of the circumstances surrounding the attack generally praised the agents on the scene but was less than laudatory about the intelligence work of both the

Secret Service and the FBI in identifying threats in advance. "The Secret Service's protective capabilities have been impaired by the decline in the quantity and quality of intelligence collected by the FBI," the review stated. It attributed the decline to restrictions placed by the Justice Department on the intelligence information the FBI was permitted to collect and share with the Secret Service. The review concluded that the Secret Service needed to "make use of advances in statistical methods and data processing to improve its analytic abilities."[12]

The Treasury Department also criticized the poor communications among Secret Service agents during the assassination attempt; the Service's failure to have a hospital security plan and Reagan's medical records handy; and a lapse of duty of several agents who stayed at the crime scene instead of accompanying the president to the hospital.[13]

During Hinckley's trial, prosecutors learned more about his pathologies. The assassination attempt resembled a scene in Hinckley's favorite movie, *Taxi Driver*, in which actor Robert De Niro tells a woman that if she rejected him he would carry out an assassination. De Niro then goes to a political rally in New York City carrying three guns but does not get close enough to the presidential candidate to shoot him. The FBI also discovered that Hinckley had become fascinated with previous assassinations or assassination attempts. Following his arrest, Hinckley emulated Robert F. Kennedy's killer, Sirhan Sirhan, by telling police he knew nothing about the assassination attempt. He also emulated Sirhan by asking the arresting officers if his act had been broadcast by the media. Police officers said Hinckley was excited about appearing on television.[14]

In 1982, a District of Columbia jury found Hinckley not guilty by reason of insanity. Jurors had accepted the judgments of Hinckley's psychiatrists that the would-be assassin had been suffering from psychosis, delusion, and depression when he shot Reagan. Hinckley was committed to St. Elizabeth's Hospital for treatment of his mental illness. The verdict provoked an outcry.

Two years after the assassination attempt, President Reagan wanted to meet his would-be assassin face to face. In 1983, Reagan asked the White House physician, Daniel Ruge, to see whether a meeting with Hinckley would be possible. Reagan wanted to know what Hinckley's caregivers thought. But Roger Peele, then-head of psychiatry at St. Elizabeth's who oversaw but was not directly involved in Hinckley's treatment, told Reagan that it would not be wise for him to meet with Hinckley. "I was concerned that it would diminish Mr. Hinckley's sense of responsibility … I didn't want him to feel rewarded in any way for what he did," Peele said.[15]

In 2009, twenty-eight years after the shooting, a judge allowed Hinckley multiple ten-day visits to his mother's home in Williamsburg, Virginia. Hospital authorities told the press they wanted the visits increased to seventeen and twenty-four days and also be allowed to decide if the fifty-six-year-old Hinckley was fit to live full-time with his mother. But Dr. Robert Phillips, a former director of forensic services for the Connecticut Department of Mental Health, and Dr. Raymond F. Patterson, a former medical director of St. Elizabeth's, doubted that the symptoms leading to Hinckley's violent behavior had disappeared. They said Hinckley "continued to have a sense of grandiosity and self-importance" and "did not understand the distinction between famous and infamous."

Dr. Phillips also said he was troubled by supervised visits Hinckley made to four bookstores in 1999. Secret Service agent Jason Clickner secretly watched Hinckley in a Williamsburg, Virginia, bookstore. He said he got "goose bumps" when he realized Hinckley had briefly looked at books about presidential assassination. During a 2011 visit to a Barnes and Noble bookstore in Williamsburg, Clickner said Hinckley became "momentarily fixated" on two books dealing with the murder of presidents and a biography of President Reagan.

Nancy Reagan also objected to the idea that Hinckley might be paroled. "Although the judge limited Mr. Hinckley's travel to the Washington, D.C., area, we continue to fear for the safety of the general public," she said. "Our thoughts are with all of Mr. Hinckley's victims … especially Jim Brady and his family, as they must continue to live with the tragic consequences of the assassination attempt."[16]

— — —

At the time of the Hinckley shooting, the Secret Service was investigating around 14,000 threats, most of which, according to former agent Dennis McCarthy, were nothing more than "some guy sounding off in a bar that the president is such a jerk, someone ought to shoot him."[17] Around four hundred of the threateners were considered serious, but only around three percent were classified as "dangerous," and many of them were incarcerated in mental institutions or prisons.

Ronald Reagan was subjected to threats against his life long before the Hinckley assassination attempt. Reagan was governor of California when Robert Kennedy was killed in Los Angeles in June 1968. When Reagan ran for president that year, he was assigned

Secret Service protection. In July 1968, the agent on duty at the governor's mansion saw two men moving stealthily up the driveway toward the house. The agent shouted for them to halt, and when the men turned and ran he fired a warning shot. Although the two men escaped, they left behind two petrol bombs that had been found smashed on the pavement.[18] According to former Secret Service agent Michael Endicott, the attackers were members of the Black Panther party. "One night we got an anonymous tip that there might be some type of terrorist activity about to go down," Endicott said, "courtesy of the Black Panther Party. As it turned out, they tried to firebomb Reagan's home with all manner of weapons. I'll never forget it, I was on the point and saw one of the attackers in the car lighting a Molotov cocktail and then tossing it toward the house."[19]

The Hinckley shooting provoked an upsurge in threats against the president. The agency, as per their normal procedures, declined to say how many threats there were, but UPI reported that there were as many as three hundred in the two weeks after the shooting.[20]

According to Robert Fein, a Secret Service psychologist, "In the space of 18 months, four situations came to the attention of the Secret Service. In two of these incidents, people [came armed] with weapons and an intent to kill [when they] appeared at public events. In the two other incidents, the would-be assassins were intercepted before the events. Ultimately, all four cases were prosecuted. Two were convicted, and two were sent to psychiatric facilities, though the government didn't exactly advertise it." Fein added, "These were not stories that hit the news but they were situations that caused great concern for protectors.... So after these incidents, the Secret Service leadership got together and said, 'We really would like to know more about the behaviors of these people.'"[21]

Among the "copycat" threateners who followed Hinckley was a farmer who was arrested after telling television broadcaster Jessica Savitch that he would shoot Reagan to win her love.[22]

The threats continued. On March 30, 1981, the day of the shooting, an anonymous caller informed a Michigan Bell telephone operator that another attempt would be made on the president's life. The call was traced to Linden, Michigan, about 170 miles northwest of Detroit. Secret Service agents were dispatched to investigate, and when they arrived at the caller's home, twenty-year-old James Anthony Vincent met them in the yard. After a heated argument, Vincent struggled with the officers, seriously injuring one of them. As Vincent was arrested, he made several verbal threats to kill Reagan. Vincent was later found guilty of threatening the president. The district judge imposed concurrent sentences of three years for assaulting the federal agents and five years for threatening the president.[23]

On the day after the Hinckley assassination attempt, twenty-one-year-old Douglas Bolomey, a patient at the North Florida Evaluation and Treatment Center, a psychiatric facility, sent a letter to President Reagan threatening to "complete the job Hinckley started." When he was interviewed by agents, he repeated his threat and was arrested. A government psychiatrist testified in court that Bolomey legally knew what he had done when he made the threat. The jury concurred, and he was sentenced in a Tallahassee federal court to four years in prison.[24]

On April 1, two days after Reagan was shot, Mary Frances Carrier was stopped by local police on harassment charges. In Carrier's car they found an envelope that bore several phrases threatening President Reagan and others, including the phrase "Murder the President." Police informed Secret Service special agent Kevin Mitchell, who interviewed Carrier in the Broome County, New York, jail where she was held. As Mitchell displayed his credentials and showed the envelope to Carrier, she interrupted, saying, "Yes, I know why you are here. The President should be murdered. Yes, I wrote that.... Yes, I threatened the President."

When Carrier was booked at the police station, she repeatedly made remarks about wanting to shoot Reagan. "It is too bad Hinckley wasn't successful in killing that son of a bitch," she said. "He deserved what he got ... if need be I would shoot him.... The only thing I will do is blow the president's head off, the President of the United States." Carrier also said she was very familiar with the use of firearms, was a successful hunter, and owned rifles, shotguns, and a .32 caliber pistol. Agent Mitchell said Carrier appeared to be very serious about her remarks. He also learned that Carrier traveled extensively, including to Dumfries, Virginia, a location where President Reagan rode horses.

Carrier was found guilty of threatening the president. An appellate court rejected her appeal, stating that even if a threat is "made with no present intention of carrying it out," it could cause harm because "[it] may still restrict the President's movements and require a reaction from those charged with protecting the President."[25]

On April 6, the Secret Service arrested fifty-eight-year-old Steven E. Seach in Philadelphia. Seach was a drifter who worked as a kitchen employee at a boarding school in Paoli, Pennsylvania. During his stay at the school, Seach told a colleague he wanted to go to Washington "to finish the job" on Reagan. He also said if he had been in Washington during the Hinckley shooting, he "would not have missed." The Secret Service was notified and Seach was arrested on a charge of threatening Reagan's life.[26]

Another copycat would-be Reagan assassin was twenty-two-year-old Edward Michael Richardson, a jobless drifter from Drexel Hill, Pennsylvania. A week after the Hinckley shooting, Richardson left .32 caliber bullets and two letters in the Park Plaza Hotel in New Haven, in which he said Reagan was "targeted for death." Richardson was arrested as he was about to board a Philadelphia-bound bus in Manhattan's Port Authority terminal. He was carrying a .32 caliber revolver.[27]

Richardson had lived in Lakewood, Colorado—Hinckley's hometown. He was also obsessed with *Taxi Driver* actress Jodie Foster and had seen her perform at a Yale University theater that was heavily guarded following the investigation into the Reagan assassination attempt. The deranged stalker sent Foster a letter in which he wrote: "I will finish what Hinckley started. Ronald Reagan must die. He [Hinckley] has told me so in a prophetic dream.... Sadly, though; your death is also required. You will suffer the same fate as Reagan and others in the fascist regime. You cannot escape. We are a wave of assassins throughout the world."[28]

Richardson, who had a history of drug use, was ordered to undergo one year of mental health treatment in a Morgantown, West Virginia, federal prison after he pleaded guilty. He told the judge he had no intention of carrying out his threats. "I'm not some political fanatic," he said, "but an American who believes in his country. I have a lot of regret, a lot of remorse for all the trouble I've caused."[29]

Harold Thomas Smith may have the distinction for being the most incorrigible presidential threatener. In 1967, Smith was sentenced to two years in prison for threatening Lyndon Johnson, and in 1971 he was sentenced to four years for making threats against

Richard Nixon. On April 7, 1981, Smith was eating dinner at the Raleigh Greyhound bus depot when he struck up a conversation with a police officer, Randy L. Carroll, who had been working part time at the bus station. "If I ever get my hands on [Reagan] I'm going to blow his brains out," Smith boasted. "The president ought to be killed and the only thing that Hinckley did wrong was that he didn't kill him." Like Hinckley, Smith wanted to be famous. "One day you're going to know who I am. What you'll say is you sat beside Harold Smith while he was eating a bowl of soup … when I become famous for killing the president," he told Carroll. Smith was found guilty of threatening to kill President Reagan and sentenced to a five-year prison term.[30]

Copycat threats continued throughout Reagan's presidency. On October 24, 1984, two high school students sent ten letters to movie actress Brooke Shields, who was a student at Princeton University. A Princeton student found one of the letters and took it to campus security. The letter read, "Dear Brooke Shields, I love you, if you don't make love to me I will kill President Reagan in one week if you don't meet me at David's Cookie Shop." The students viewed the incident as a prank, but the Secret Service took it seriously. The students were charged and pleaded guilty. The seventeen-year-old boy was given three months' probation and dismissed from his school. The sixteen-year-old was suspended from school. Both were ordered to undergo psychiatric treatment.[31]

Reagan was also the victim of repeat offenders. Carlos Valle had threatened the life of former president Nixon and received a three-year prison sentence. On July 18, 1981, Valle wrote and mailed a letter to *Playboy* magazine, threatening to kill President Reagan. He was arrested by Secret Service agents and indicted by a federal grand jury on November 18, 1981. Valle was found guilty and received a prison sentence.[32]

One of the most dangerous "repeat threateners" was Edward Joseph Patterson, a thirty-eight-year-old drifter who had a record of fifty arrests on charges of attempted robbery, drug offenses, and other crimes in New York, New Jersey, Chicago, and Florida. He had also been hospitalized repeatedly for treatment of mental illness.

Patterson had been arrested at least four times for threatening Presidents Nixon, Ford, and Carter, and had served a prison sentence for threatening President Reagan in 1981 and 1982. He was released July 2, 1986, from a federal prison in Ray Brook, New York, and instructed to go to a halfway house in Camden, New Jersey, but he never arrived.

Patterson was a ticking time bomb, but when he finally did blow it was not against a president but against Robert Burdick, a seventy-eight-year-old retired teacher. Burdick's body was found lying in his kitchen, stabbed at least ten times in the chest. Patterson had corresponded with Burdick from prison, given Burdick's address as his own when he was released, and lived in Burdick's apartment in Manhattan for three weeks before the murder. Patterson was arrested in a Baltimore bus station after he told a television news editor about the murder. He said he killed Burdick because the retired teacher had abused children.[33]

— — —

President Reagan's security cordon was breached several times during his presidency.

On October 22, 1983, Reagan was enjoying a golfing weekend at the Augusta National Golf Club when forty-five-year-old Charles

Raymond Harris drunkenly crashed through Gate 3, an exterior gate, in his four-wheel-drive pickup truck. Harris, who lived in Augusta, had lost his job for turning up for work drunk. He was described by a friend as a "Reagan voter, coon hunter and good ole boy with a drinking problem."[34] Another friend, a lieutenant with the Augusta police, said Harris was "fine when he's sober, but when he's drinking, there's no reasoning with him. He's got a negative attitude. He's right and everyone else is wrong."[35]

Harris exited his vehicle brandishing a .38 pistol and shouted, "Perhaps someone will be killed" if authorities did not allow him to "see the president." Harris ran to the golf club shop, took two White House aides and five others hostage, and told police and Secret Service agents he wanted to talk to Reagan about "foreigners taking American jobs." He also demanded whisky and food be brought to him. Reagan was informed of the hostage crisis while on the sixteenth hole. The president called Harris twice but each time Harris hung up on him because he wanted to talk to Reagan "face-to-face." The president was then evacuated by helicopter away from the course.

Police soon brought Harris's mother and a brother to the golf course to reason with him. Within two hours, four of the hostages were released and a fifth hostage had run to safety. Harris then released the remaining hostages and surrendered. He was charged with making threats against the president, assault of or resistance to a federal officer, and possession of a weapon during the commission of a felony. But the federal charges were dropped in favor of state kidnapping charges.[36] Harris pleaded guilty and was sentenced to ten years in prison and ten years' probation. In 1987, he said that though he probably would not repeat his actions when released from prison, he "did not regret them."[37] As a result of the hostage crisis, President Reagan gave up playing golf anywhere but a friend's private estate. He thought that playing on public courses put others at unnecessary risk.[38]

The following year, twenty-five-year-old high-school dropout David A. Mahonski arrived at the White House carrying a sawed-off shotgun. Mahonski, who had been hospitalized for psychiatric treatment, had made threats against President Reagan and was under surveillance by both the FBI and the Secret Service.[39]

Mahonski's uncle, Howard Engel, said his nephew had repeatedly talked about "going to see the president and straightening him out," adding that Mahonski had been treated for drug use, particularly cocaine. "When he was high," Engel said, "he blamed the establishment for everything."[40]

Mahonski traveled to Washington, D.C., several times in March 1984 and frequently visited the White House. During this time, he also bought a shotgun at a York, Pennsylvania, store.

On the evening of March 15, 1984, Mahonski was observed by two Secret Service uniformed officers walking along a sidewalk outside the South Lawn of the White House. They determined that he was acting in a "suspicious manner." When the officers approached Mahonski, he "wheeled around" and pointed his 16 gauge shotgun at them. The gun, which had been concealed under his coat, had one live round of ammunition. The two officers told Mahonski to hand over his weapon. When he failed to respond, one of the officers shot him in the right forearm. Mahonski was taken to District of Columbia General Hospital, where he was treated for a fracture of the right forearm then held in a special hospital cell. President Reagan was in the White House at the time of the shooting.[41]

When Mahonski was arraigned before a judge, he insisted that he had been drugged by President Reagan, the CIA, the FBI, and the Air Force. He also said government agents "had put a bug" in his head that transmitted "everything I think across the country. I don't need another nut ward. The president has had me in three already. The President of the United States and certain elements of the society fill me with drugs and ruin my life, like the communists would. I have had just about enough." He added that he had been "down to the White House to ask the president to order the FBI to take that bug out of my ear."

In September 1984, a federal jury found Mahonski guilty of assault on a federal officer and carrying a sawed-off shotgun outside the White House. He was committed to St. Elizabeth's Hospital until ruled competent. He was diagnosed with schizophrenia and bipolar disorder and spent nine months in the hospital before he was released.[42]

Two years later, the Secret Service investigated two mentally unbalanced men. James Neavill was a thirty-year-old man who had been hospitalized for mental problems thirty-eight times over the preceding ten years. The Social Security Administration had determined he was unfit for work due to his mental impairments. In 1982, he had been investigated for making threats to kill Reagan but no action had been taken.

On April 28, 1987, eight days after discharging himself from the Missouri State Hospital, an intoxicated Neavill walked into the Festus, Missouri, police station and told police officers he had been paid $35,000 to assassinate the president with an Uzi submachine gun. The purported assassination plan was to take place sometime in May. The local police reported Neavill to the Secret Service. When he was interviewed at the Festus jail, he repeated his threats. When he was asked what he would do if he were released from custody, he replied, "put a bullet in the President's head."

Neavill was indicted by a grand jury on the charge of threatening the president. He was found competent to stand trial. Neavill pleaded insanity, but the jury returned a guilty verdict and Neavill was sentenced to five years' imprisonment. In lieu of incarceration in a federal prison, he was committed to a psychiatric facility.[43]

Reagan was the recipient of numerous lethal devices during his eight years in office. On August 31, 1981, Earl S. Bruton, a fifty-four-year-old man from Detroit, sent Reagan a threatening letter wrapped around six sticks of dynamite. He was angry at being denied loans through the federal Small Business Administration. Bruton had sent similar devices to local Detroit newspapers. He was arrested and sentenced to twelve years in prison.[44]

In 1986, Reagan visited Spokane, Washington, to campaign for Republican senator Slade Gorton. Before the visit Secret Service agents had been informed that notes found in an elevator of a local motel gave details about security personnel around the Spokane Coliseum where Reagan was due to give a speech. The notes included the descriptions of security vehicles, including license numbers and the notation "10-28-86 at 1:23."

After checking the motel's registration records, agents compared the handwriting on the note and matched it to a guest, twenty-three-year-old ex-con Robert W. Nelson.

Agents entered Nelson's motel room and questioned him about the note. They found a bullet attached to a note in on a dresser. The note said "Reagan Will Die" and "If I miss, Carlop won't." "Carlop" was a nickname for Libyan leader Colonel Muammar Gaddafi.

The other side of the note read, "For you Mr. President." When agent Pete Dowling searched Nelson's car, he found a loaded five-shot revolver and a box of ammunition. He also discovered stolen credit cards in a litter bag. Nelson was arrested and charged with threatening the life of President Reagan. He told Dowling his "assassination plot" was designed to return him to prison so he could be with his homosexual lover.[45] In May 1987, Nelson pleaded guilty and was sentenced to three years in prison.[46]

President Reagan was also the target of stalkers. According to Robert L. DeProspero, who headed the White House presidential detail for six years, the president received a threatening letter from a man who called himself "Catman." Catman had been stalking Reagan and Senator Alphonse D'Amato since 1981. He had called the White House numerous times and sent letters to the president that mentioned security details that were unknown to the general public. He also sent close-up photographs of his intended victims when they appeared at political events and "lots of photos of cats." When Secret Service agents eventually caught Catman on a New York subway in 1983, they discovered photographs that revealed he had positioned himself outside the fence at the New York City mayor's residence, Gracie Mansion, during a presidential visit. Catman had been close enough to shoot President Reagan, but his shot had apparently been blocked by agents.[47]

Threats to President Reagan continued after he left office. Reagan and his wife moved back to California and bought a single-story, three-bedroom flagstone mansion. The house stood behind a wall and a security fence on a hillside dotted with orange palms. In 1981, thirty-three-year-old Gregory Stuart Gordon came to the attention of the Secret Service when he made several threats to kill the president.

He had been committed to mental institutions for the offenses. On his release, Gordon was still obsessed with killing Reagan.

In July 1990, he climbed over the fence of the Reagan home and ran up the driveway, through the house, and out a back door. At the time President Reagan was sitting beside the swimming pool. Nancy was in the bedroom and witnessed Secret Service agents chasing the attacker. Agents soon caught up with Gordon, who was unarmed, and arrested him. Gordon told agents he wanted to strangle the president and that he was "Christ in the second coming." He said Reagan was the "anti-Christ" who "must be killed and I must kill him."[48]

Gordon was sentenced to two years in prison. During his trial Secret Service agents said Gordon's statements about killing Reagan were "coherent" and "serious." His lawyer said his client had simply been trying to draw attention to himself so he could end up in a rehabilitation center. But Gordon insisted he had been trying to kill Reagan for ten years and would return to finish the job after he was released from prison. In 1992, his appeal was rejected.[49]

In 2012, eight years after Reagan's death, it was revealed that singer John Lennon's assassin, Mark David Chapman, had planned to threaten Reagan. Like Hinckley, Chapman lusted for notoriety and had a list of people he wanted to kill, including Elizabeth Taylor, Johnny Carson, Jacqueline Kennedy, and George C. Scott. He chose them simply because "they were famous," and he expected to attain "instant notoriety." In a 2012 prison confession, the fifty-five-year-old Chapman said he targeted Lennon on December 8, 1980, because the forty-year-old Beatle just happened to be "more accessible" at the time. Although Chapman said he did not really want to shoot Reagan, he did confess his plan was to "disrupt his inauguration by firing a few shots."[50]

— — —

In January 1989, President Reagan concluded his second term as president. He said there were two things he was proudest of: "One is the economic recovery.... The other is the recovery of our morale. America is respected again in the world, and looked to for leadership."[51]

Five years after leaving office, the former president announced he was suffering from Alzheimer's, an incapacitating brain disease. In 1994, he said farewell to the American public in a handwritten letter released to the press. He said he was setting out on "the journey that will lead me into the sunset of my life." In May 2004, a month before his death, Nancy Reagan said her husband's disease was worsening. "Ronnie's long journey," she said, "has finally taken him to a distant place where I can no longer reach him."[52]

FDR's Plymouth Phaeton automobile. The president often drove around in his open-top cars—becoming a target for any would-be assassin. It is the last car he drove shortly before his death and is kept in Warm Springs, Georgia, where it can still be seen. *(Photo: Mel Ayton)*

February 9, 1945: Winston Churchill, Franklin D. Roosevelt, and Joseph Stalin at the Yalta Conference, Livadia Palace, Yalta, USSR. A German attempt to kill the Allied leaders at Yalta in February 1945 was planned and considered by the Secret Service to be "dangerous," but the plot never materialized. *(White House photo, Public Domain)*

President Truman returns to Washington, D.C., after his 1948 presidential win accompanied by Secret Service agents on the limousine's rear running boards. *(Copyright Unknown, Courtesy of Harry S. Truman Library)*

March 2, 1960: Eisenhower motorcade in Uruguay. A Secret Service agent in front of President Eisenhower monitors the crowd. *(Public Domain)*

June 1961: The new presidential limousine built by the Ford Motor Company arrives at the White House. Director of the U.S, Secret Service U. E. Baughman sits in the rear seat. It is the limousine JFK was riding in when he was assassinated in Dallas, Texas. *(White House photo, Public Domain)*

1962: White House Secret Service agent Gerald "Jerry" Behn stands next to President Kennedy. Astronaut Lieutenant Colonel John H. Glenn sits on the back of a convertible as his motorcade prepares to depart the White House for the Capitol following a reception in his honor. *(White House photo, Public Domain)*

June 28, 1963: President Kennedy stands in his limousine to greet a crowd of well-wishers on his visit to Ireland five months before his assassination. To his rear Secret Service agents scan the crowd. Kennedy received assassination threats during his short stay. *(White House photo, Public Domain)*

President Johnson guarded by Secret Service agent Rufus Youngblood. Youngblood was the agent who threw himself over Vice President Johnson when shots rang out in Dallas's Dealey Plaza on November 22, 1963. *(Public Domain)*

Mexican president Gustavo Diaz Ordaz (left) and President Richard Nixon (right) riding a presidential motorcade in San Diego, California, September 4, 1970. There was a consensus among Secret Service agents that Nixon was reckless about his own safety during his eight years as vice president and six years as president. *(White House photo, Public Domain)*

Secret Service chief U. E. Baughman described Nixon as "an assassin's delight," who had "delusions of personal safety," and was "an assassin's dreamboat." Secret Service agent Rufus Youngblood said that Nixon "seemed oblivious to personal danger." *(Public Domain)*

Secret Service agents rush President Ford toward the California State Capitol following the attempt on the president's life by Lynette "Squeaky" Fromme, in Sacramento, California, September 5, 1975. A plot to assassinate Ford by two men, planned for the day of the Lynette Fromme attack, was foiled by California law enforcement officers. *(Gerald R. Ford Presidential Library and Museum)*

President Ford winces at the sound of the gun fired by Sara Jane Moore during the assassination attempt in San Francisco, California, September 22, 1975. *(Gerald R. Ford Presidential Library and Museum)*

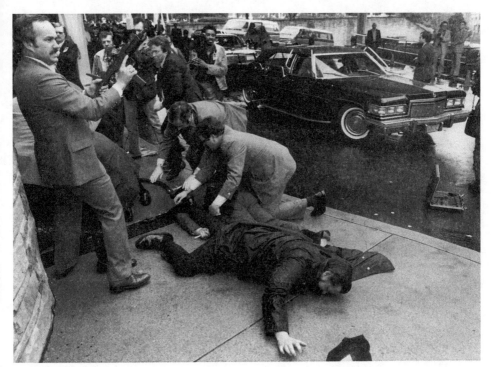

March 30, 1981: Just after the assassination attempt on President Ronald Reagan, outside the Washington Hilton Hotel, White House press secretary James Brady and Washington, D.C., police officer Thomas Delahanty lie wounded on the ground. Hinckley was subdued by Secret Service agents and taken to Washington police headquarters. Following the shooting, numerous individuals across the United States made "copycat" threats to assassinate the president. *(Courtesy, Ronald Reagan Library)*

Secret Service agents accompany President George W. Bush as he enters the presidential limousine. Bush was the target of numerous would-be assassins, including al Qaeda terrorists and home-grown supporters of the terrorist organization. *(Public Domain)*

Secret Service agents surround the presidential limousine during President George W. Bush's second inaugural parade down Pennsylvania Avenue, Washington, D.C., in January 2005. Following the war in Iraq and the ongoing war in Afghanistan, the Secret Service were especially alert to the dangers inherent in the president's public appearances. *(Public Domain)*

March 6, 2009: President Barack Obama arrives at Port Columbus International Airport, Columbus, Ohio, on Air Force One. Accompanying the president are Senator Sherrod Brown, Representative Mary Jo Kilroy, and his Secret Service detail. The Secret Service uncovered many plots to assassinate America's first black president, including those organized by U.S. right-wing groups, al Qaeda terrorists, and individuals who expressed their hatred of the president on the internet. *(White House photo, Public Domain)*

CHAPTER TEN

TIMBERWOLF

A lot of people were saying don't go there [Colombia].
The drug lords are out of control down there and [I said] we got
the Secret Service, so we don't have to worry about that.
—President George H. W. Bush

You don't read about them, you don't hear about them, you
don't discuss them because it may encourage others but
there's always threats on the lives of presidents.
—President George H. W. Bush

George Herbert Walker Bush was one of the most qualified candidates to become president. Before ascending to the Oval Office, Bush had been a congressman, U.S. envoy to China, ambassador to the United Nations, CIA director, and vice president.

During his one term as president, Bush oversaw the end of the Cold War. He also successfully removed Panama's Manuel Noriega from power when he ordered a military invasion of Panama, and he built an international coalition to expel Iraq's Saddam Hussein from Kuwait.

But during his 1992 reelection campaign, Bush was seen as out of touch with ordinary voters and unable to rescue the floundering economy. He also alienated many conservatives by breaking his famous pledge not to raise taxes. Bush lost the election to Arkansas governor Bill Clinton.

— — —

By the time he became president, Bush was used to Secret Service protection, having served eight years as vice president under Reagan. He had a close relationship with his agents, and he treated them with civility and respect. "I always will [respect them]," Bush said, "because we kept total trust in their professionalism and their discipline...."[1] One of the reasons agents respected Bush was that the president was aware that they wanted to spend time with their families during holiday periods.[2] One agent recalled that President Bush was, "a great man, just an all-around nice person.... Both he and Mrs. Bush are very thoughtful, and they think outside of their own little world. They think of other people."[3] Another agent said, "George was a straight shooter," and "Barbara Bush was a sweetheart ... one of the nicest first ladies we have ever had."[4]

According to Agent Pete Dowling, "[Bush] made it clear to all his staff that none of them was a security expert and if the Secret Service made a decision, he was the one to sign off on it, and they were never to question our decisions or make life difficult. So consequently it was kind of a moment in time because all the entities really worked well together to make his protection and the activities that he participated in successful."[5]

The only downside to protecting Bush, agents said, was his "hyperactivity." Agents nicknamed him the "Mexican Jumping Bean."[6] He would often leave the Oval Office spontaneously and walk to the White House fence on Pennsylvania Avenue to greet tourists. On one occasion Agent Glenn Smith spotted a suspicious-looking man, eyes darting, walking backward and forward outside the fence; they searched him and found he was carrying a 9 mm pistol. Agents believed he intended to use it to assassinate the president. Following the incident, Bush allowed that in the future his detail should be given time to set up a security cordon at the fence.[7]

— — —

As vice president, Bush was targeted by left-wing guerrillas during a 1982 visit to Colombia. In the days before Bush's arrival, the plotters buried dynamite under the single runway at Bogota's airport. The dynamite connected to wires running to an electrical generator three hundred yards away and was primed, ready to explode. But because of the strong security force around the airport during Bush's visit, the assassins were unable to enter the area to detonate their bomb. The plot to kill Bush was unmasked only hours after his plane left.[8]

When President-elect Bush was vacationing in the Florida Keys, thirty-seven-year-old George Hicks, an out-of-work musician who believed he was "Jesus Christ," made telephone threats to the White House. Hicks said about Bush, "If I see him I'll kill him." Hicks was arrested in his apartment by agents and charged with threatening the president.[9]

As president, Bush received about three thousand threats a year. The Secret Service was open to receiving tips about presidential threateners from just about any source. During the 1992 presidential reelection campaign, a psychic who had worked with police on homicide cases, told her police contact of a vision in which President Bush was going to be assassinated by a sniper during his visit to the civic auditorium in Enid, Oklahoma. The detective assured the Secret Service that this psychic's visions had helped police find buried bodies and had provided useful leads in other criminal investigations. The investigating agent asked the psychic where the president's limousine was at that time. She correctly told him that it was at the air force base near Enid and agreed to be taken there. As they drove past airport hangars, she told agents that "something important" was in the hangars—which turned out to be the places where the president's helicopter and limousine were parked up.

The psychic said that in her vision Bush was sitting on the left-hand side of the limo, wearing an open-neck shirt and light jacket, and that the sniper was shooting from an overpass. These statements cast considerable doubt on her psychic ability, since the president normally wore a suit and tie, and he always sat on the right-hand side of the vehicle. But when Air Force One landed at the Enid base, President Bush stepped off wearing an open-neck shirt and light jacket. And when he climbed into the limo, he slid across to the left side. The Secret Service advance team leader decided to change the route away from the overpass, just to be safe. Bush was unaware of the change in plans.[10]

In 1990, twenty-one-year-old Otto Lakas, an architecture student at Lubbock Christian University, visited a pawnshop in Lubbock, Texas, to buy a .357 Colt revolver. During the purchase, the pawnbrokers teased Lakas, whose father was a former president of Panama, about the 1989 invasion of Panama, taunting him when Lakas told them U.S. soldiers had confiscated his father's guns during the invasion. Lakas then allegedly threatened to kill President Bush, saying, "I have a bullet with Bush's name engraved on it." The pawnbrokers also said he was "planning to blow Bush's head off" when

the president visited Dallas, Houston, and Austin in May 1990. They
notified the police about Lakas's remarks. The police passed on the
information to the Secret Service. Lakas was arrested on April 17,
1990, and charged with making threats against the president. Agents
found a .223 caliber rifle, a stun gun, and a BB gun in his home.[11]

During Lakas's trial, his father, Demetrio Lakas, said that in
Panama death threats "are a way of expressing ourselves." Lakas Jr.
admitted he made the remark to the pawnbrokers and apologized
for it. His lawyer told the jury his client had "used an exaggeration
to make a point. But you can't throw a man in jail for shooting his
mouth off." The jurors sympathized with Lakas and found him not
guilty after deliberating for fifteen minutes. Lakas refused to discuss
the incident with local reporters. "Talking is how I got into this
mess," he said.[12]

Ronald Tanur was another threatener who later regretted his
impulsive remarks. In 1990, the forty-year-old former mental patient
was serving a five-year sentence on narcotics charges at the Pittsburgh State Correctional Institution. On July 7, bitter about prison
conditions, he sat down and wrote a letter to President Bush, stating,
"Dear President Bush, I'm going to kill you. Sincerely, Ronald
Tanur." President Bush was due to visit Pittsburgh on August 14,
1991, to attend the National Convention of the Fraternal Order of
Police.

Secret Service agents had no trouble in tracking down Tanur as
he had included his prison address in the letter. He was interviewed
by agents, and he told them he sent it to draw attention to prison
conditions. He was charged with threatening the life of the president.
In August 1991, he was found guilty and sentenced to six months in
prison. The judge told Tanur he did not believe he had any intention

of carrying out his threat but warned him he should think twice "before putting pen to paper."[13]

Tanur was one of many prisoners who wrote letters to the president expressing anger at prison conditions. Sometimes prisoners made threats because they wanted a transfer to a federal institution, where conditions were often superior to those in state facilities. Many prisoners had no idea that their threats would land them in trouble, clearly unaware that U.S. law forbade threats against the president even if the threatener is in no position to carry it out.

President Bush attracted many threats from men with mental health problems. In August 1989, twenty-two-year-old Paul Michael Rodda was incarcerated in the Morgan County jail in Decatur, Alabama, on charges of auto theft. He was described by his lawyer as a "drifter" who had "many family problems" and could not function "outside a structured environment." On August 3, Rodda telephoned the White House and threatened to kill President Bush and Vice President Dan Quayle. Rodda was arrested by Secret Service agents and charged. In November 1989 he pleaded guilty and was sentenced to twenty months in prison and three years' probation.[14]

The following August, forty-three-year-old Eugene Hains, who suffered from post-traumatic stress disorder after serving in Vietnam, sent a threatening letter to President Bush, informing him he would "punch his lights out" if the president visited the Northwest. He was arrested by Secret Service agents and later found guilty. His defense lawyer criticized prosecutors for not advocating that Hains receive psychiatric help instead of trying him for a criminal offense.[15]

In 1992, Frank Paul Jones, a thirty-three-year-old man who suffered from a bipolar disorder, had become obsessed with singer Michael Jackson's sister, Janet Jackson, and believed he was married to her. Jones, who bizarrely claimed he was the son of mafia mob boss John Gotti, said he was entitled to half of Michael's estate and that he would kill the singer. But the threat was apparently a ruse to gain the attention of Janet Jackson. Jones also had a history of threatening to kill the president and had been arrested numerous times outside the White House.

Jones wrote dozens of threatening letters to, among others, his estranged wife and singer Michael Jackson. When there was no response to his letters from Jackson, he threatened to kill President Bush. In a May 18 letter to the *New York Daily News*, he wrote, "I decided to go to the FBI today, if that doesn't work I'll go to the CIA, military intelligence on up to the President of the United States of America and if the chain of command doesn't work, I will resort to violence, to bring attention to my problem. I'll commit mass murder at a Michael Jackson concert if necessary, in an attempt to murder Michael, and then you will have to deal with my problem in the public eye."

In another letter, dated May 21, 1992, and sent to the U.S. Secret Service among others, Jones wrote, "To all concerned parties, I hope you receive this letter in good health and in good spirits. I decided that because nobody is taking me serious[ly] and I can't handle my state of mind that I am going to Washington DC to threaten to kill the President of the United States, George Bush. If they do not arrest me or solve my problem I'm gonna attempt to kill President George Bush … I dare you to call this a bluff." The Secret Service and FBI investigated Jones's threats. According to the FBI file, Jones "was arrested by the U.S. Secret Service on 22nd May 1992 as he attempted to get on the White House grounds. Apparently, this was a ploy by [Jones] to attract attention to his 'problem' with [Michael Jackson]."[16] Jones was not prosecuted and he was released even though an FBI agent, in a sworn affidavit, said Jones had told him he had "tried to kill the President."[17]

Jones was arrested on June 22, 1992, for trespassing in the driveway of the Jackson family compound in Encino, California. In 1992, he was initially judged to be incompetent to stand trial, but after treatment at a federal corrections institution in North Carolina, doctors determined he was fit to be tried. In 1993, he was sentenced to two years in prison for "mailing a threatening communication," but no charges were made in relation to the threats against President Bush.

On December 26, 1989, LeRoy Johnson Jr. was convicted of burglary and sent to the Auburn Correctional Facility in Auburn, New York. While there, Johnson claimed to be depressed, suicidal, and hearing voices. As a result, he was sent to the Central New York Psychiatric Center in Marcy, New York. On June 28, 1991, he told recreational therapist Tina Fahringer that he was a Shiite Muslim and intended to kill President Bush for waging an "unnecessary" war in the Persian Gulf. The Secret Service was informed and Special Agent Alan Kolwaite interviewed Johnson. During the second interview, Johnson told Kolwaite that he intended to kill President Bush because the president was trying to take over the oil in the Middle East. He also said he wanted to kill former president Ronald Reagan because he had killed Colonel Gaddafi's son during the U.S. bombing of Libya in 1986.

Johnson was charged with threatening the president. The government presented two psychiatric experts who testified that Johnson was able to appreciate the quality and wrongfulness of his acts. The defense presented two experts who testified to the contrary. The jury found Johnson guilty, and he was sentenced to fifty-one months' imprisonment and two years of supervised release. After he appealed his conviction, the courts concluded that there was abundant evidence "from which a rational fact finder could conclude beyond a reasonable doubt that Johnson was sane at the time he made the threats for which he was indicted."[18]

Two of the most dangerous individuals ever to threaten Bush's life were lone-wolf terrorists who offered their services to Iraqi intelligence. Thirty-four-year-old Stephen Ashburn's threat was discovered through electronic surveillance under the Foreign Intelligence Surveillance Act. In January 1991, Ashburn, who had a doctorate in organic chemistry, contacted Iraqi Embassy officials and offered to kill Bush using Serin, a potent nerve gas. Ashburn was arrested and tried in a Baton Rouge federal court. Neil Gallagher, chief of the FBI's counterterrorism section, said Ashburn was "quite capable" of developing the gas. He would have used an aerosol delivery system to attack the president. On February 22, 1991, Ashburn pleaded guilty to federal charges of threatening to kill the president. After entering his plea the judge asked him if he had been joking. Ashburn replied, "No."[19]

Another threat came from Jamal Mohammed Warrayat, a Palestinian and naturalized American citizen living in New Jersey with his wife and children. His parents lived in Kuwait, and other relatives lived in Iraq. He came to the United States in the early 1970s and served four years in the army until 1979. After leaving the army, he became unemployed.

On April 16, 1990, the thirty-two-year-old Warrayat telephoned the Iraqi Embassy in Washington, D.C., and offered to kill Bush. The threat to the president's life was discovered through U.S. intelligence agencies' electronic surveillance. Responding to the threat, the FBI, through undercover work, organized a meeting between Warrayat and an FBI agent posing as an Iraqi intelligence officer. The would-be assassin met the undercover agent on November 8 at the Newark International Airport.[20]

Speaking in Arabic, Warrayat told the agent that he and the seven members of his group had weapons and materials to carry out small terrorist operations. During the conversation Warrayat said his group was ready to attack President Bush, Secretary of State James Baker, and members of Congress. They were looking for help in obtaining explosives, money, and technical training. Warrayat also said he had drawings and diagrams of military targets in Texas, Kansas, and North Carolina that he had made while in the U.S. Army.

On November 27, 1990, Warrayat was arrested at his home. A small amount of marijuana and a .357 Magnum handgun were found. He was sentenced to a year in prison and three years of supervised release.[21] FBI counterintelligence determined that Warrayat was not part of a terrorist network.[22]

The Secret Service investigated several armed presidential stalkers during the Bush years.

On September 27, 1988, twenty-two-year-old David Russell attended a presidential campaign rally in Owensboro, Kentucky, concealing a loaded semiautomatic .45 caliber handgun. As Bush shook hands with campaign supporters, Russell took photographs of him, coming within forty feet of the vice president. Two days later, Russell wrote a threatening letter to the White House in which he said he would kill Bush unless the vice president dropped out of the race. The letter also contained the photographs he had taken at the campaign rally documenting how close he came to Bush. Russell wrote another letter on October 10 addressed to President Reagan in which he again threatened the vice president's life.

On October 18, Russell was arrested by Secret Service agents and charged with threatening the life of the president. The following March he pleaded guilty in exchange for dismissal of two counts of extortion. During the trial Russell told the judge, "What I did was stupid and it was wrong and I'm sorry." But his contrition did not sway the judge, who said Russell "obviously intended to carry out his threats." The judge came to these conclusions because Russell had purchased a handgun, ammunition, and film for his camera, and he had come close to his intended target. In May 1989, Russell was sentenced to twenty-two months in prison, fined $5,000, and sent to a minimum-security federal prison. Under the sentence Russell was required to undergo mental health treatment.[23]

In 1991, forty-five-year-old Oxnard, California, resident Robert Thomas Ward had assembled a stockpile of weapons that included thirty-four firearms; twelve automatic weapons, including an Uzi submachine gun and several AK-47 assault rifles; silencers; hand grenades; and twenty-seven thousand rounds of ammunition. In October 1991, an informant for the Santa Barbara office of the Secret Service told agents that Ward had "made remarks threatening Bush." The informant also said Ward had been scouting the area around the Ronald Reagan Presidential Library and Public Affairs Center in Simi Valley, some fifty miles northeast of Los Angeles, for a place where he could get a clear shot. Bush was due to visit the presidential library just a few weeks later for the dedication ceremonies. During their investigation, agents also learned that Ward's neighbors said he was "considering killing the president." Ward was arrested and charged with threatening the president. During his interrogation at the Ventura County Jail, Ward said if he did make the threats against Bush, he "regretted" it.[24] The charges of threatening the president were later dropped "due to insufficient evidence with which to present at a trial." But Ward was charged with possessing ten unregistered machine guns and two silencers without serial numbers. In February 1992, he was found guilty of illegally stockpiling weapons.[25]

On January 13, 1992, thirty-five-year-old Roger Hines stole a .357 Magnum revolver and fifty rounds of ammunition in Oregon before traveling to Washington, D.C., with the intention of killing President Bush. Hines was a six-foot-four-inch, 457-pound man who had been convicted of crimes four times, hospitalized for mental problems five times, and had once entered a hospital with an ax, threatening patients and staff. His psychiatrist said that when Hines was off his medication, he was "dangerous." Several relatives had received postcards from Hines, one of which depicted a Derringer gun and a newspaper article about the assassination of Abraham Lincoln. Hines said he wanted "to become famous." He also kept a diary in which he recorded his fantasies about killing George Bush and molesting and killing young boys.

Shortly after arriving in D.C., Hines took his gun to a school where he believed the president would be making an appearance. But Hines chose the wrong school. The president was forty-five miles away at the Emily Harris Head Start Center in Catonsville, Maryland, southwest of Baltimore.

Hines left Washington, D.C., at the end of January and traveled west. On February 12, 1992, he sold the .357 Magnum at a gun shop in San Francisco. Four days later, while in Salt Lake City, he mailed a letter to Walt Dillman, his state probation officer in Oregon, in which he stated that he had been close to killing President Bush and that he "need[ed] to be stopped. I will kill someone a boy, yes for sex. Maybe I need help 1) by going to jail 2) kill myself 3) being killed by police, I want to die and you need to do so right now I am going after President Bush to do the job the right way."[26] The letter triggered a nationwide Secret Service and FBI manhunt.

On February 28, 1992, Hines was arrested at a bus depot in Portland, Oregon. When he was searched, police found a butcher knife, a hunting knife, and a handwritten diary. Hines told agents that he would "kill President Bush some other time." He admitted sending postcards and letters threatening to kill the president, and while in custody he also confessed his assassination plans to a local television station. He said he would do it again in a "hart [sic] beat" if he could get out of jail. He explained that he wanted to kill President Bush to get attention. Hines also sent a letter to a female acquaintance and wrote, "I was on a killing roll and you could have been next. I was going to rob you and cut you up into parts … you should hope I don't get out of jail for about ten years, because you could be next."[27]

On June 1, 1992, Hines pleaded guilty to making threats against the president and being a felon in possession of a firearm. The court noted Hines's "extraordinarily dangerous mental state" and "significant likelihood that he will commit additional serious crimes." The court sentenced Hines to a hundred months in prison for being a felon in possession of a firearm and a concurrent sixty months for making threats against the president, followed by three years of supervised release.[28]

Deborah Butler was a thirty-two-year-old legal secretary who lived in Denver, Colorado. She kept a diary in which she wrote of her admiration for President Ford's would-be assassin, Sara Jane Moore, and of her plan to kill President Bush. Although Butler had had no previous psychotic episodes in her life, she had lately been having mental problems. She decided to shoot the president "to draw attention to herself and her need for help."[29]

On September 15, Butler drove to a Denver suburb for a Bush reelection campaign rally. Concealing a .32 revolver in the back waistband of her pants, she joined a campaign crowd awaiting Bush's motorcade. Butler was ready to take a shot at the president, but "[a] man diverted her attention long enough so that the motorcade was right in front of her before she knew it," according to a Secret Service agent.

The president's limousine drove by before Butler was able to fire her revolver. She contemplated going to the cordoned-off area where Bush was to speak but changed her mind when she found she would have to go through a metal detector. Butler drove home. After she told her husband of her aborted assassination attempt, he took her to a psychiatric hospital. She told staff at the hospital that she "had just tried to shoot the president." After the staff informed the FBI of her plans, Butler was taken into custody. Police found her diary detailing her assassination plans.[30]

On December 8, 1992, Butler was found competent to stand trial and pleaded guilty to threatening the president. The next month she was sentenced to twenty-seven months in prison and ordered to receive psychiatric treatment. She was also fined $2,000 and put on probation for three years after she had served her term at the federal penitentiary in Rochester, Minnesota.[31]

During his time as president, and later as a former president, Bush was the target of terrorist plots by Colombian drug cartels, Iraqi intelligence officers, and Hezbollah terrorists.

In 1990, Bush visited Colombia despite warnings that a bounty had been placed on his head by a drug cartel angry at the president's determined efforts to aid South American governments in their crackdown on illegal drug distribution. In a September 1989 speech, Bush said, "Our message to the drug cartels is this: The rules have changed. We have a responsibility not to leave our brave friends in Colombia to fight alone."[32]

Jerry Parr, who headed President Reagan's protective detail, said Bush's visit in terms of risk was "probably a seven or eight" on a scale of 1 to 10. "It's risky to be president" he said. "You can't reduce all the risks." Chuck Vance, who was on President Ford's protective detail, said, "There's going to be some razzle dazzle so people aren't quite clear about who to attack. They'll have military personnel everywhere: frogmen, ships, and aircraft. I called in a whole [naval] fleet one time in a Moroccan visit for [Vice President] Agnew because of political uncertainties."[33]

In September 1989, the Secret Service had received information from a "reliable government informant" that ten assassins from Colombia's Medellin cocaine cartel planned to assassinate Bush during his 1990 visit. The threat was considered by the Secret Service to be extremely dangerous, as the year before the drug cartel had hired assassins to kill Reagan's secretary of state, George Schultz, who escaped injury when an explosive device was hurled at his car in Bolivia. The cocaine lords allegedly placed a $3 billion bounty on Bush's head. The assassins were hired by the cartel leaders, including Carlos Lehder, who was already serving a life sentence in a U.S. prison. The assassins allegedly hid out on a ranch in the Chihuahua Mexican border state, waiting for false identification to carry into the United States.

On February 15, 1990, Bush met with the leaders of Colombia, Peru, and Bolivia to discuss the mounting drugs problem in the Western Hemisphere. Before the visit the Secret Service investigated intelligence reports that drug lords were smuggling SA-7 shoulder-fired missiles into Colombia to shoot down Bush's plane when he attended the meeting, which was held in the Colombian city of Cartagena, the heart of cocaine country.[34] The information concerning the alleged attempt to shoot down Bush's plane was confirmed when Colombian authorities discovered ten French-made anti-aircraft missiles in the hands of cocaine traffickers on February 12. Two men were also arrested in Florida attempting to buy 120 Stinger missiles and other arms. According to the FBI, the weapons were to be used to attack Colombian government aircraft.[35] Despite the danger the threats posed, Bush's visit to Colombia went off without incident.

Perhaps the greatest danger to President Bush's life occurred shortly after he left office. On April 14, 1993, three months after Bill Clinton's inauguration, Bush traveled to Kuwait to take part in a three-day celebration marking the victorious U.S.-led invasion to expel Iraqi occupation forces two years earlier. Bush had orchestrated the thirty-three-nation coalition and the forty-three-day Persian Gulf War that ended the seven-month Iraqi occupation of Kuwait.

Shortly before Bush's arrival, Kuwaiti authorities seized seventeen people, including at least two Iraqis, and accused them of plotting to kill Bush by using a 180-pound bomb connected to a remote-control detonator that had been packed into a Toyota four-wheel-drive vehicle. Two of the would-be assassins, ringleaders al-Ghazali and al-Assadi, admitted during the FBI interviews that they had participated in the plot organized by the Iraqi Intelligence Service (IIS). Ghazali told the FBI that he was recruited specifically to kill

Bush. Assadi told the FBI that he was to guide the car bomb, driven by his partner, to Kuwait University, where Bush was to be honored by the emir of Kuwait for his leadership in the Gulf War. The terrorists told the FBI that the bomb was to be parked near the motorcade route. From a vantage point 300 to 500 yards away, Ghazali would set off the bomb using a remote control. FBI bomb specialists estimated the bomb would have been lethal for nearly a quarter mile.

Al-Ghazali and al-Assadi told FBI agents that if the remote control device failed, the bomb was to be detonated by a timing device on a street in Kuwait City named for Bush. Ghazali had a "bomb belt" he would use if all else failed; he was to wear it, approach Bush, and blow them both up. The would-be assassins chose two locations—either at the airport or the ceremony at Kuwait University.

The alleged plot ended in a trial and conviction of eleven Iraqis and three Kuwaitis. On June 4, 1994, the state security court of Kuwait sentenced six of the plotters to death and handed out lengthy prison sentences to seven others. One defendant was later acquitted. On March 20, 1995, a Kuwaiti appeals court commuted the death sentence of four of the convicted conspirators while upholding the death sentences of al-Ghazali and al-Assadi.

The FBI and the CIA concluded that the assassins had indeed been hired by the Iraqi Intelligence Service, as the two would-be assassins alleged. The investigation unearthed "compelling evidence that there was in fact a plot to assassinate former president Bush." In retaliation President Clinton ordered two U.S. warships to launch twenty-three cruise missiles against the Iraqi intelligence headquarters in Baghdad on June 26, 1993.[36]

Several journalists have alleged that the plot never happened. Investigative reporter Seymour Hersh said a classified CIA study was highly skeptical of the Kuwaiti claims of an Iraqi assassination attempt. The study, prepared by the CIA's Counterterrorism Center, suggested that Kuwait might have "cooked the books" on the alleged plot in an effort to play up the "continuing Iraqi threat" to Western interests in the Persian Gulf.

In 2008, *Newsweek*'s Michael Isikoff cited a Pentagon study that "combed through Iraqi intelligence documents seized after the fall of Baghdad, as well as thousands of hours of audio and videotapes of Saddam's conversations with his ministers and top aides" and found "no documents that referred to a plan to kill Bush. The absence was conspicuous because researchers, aware of its potential significance, were looking for such evidence."

Isikoff quoted a source familiar with the Pentagon report, who said "It was surprising, [given how much the Iraqis did document] ... you would have thought there would have been some veiled reference to something about [the plot]."[37]

Bush said the plot to assassinate him was "real" and that he did not learn about it until he returned to the United States. "Some of you probably read about the attempt in Kuwait," Bush said. "We didn't know about it until after the fact after we got back to the states but had I known ... I still would have gone. It's not a macho thing. But that's how much confidence I have in the men and women who dedicate their lives to the Secret Service of the United States."[38]

In 1996, former president Bush was the target of a yet another alleged terrorist attack. Bush planned to visit Beirut, Lebanon, with a scheduled stopover in Cyprus. The CIA received information from an informant that plotters would attempt to shoot down Bush's helicopter. The agency took the information seriously. Bush insisted on going to Beirut anyway, so the Secret Service changed the itinerary, flying him to Damascus instead, and then traveling by motorcade to Lebanon's capital city.[39]

— — —

When George Bush was interviewed in 2012, the eighty-eight-year-old former president said that losing the 1992 election to Bill Clinton was a "terrible, awful feeling.... I really wanted to win and worked hard. Later on, people said, 'Well, he didn't really care,' which is crazy ... I worked my heart out."[40]

CHAPTER ELEVEN

EAGLE

We ... didn't want to be perceived as flies on the wall.
When sensitive family issues were discussed and
as much as possible I didn't want to hear. I didn't want
to know. I felt awkward being present....
—Larry Cockell, head of President Clinton's
White House detail, 1998–2000

Bill Clinton was forty-six years old when he was inaugurated in January 1993, making him the youngest U.S. president since John F. Kennedy. Clinton based his candidacy on his promise to follow a different path from traditional Democratic Party liberals. He appealed to the middle class and to political moderates and independents, and he promised to both promote job growth and reduce the national debt.

Once in office Clinton prioritized law and order, individualism, and welfare reform. Clinton left a complicated legacy. He presided over a booming economy, balanced the budget, and established several new free-trade regimes. He also intervened to prevent genocide in Kosovo, and, in September 1993, he orchestrated a historic peace treaty between Israeli prime minister Yitzhak Rabin and Palestinian leader Yasser Arafat.

Clinton was reelected in 1996, but scandal soon followed. During his second term, Clinton lied about having an affair with White House intern Monica Lewinsky, which led to only the second impeachment, for perjury and obstruction of justice, of an American president. Though he was cleared of all charges in a U.S. Senate trial, many Americans believed Clinton severely damaged the office of the presidency.

--- --- ---

By the time Clinton took office, the Secret Service had begun introducing innovative measures to protect the president. When the president went swimming in the sea, agents were fitted with snorkeling equipment, and when he appeared in public, they'd sometimes dress up as firefighters or rescue workers to offer better protection. When Clinton went on a safari in Africa, they carried weapons that could bring down elephants and rhinos.

Clinton appreciated that his agents worked in a way that allowed him to avoid the suffocating atmosphere of round-the-clock protection. "They were really good about trying to be flexible," Clinton said. "Sometimes Chelsea [Clinton's daughter] and I would be walking down in Washington and go to a bookstore or something like that but I tried to give them enough notice so they could prepare."[1]

But some observers believed Clinton's relationship with the Secret Service was less than congenial. Some agents were bothered by Clinton's avoidance of the draft during the Vietnam War, and others did not like his "informal lifestyle,"[2] which involved having to follow

"Clinton Standard Time," a reference to the fact that Clinton was often "one or two hours late." Speaking about himself, Clinton acknowledged problems with his protectors when he said, "You're impatient because you're tired and you've got a headache and you take it out by being a little short [with agents].... They have to put up with it."[3]

Although most agents did not condone Clinton's philandering, they believed he was "decent" and had a good attitude toward most people he came into contact with. Many of the problems agents encountered were not caused by Clinton, some agents believed, but by the president's staff, who were "difficult and arrogant."[4] Agents held particular contempt for Bill's wife, Hillary. One agent said she had an "explosive temper and constantly belittled everyone.... She's very angry and sarcastic and it is very hard on her staff. She yells at them and complains." Another said, "She did not speak to us. We spent years with her. She never said thank you."[5] This view was also held by many members of the permanent White House staff, who characterized the Clintons as "haughty and arrogant."[6]

Hillary Clinton allegedly "hated" the Secret Service. She once ordered her agents to "stay the f*ck back, stay the f*ck away from me! Don't come within ten yards of me, or else!" On another occasion she remonstrated with an agent who refused to carry her luggage. "If you want to remain on this detail, get your fucking ass over here and grab those bags," she shouted at him.[7] She also ordered agents never to speak to her if she was walking through the White House grounds. When agents reminded her that keeping a distance of ten yards made it difficult for her detail to protect her, she "didn't seem to care what the Secret Service said." Her response was simply, "Just f*cking do as I say, okay?"[8] During a trip to Little Rock, she left her agents standing as she got in her car and drove away and stayed away for several hours. She later laughed about it, but her detail was not amused, believing the first lady had placed her life in jeopardy.[9] Another agent told author Gary Aldrich that the president's daughter referred to her protectors as "personal trained pigs" and described them as such to some of her friends. When an agent scolded her, Chelsea said her parents referred to agents in the same way.[10]

The Secret Service was virtually omnipresent during the Clinton presidency. Except for the upstairs family quarters of the White House, agents were always present except when Clinton met with close advisors, and even then an agent would be posted on the patio just outside the Oval Office's glass-paneled doors. Agents were present when Clinton walked his dog, Buddy, on the South Lawn and when he went swimming in the White House pool.[11] As Clinton observed, "The Secret Service is in the front seat of the car when the president is riding with people talking about anything from national security to sensitive political matters … to personal family matters."[12]

It was because of their close proximity to the president that Kenneth Starr, an independent prosecutor appointed by Congress to look into allegations of corruption in the Whitewater scandal, wanted to subpoena some agents in Clinton's White House detail. He also asked them to appear as witnesses in his investigation into whether Clinton obstructed justice in the Paula Jones sexual harassment case. Jones had accused the president of making improper sexual advances toward her when he was governor of Arkansas. Her lawsuit was later settled. Effectively, Clinton admitted guilt.

When Starr subpoenaed several agents, including the head of Clinton's detail, Larry Cockell, to question them about the alleged romantic affair with Monica Lewinsky, the agency objected. "We, internally in the agency didn't want to be perceived as flies on the wall," Cockell said. "When sensitive family issues were discussed ... as much as possible I didn't want to hear. I didn't want to know. I felt awkward being present but I know my presence was compelled by law."[13]

The Secret Service felt very strongly that agents should not have been summoned to testify before the grand jury investigating the Jones incident. The issue was argued all the way to the Supreme Court, which ruled that the Secret Service was not immune to subpoena power. Cockell and other agents were compelled to testify. It was one of the few times in history that the agency was forced to break the unwritten rule of confidentiality.

In fact, Clinton's womanizing caused problems with the Secret Service throughout his presidency. Agents were concerned about the way the president compromised their protective mission by frequently leaving the White House unescorted. According to FBI liaison Gary Aldrich, a "sensitive White House source" said that Clinton would leave late at night through the West Executive Lobby exit, "in such a way it would appear [he was] walking to the Executive Office Building." But once Clinton was out of sight, he would be driven by his aide Bruce Lindsay, covered up by a blanket on the back seat of the car, to the Marriott Hotel, where he would meet up with one of his mistresses. The Secret Service apparently knew about the trips and kept a log of the president's movements. Aldrich characterized Clinton's behavior as "one of the most serious and irresponsible breaches of security in U.S. history."[14]

— — —

During Clinton's first seven years in office, the Secret Service made arrangements for 2,500 appearances in more than eight hundred cities in the United States and abroad, as well as 450 appearances at public events in the Washington area. During this period, the Secret Service Research Division maintained a list of "several thousand" Americans who were "presidential threats." More than four hundred were on the "watch list" of "dangerous" individuals. Several hundred weapons were detected each year—almost all of them carried lawfully by people who had state permits. Those who were discovered to be carrying weapons illegally were usually taken to police headquarters and charged with a misdemeanor.[15]

There were a number of incidents that the media characterized as "threats" but were unconnected to any assassination attempt. Three incidents, in particular, received a lot of attention. In the early morning of September 12, 1994, a Cessna 150L airplane crashed onto the South Lawn of the White House, killing the pilot, thirty-eight-year-old Frank Eugene Corder, but injuring no one else. The plane came to a halt against the south wall of the White House, causing minimal damage. President Clinton and his family were not home at the time. The Clintons were spending the night across Pennsylvania Avenue at Blair House while White House workers repaired faulty duct work. There was no evidence Corder, who had been drinking and smoking crack cocaine at the time he flew the plane, ever intended to kill Clinton or had been angry with his policies. Rather, according to informed associates, he simply wanted to die crashing his plane into the White House.[16]

Another incident involved thirty-three-year-old Marcelino Corniel, a gang member with a violent criminal record. Five days before Christmas 1994, Corniel, who had been living in Lafayette Park across from the White House, ran toward uniformed White House police with a hunting knife taped to his hand. Two Park police officers and two Secret Service agents confronted him, their pistols drawn. After Corniel ignored repeated orders to drop his weapon, one of the U.S. Park police officers shot and killed Corniel. He had made no overt threats to kill President Clinton.[17]

In another incident, on May 23, 1995, Leland William Modjeski, an out-of-work pizza delivery man who had once studied for a doctorate in psychology, scaled the White House fence and was shot in the arm by a Secret Service agent. Another agent who grappled with Modjeski suffered an arm wound from the same bullet. Modjeski was carrying an unloaded .38 caliber revolver, and the Secret Service concluded that he had no intention of harming Clinton. Instead, agents believed, Modjeski wanted to be "cop-shot."[18]

Clinton was the subject of numerous written and verbal threats to his life, some serious and some not so serious. Among the nonserious threats was the case of Rob Sherick. On Christmas Eve 1996, Sherick preached from the pulpit of the Washington National Cathedral, saying, "God will hold you to account, Mr. President," referring to the president's veto of a ban on partial-birth abortions. After the service, Sherick was detained by Secret Service agents who accused him of threatening the president's life. No charges were forthcoming.[19]

Michael Shields was a twenty-eight-year-old gun dealer and president of Firearms International of Norfolk, Virginia. He was an avid student of war and sometimes donated military memorabilia to his alma mater, Virginia Wesleyan College. Shields hated President Clinton, and when he was questioned in 1993 by agents from the Bureau of Alcohol, Tobacco, Firearms, and Explosives about an unrelated gun case, he told them he wanted to kill the president. Shields assured agents he was serious about the threat and that he was recruiting accomplices. Secret Service agent Glen Garbis said he made the threat "over and over again." Shields was arrested at the

Norfolk federal building.[20] In June 1993, Shields pleaded guilty to threatening President Clinton and was placed on probation for five years and sentenced to eight months' imprisonment. But under an agreement with prosecutors, he received credit for four months he spent undergoing psychiatric evaluation and another four months for time he spent between a halfway house and home detention.[21]

The Secret Service considered the cases of Paul F. Walling and Zsolt Sass to be considerably more dangerous. Forty-six-year-old Walling, who lived in Berwyn, a suburb of Philadelphia, was an unemployed auto mechanic and gun enthusiast who had stockpiled forty guns and hundreds of rounds of ammunition. Neighbors described him as a "gun nut" and heard him talk incessantly about weapons. Local gun dealers described him as a regular customer.

Walling also had a temper. When he was angry, he sometimes threatened to shoot his neighbors. In July 1994, Walling told a friend that he was livid about the Brady Handgun Control Act and that he would "like to shoot Clinton and Attorney General Janet Reno for what they have done to the American people by trying to take guns away from them." The friend happened to be a police officer who told the Secret Service of Walling's threats. On July 19, Walling was arrested in Cape May, New Jersey, while walking toward a stolen vehicle containing handguns, semiautomatic rifles, and ammunition. In May 1995, in Philadelphia's U.S. District Court, Walling pleaded guilty to threatening the president's life. He received four years in prison.[22]

Thirty-four-year-old Zsolt Sass, an illegal German immigrant and right-wing conservative, was also gun lover. He ran a nightclub in Sarasota, Florida, and had used a variety of false Social Security numbers, including Elvis Presley's. He claimed he was a government informant who used his nightclub business to help the Secret Service gather information on criminal activity. The Secret Service confirmed the story and admitted Sass had helped them on a counterfeiting case.[23] Sass also claimed that he helped look into the sale of human organs from China, monitored a spy who had been working for the KGB, and acted as a middleman to sell plutonium to Saddam Hussein.

When Sass fell out with his girlfriend, she filed domestic violence charges against him. She also told local police that Sass had threatened to kill Clinton "numerous times." Her story was supported by three other witnesses. When Sass was arrested on September 3, 1997, Sarasota County deputy sheriffs found seven guns in his car and home, including a handgun with laser sighting. They also found eight knives and 250 rounds of ammunition. Sass waived his right to a jury trial and asked the judge to decide the case. At his three-day trial in January 1998, Sass was found guilty of threatening the president. U.S. District Judge H. Dale Cook said, "The threats were clear and concise. The circumstances were such that there was danger to the president."[24]

In June 1998, the Republic of Texas, a little-known radical separatist organization, sent a threatening email to President Clinton, along with an attached document entitled "Declaration of War." A couple of weeks later, a second email was sent to FBI director Louis Freeh that stated, "Your FBI employees and their families have been targeted for destruction by revenge. We the people are extremely mad and will not accept the inequities any longer."

The Republic of Texas believed that the state of Texas was illegally annexed by the United States in 1845 and should therefore be a separate nation. In 1997, some of the organization's members had drawn police into a week-long armed standoff.

During an investigation, the FBI learned that conspirators planned to kill the president by modifying a BIC lighter so that it would expel air instead of propane. They would glue a hypodermic needle to the opening of the lighter, and a cactus thorn would be inserted that would be coated with a biological agent such as anthrax, botulism, or HIV. On July 1, 1998, the FBI arrested three men, seventy-two-year-old Johnnie Wise, sixty-three-year-old Oliver Dean Emigh, and forty-three-year-old Jack Abbot Grebe in Olmito, Texas, near the border with Mexico. All three were former members of the military with no criminal records.

FBI agents seized several three-gallon drums and three jars with a clear liquid from Wise's trailer. The men were charged with conspiring to use weapons of mass destruction against federal officials. Later it was learned that the would-be assassins had also hatched a plot to kill U.S. attorney general Janet Reno, FBI director Louis Freeh, and other federal and local officials.[25]

During their trial it was revealed that the men apparently had not attempted to obtain any biological agent. Emigh was acquitted on all eight charges, while Grebe and Wise were each convicted on two counts of sending threatening emails to government agencies and were sentenced to more than twenty-four years in prison. According to federal prosecutor Mervyn Mosbacker, FBI agents saved lives by arresting the men. "I don't think the U.S. should have to wait for someone to cause death and destruction to respond to a threat of that kind," he said.[26]

Like presidents before him, Clinton was the intended recipient of parcel bombs. One bomber, thirty-year-old David Shane Shelby, was characterized by people who knew him as a "class clown."[27] In 1995, after serving three years in an Indiana prison for burglary,

Shelby began writing threatening letters to President Clinton. "I hate you … turn Charles Manson loose or I will kill you," Shelby wrote in one of the letters. Secret Service agents trailed Shelby to Utah. After distributing sketches of the suspect to various businesses in the Ogden, Utah, area, mail clerk Chris Ferre recognized him as a regular customer. "He looked like a hillbilly," Ferre said, "The first time he came in here he wore bib overalls. He was real nice to me. He didn't talk a lot but he didn't seem the type that would do this."[28]

Shelby picked up his mail on Wednesday January 25, 1995, and told Ferre he had some packages to send. Ferre immediately called the police, and a short while later a Secret Service agent and an Ogden police officer arrived at the post office and arrested him. Within minutes more than a hundred federal, state, and local law enforcement officers swarmed the neighborhood. A bomb squad was called, and when Shelby's packages were X-rayed, agents found a bomb made from a light bulb packed with smokeless powder. It would have exploded when screwed into a socket and switched on. Secret Service agents also found a small arsenal of guns and explosive materials in Shelby's rented van. They also learned that he tried to mail a gun to convicted killer Charles Manson. In 1996, Shelby pleaded guilty to charges of threatening the president and weapons violations. He was sentenced to twenty-four years in a federal prison.[29]

Two years later, in June 1998, Clinton was targeted once again by a would-be bomber, forty-nine-year-old Jeffrey Loring Pickering. On June 13, President Clinton visited Eugene and Springfield, Oregon, in the wake of a shooting rampage that left two people dead. The previous day a caller had told police that "bombs have been distributed" across the city. Two bombs were found in a culvert behind an air and space museum on the airport grounds about a quarter of a mile from the terminal.

Shortly before Clinton's visit, Pickering, who had a criminal record, told friends and relatives that if the president visited Eugene, Oregon, he would "blow him away." His brother contacted the FBI, which arrested and charged the would-be assassin. He was also charged with planting the bombs the day before the president's visit. He pleaded guilty and was sentenced to thirteen years in prison.[30]

Clinton was also the target of at least three terrorist assassination plots. The FBI's investigation of the 1993 World Trade Center bombing in New York produced evidence that al Qaeda leader Osama bin Laden had ordered a team of assassins to use shoulder-fired missiles or explosives against Clinton's motorcade in Manila, the Philippines, during his November 1994 visit. Later, intelligence agents learned that Ramzi Yousef, the al Qaeda terrorist who used a truck bomb to attack the World Trade Center, admitted that he plotted to assassinate Clinton during the time he spent in Manila but was dissuaded by heavy security.[31]

In November 1996, President Clinton visited the Philippines for a second time to participate in the Asia-Pacific Economic Cooperation Summit. At one point during his stay, Clinton was scheduled to visit a local politician, his route taking him across a bridge in central Manila. As the presidential motorcade set off, Secret Service agents learned that an attack was imminent. The motorcade was quickly rerouted. Agents soon discovered that a bomb had been planted under the bridge. The subsequent Secret Service investigation into the plot revealed that Osama bin Laden had been the mastermind. Terrorists came within minutes of killing President Clinton.[32]

The FBI was also convinced that Osama bin Laden had organized a team of jihadists to fire a shoulder-launched missile at Clinton's helicopter when he visited Bangladesh in March 2000. The Secret Service abruptly canceled a scheduled trip to a remote village when it received information about the plot.[33]

President Clinton loved to jog on the streets of Washington, D.C., usually three eight-minute miles, three to five days a week. A quarter-mile running track had been constructed on the south grounds of the White House, but Clinton preferred running on the streets of Washington to see people and shake their hands. The president ran through crowds, crossed city streets outside of the crosswalk, and stood in the open. He was accompanied by a ten-car motorcade, a Secret Service SWAT team vehicle, a communications truck, an ambulance, a press van, and cars for guests. Clinton's detail required four armed agents and a supervisor with a radio.

Some of Clinton's agents were so unfit that they could not keep up with the forty-six-year-old president, according to former agent Dan Emmett. During one run agents lost sight of Clinton as he disappeared over the crest of a hill at the Washington Monument. Clinton was out of sight, without protection, and in the midst of tourists before his agents caught up with him. "To run with the president of the United States through downtown D.C.," Emmett said, "and then have him stop and shake hands with the man on the street was unwise on Clinton's part—dangerous as hell, in fact." Clinton put himself and his agents in harm's way, according to Emmett.[34]

President Clinton's stubborn insistence on jogging in public also nearly got him assassinated, and it would likely have happened, Dan Emmett said, "were it not for an overseas trip." Clinton's would-be assassin was Ronald Gene Barbour, a forty-five-year-old veteran and unemployed limousine driver who lived in Orlando, Florida, and suffered from severe depression. Barbour hated Democratic politicians and wanted to kill Clinton to embarrass the administration. Barbour didn't much like Hillary either, once telling a neighbor, "I have this vision of stomping that woman [Hillary Clinton] to death with hobnail boots." He then told her he was the man who would be known as Clinton's assassin.[35]

On January 11, 1994, before he put his plans to kill Clinton into effect, Barbour attempted suicide at his apartment in Florida. After the attempt failed, he put his gun and clothes in his car and drove toward West Virginia, where he intended to try again. But Barbour missed his exit and decided instead to drive to Washington, D.C., to kill Clinton. He also wanted to get himself killed, or "cop-shot" as police officers call it.

In Washington, Barbour roamed the National Mall every day for a week with his .45 handgun, intending to shoot Clinton while the president was jogging. "I never got stopped by the police," Barbour said. "I am a very orderly person. I just played Joe Tourist."[36] He also walked around the White House several times. But then Barbour learned that the president was in Russia, so he headed back to Florida and sold his gun.

On January 29, 1994, Barbour invited a neighbor into his apartment and told him about his aborted plans to assassinate the president. Intrigued, the neighbor returned with his fiancée and a tape recorder. Barbour told them that he planned to kill Clinton then travel to Virginia to commit suicide at St. Mary's Hospital, his birthplace.[37] Over the next few days, Barbour related his story to several other people. At the urging of some of his neighbors, Barbour visited the Veterans Affairs Medical Center on February 3, 1994, for psychiatric treatment.

The Secret Service soon learned about Barbour's confession and began an investigation. Agents found Barbour's suicide note and tracked him to the medical center. While Secret Service special agents met with Daniel Doherty, head of the hospital administration, they saw Barbour in the lobby awaiting treatment. After a doctor's evaluation, Barbour was involuntarily committed to a private mental health facility. He was also eventually charged with threatening to kill the president. The president's head of detail told Clinton about Barbour's plot and warned him that his jogging habits had left him extremely vulnerable.

On May 27, 1994, Barbour was found guilty by an Orlando jury and sentenced to five years in prison and three years' probation on his release.

A few months later, Clinton was stalked by twenty-six-year-old New Mexico native Francisco Martin Duran. Duran was an army veteran who was dishonorably discharged for aggravated assault with a vehicle and drunk and disorderly conduct.

He had fantasies of killing President Clinton with "his hands, very privately and very intimately."[38] In mid-September 1994, he began to purchase assault weapons, including an SKS assault rifle and about a hundred rounds of ammunition. Two days later, Duran bought a thirty-round clip and had the rifle equipped with a folding stock. Soon thereafter he bought a shotgun and more ammunition.

On September 30, Duran left work and, without contacting his family or employer, drove to Washington, D.C., in his 1989 Chevrolet S-10 pickup truck. His wife filed a missing person's report with the sheriff's office on October 1, the day after her husband disappeared. By October 10, Duran was in Charlottesville, Virginia. The following day he bought a large trench coat and another thirty-round ammunition clip in Richmond, Virginia, before driving to Washington, D.C., and checking into a hotel. Duran moved around various hotels in the Washington area between the tenth and the twenty-ninth of October.[39]

On the morning of Sunday, October 29, Duran checked out of the Embassy Suites Hotel in Tysons Corner, drove to downtown Washington, and parked his truck on 17th Street, between D and E Streets. He walked to the White House and watched President Clinton return to the executive mansion from his Middle East visit via a helicopter that landed on the White House lawn. By early afternoon Duran was in front of the north side of the White House, wearing the overcoat he had purchased earlier.[40]

Around 3:00 p.m., as Duran stood by the White House fence, sightseers and tourists walked along Pennsylvania Avenue in front of the White House. Two boys who had been standing at the fence remarked aloud that one of the men standing near the North Portico of the White House looked like President Clinton. Within seconds Duran, who by then had been staring at the executive mansion for more than an hour, pushed the boys aside, slipped a semiautomatic assault rifle from beneath his coat, extended its folding stock, and began firing at the person he mistakenly believed was Clinton. "I watched him place it between the bars of the fence," said corrections officer trainee Kenneth Alan Davis, "and he just opened fire."[41]

Running back and forth along the fence as he fired, Duran quickly emptied a clip of thirty rounds at his intended victim as bystanders scattered in panic. Five bullets hit the mansion's four-foot-thick sandstone wall, and three shattered a window and chipped the stone of the Press Briefing Room near the West Wing. No one was injured. When Duran stopped to insert another thirty-round clip, a bystander, security expert Michael Rokosky, tackled him from behind as the gunman tried to reload his rifle. "I thought, 'I'm probably not going to get a better opportunity to tackle him,'" he said, "so I did." As they struggled on the sidewalk, two other bystanders joined Rokosky and helped him to subdue Duran before uniformed Secret Service officers arrived.[42]

Duran fired at least twenty-nine rounds before he was subdued. As he was being handcuffed by Secret Service agents, Duran said, "I wish you had shot me." President Clinton was watching a televised football game on the opposite side of the White House, unaware of the shooting.[43]

During their investigation of Duran's attack, Secret Service agents impounded his brown pickup near the White House and found one of the rifles he had purchased en route to Washington, several boxes of ammunition, a nerve gas antidote, a handwritten document with the heading "Last will and words," an order form for the book *Hit Man*, and several books about out-of-body experiences. They also found a number of items that clearly revealed his intention to assassinate Clinton, including a letter in which he had written, "Can you imagine a higher moral calling than to destroy someone's dreams with one bullet?" a road atlas on which he had written "Kill the Pres," and a cover torn from a telephone book that bore a picture of President Clinton with a circle drawn around his head and an "X" on his face.

Duran was charged with attempting to assassinate President Clinton. He pleaded not guilty and mounted an insanity defense, claiming that he was trying to save the world by destroying an alien "mist" connected by an umbilical cord to an alien in the Colorado Mountains. He also claimed to be incited by ultraconservative talk show host Chuck Baker, who spoke on air about "armed revolution" and "cleansing" the government.[44]

But the jury wasn't buying it. In April 1995, after deliberating nearly five hours, jurors convicted Duran of trying to assassinate President Clinton. They rejected the insanity defense, and he was sentenced to forty years in federal prison. U.S. District Judge Charles R. Richey said such crimes "cannot be tolerated in a free society." Before imposing the sentence, Richey read parts of a letter that he had received from Ronald K. Noble, a Treasury Department official with supervisory authority over the Secret Service. The semiautomatic rifle shots fired by Duran, Noble's letter said, marked "the first shooting directed at the White House in over 150 years." Noble told Richey that Duran's actions "were an assault on all people of the United States, as well as on the President."[45]

Duran's shooting spree and the 1995 Oklahoma bombing atrocity committed by Timothy McVeigh prompted Clinton to tighten security around the White House, including closing a two-block stretch of Pennsylvania Avenue to vehicular traffic. He was disappointed that such measures were necessary. "I felt that on occasion giving in to the security requirements did isolate me from the public," Clinton said, "After a man with an assault weapon shot up the White House the Secret Service asked me to stop running in the Mall so I did but I hated it because it was my one daily contact with ordinary citizens."[46]

— — —

Despite having been impeached and receiving low public-approval ratings of his personal character, Clinton left office with the highest-average job-approval rating of any president in the twentieth century. His popularity did not help his vice president, Al Gore, who lost the 2000 election to George W. Bush.

CHAPTER TWELVE

TRAILBLAZER

*I know [President Bush] has been getting a lot of threat letters.
There are a lot of people out there who think very strongly
about him in one way or another.... He is the only president
that invaded a country without provocation and without it
being started by the other side. I think he has gained a lot of
enmity.... There are a lot of people who resent this president,
both externally and internally, some of whom have lost sons
and daughters and had people injured in the war in Iraq.*
—Chuck Vance, former Secret Service agent

George W. Bush, the son of the forty-first president, ascended to the presidency preaching what he called "compassionate conservatism." Bush had some significant accomplishments at home, including signing a law to expand Medicare and another to require regular testing and achievement standards for public schools. In 2003, he persuaded Congress to pass a significant tax cut.

But national security issues and foreign affairs dominated Bush's eight years as president. Bush had been in office less than eight months when al Qaeda struck on September 11, 2001. Bush won praise for the way he rallied the nation and defended the homeland in the dangerous years following the 9/11 attacks. Bush received bipartisan support to pass the Patriot Act to better protect Americans at home and abroad, and to support the war in Afghanistan to root out al Qaeda. Bush also introduced new laws to give wider powers to the FBI, the Secret Service, and the CIA.

President Bush introduced the "Bush Doctrine," which sought to implement preemptive action against terrorist states, unilaterally if necessary. But Bush's invasion of Iraq in 2003 left him mired in controversy, not least because he relied on faulty intelligence to help persuade the public to go to war to topple Iraq's Saddam Hussein.

— — —

President Bush had two Secret Service codenames: "Tumbler" and "Trailblazer," the former being his codename while his father, George H. W. Bush, was president. His agents found him to be "down-to-earth" and "caring." One agent said, "[The family] are always thinking of people around them."[1]

Agents enjoyed chopping wood with Bush and appreciated that he was always punctual. They remarked on how the media failed to represent Bush's true personality to the public, noting that there was a difference between the President Bush who appeared at press conferences or public forums and the one they came to know. "With us he doesn't talk like that, doesn't sound like that," one agent said. "He's funny as hell. Incredible sense of humor, and he'll joke around. He's two different personalities."[2] Agents also thought highly of Bush's wife, Laura. She had the "undying admiration of almost every agent. I've never ever heard a negative thing about Laura Bush ... nothing," one agent said. "Everybody loves her to death and respects the hell out of her."[3]

George W. Bush became the most guarded president in American history, especially after the 9/11 attacks. Tours of the White House were suspended in the wake of the attacks. They resumed two years later, but on a limited basis.

The Secret Service introduced new measures to protect the president from public demonstrations. It developed a system of "free speech zones" and "protest zones" where people opposed to Bush's policies could demonstrate when the president gave a speech in public. The zones were successful in keeping protestors out of presidential sight and outside the view of the media.

As a wartime president, Bush received many threats, and with the advance of the internet, many of them were made online. For example, in 2003, Vaughn Alan Clark wrote on an America Online chat room website, "I am going to kill President Bush tomorrow." His comments came about a month before U.S. forces began invading Iraq and at a time when the Secret Service was acutely alert to any type of threat. Another chat room participant reported Clark to the authorities, and he was arrested, tried, and found guilty of threatening the president, even though the federal prosecutor never considered Clark's "threat" to be serious. "It's one of those typical threats against the president," Boise, Idaho, federal prosecutor Terry Derden said. "The U.S. Secret Service investigates every one. But I don't think he [Clark] represented a serious threat against the president."[4]

As with every president, Bush received many threats from people with mental illnesses. Forty-seven-year-old Timothy Wade Pinkston was a homeless man who had been involuntarily committed to the psychiatric unit of St. Joseph's Hospital in Florida. Secret Service agents were called to the hospital when Pinkston told staff that he

planned to go to Washington to shoot the president. When agents
interviewed him, Pinkston repeated the threat, explaining that he did
not like Bush's foreign policy or his handling of the war in Iraq.
Pinkston was given multiple opportunities to recant. But he didn't,
and agents said he gave the impression that he could obtain a weapon
and transportation. They were also aware that the homeless man
had threatened to kill Bush's father in 1991.[5] Pinkston was arrested
by the agents and charged.

Pinkston's lawyer appealed, but the appeal was rejected. The
judges concluded, "There was sufficient evidence for the jury to
conclude that Pinkston's statements were not just political argument,
idle talk or jest, and that Pinkston intentionally made a true threat
against the president under such circumstances that a reasonable
person would construe it as a serious expression of an intention to
inflict bodily harm upon or take the life of the president." Pinkston
was sentenced to five years in prison.[6]

Some threats against Bush were not prosecuted, and several convictions were overturned on appeal. In 2002, thirty-five-year-old
Cleveland police officer William David was distraught and angry
because his girlfriend had left him for another man. Looking for
revenge, David wrote letters threatening to kill the president "JFK-
Style" and signed the new boyfriend's name and put his return
address on the envelope. But the Secret Service traced the letters to
David through his fingerprints. He was charged with lying to Secret
Service agents but not with threatening to kill the president. He
pleaded guilty in January 2002. In a reply to a reporter's question
about why David had not been charged with threatening the president's life, Cleveland Assistant U.S. Attorney William Edwards said,
"I'm not going to get into that. We get all kinds of threats. Some we

prosecute and others we don't. It depends on the totality of the circumstances of each case."[7]

In 2005, Oregon prison inmate Jonathan Lincoln wrote a letter threatening President Bush and endorsing the 9/11 attacks. A court found Lincoln guilty of threatening the president's life. But a three-judge panel of the U.S. Court of Appeals for the Ninth Circuit overturned the conviction, ruling that the letter was "protected speech." The judges decided that while the letter's language might have been disturbing, it broke no laws. "Lincoln was exercising his constitutional right to endorse the actions of bin Laden and al Qaeda, which is protected speech," the judges wrote.[8]

In a similar case, a court ruled that a man who had made threats against the president was not exercising his free-speech rights. Thirty-five-year-old Vikram Buddhi, an Indian national who was attending advanced engineering classes at Purdue University, posted threats against President Bush on internet forums. He hijacked online identities of other Purdue students to post messages that endorsed the murder of Bush and Cheney and the rape of their wives. He also made threats against then-defense secretary Donald Rumsfeld.

In a three-day trial, Buddhi never disputed writing the online messages. But the jury had to decide whether Buddhi's comments were true threats or part of a crude online protest of the Iraq War that should be protected by free speech. Buddhi's lawyer said his client had no intention of actually harming anyone. "Where does it say Mr. Buddhi is going to kill the president, the vice president?" he asked. "It doesn't." But the jury decided Buddhi had made a clear intention of harming the president and had not simply been "exercising his free speech rights." He was convicted of "making threats against the president and successors to the president, making threats against former presidents and their families, making threats by inter-state communications and use of the Internet to threaten destruction by fire." The prosecutor, Assistant U.S. Attorney Philip Benson, said, "I hope this will serve as a deterrent to other people who want to kill human beings [and] blow up power plants."[9] In 2009 Buddhi was sentenced to fifty-seven months in prison.

On January 28, 2008, New Jersey resident Aleksander Aleksov told uniformed officers outside a White House gate that he wanted to kill the president. Bush was at the White House preparing for his final State of the Union address at the time. When challenged by the officers about his remarks, Aleksov quickly began to walk away. But a uniformed Secret Service agent caught up with him, searched him, and found a small knife in his suitcase.

During a court appearance in Washington, D.C., Alexsov admit-ted making the threats. But he was found not guilty by reason of insanity after two doctors determined that he was suffering from a mental illness at the time of the incident. Aleksov remained in a federal medical center for treatment as the courts ordered compul-sory medication.[10]

Bush, like presidents before him, was subjected to numerous threats from prison inmates. Charles E. Fuller was a career criminal who in 2002 was serving a forty-six-month sentence at the federal penitentiary in Terre Haute, Indiana, for sending three letters threat-ening President Clinton in 1998. Not long before he was due to be released, Fuller decided to threaten President Bush and sent a hand-written letter to the FBI headquarters in Washington, D.C. In the letter, Fuller expressed anger toward U.S. government leaders and made references to five bombs at five separate locations. He also indicated that he possessed a canister of Serin nerve gas. "I will be released soon! Me and my friends are going after all of America's rulers!" he wrote. "They will pay! Bush is first! He will die first! I will not have a president that is criminal in office! I will kill him myself!"[11]

Fuller's name, inmate number, and the words "Special Mail" were written on the envelope, along with his return address. He had also written on the envelope a designation normally used for privileged communications so that prison officials would not read the contents. But prison staff read the letter anyway, and it was turned over to the Secret Service. Fuller was interviewed by agents and charged with threatening to kill the president. He pleaded guilty but appealed his conviction and argued that his letter was not a "true threat," as he suffered from a mental disorder known as "institutionalization" or a desire to stay in prison. But the appeals court ruled that even if Fuller threatened President Bush because of his "institutionalization," his letter constituted a real threat, and the court affirmed his conviction.[12]

In 2007, Daniel Cvijanovich was serving a prison sentence for throwing a rock at the federal building in Fargo, North Dakota, and threatening a federal officer. He told fellow inmates Robby Aldrich and Kyle White that he planned to kill Bush after he was released from prison. Aldrich and White informed the authorities about Cvijanovich's threats, and he was charged with threatening the life of the president. In court Cvijanovich's lawyer characterized his client's comments as "jokes, lies and exaggerations" and "the kind of big talk that goes on in prison." But a jury disagreed and found Cvijanovich guilty, sentencing him to nineteen months in prison.[13]

The Secret Service was well aware that for decades many prison inmates had used the ruse of threatening the president to facilitate a move from a state prison to a federal institution, where they believed living conditions were superior.

Twenty-seven-year-old Gordon L. Chadwick had been in and out of jail for most of his adult life for crimes including indecent exposure, assault, and theft. He was a tall man with a star tattoo on his face, a spider web tattoo on his neck, and other tattoos going down his arms. While he was in solitary confinement in Montgomery County Jail in Houston, Texas, serving a four-year prison term for threatening a jail official, he wrote several threatening letters, including letters threatening to kill President Bush and the judge who presided at his trial. The threats were likely a ruse to get Chadwick transferred to a federal prison. It didn't work. Chadwick was sentenced to thirty months in a federal prison, but that time was added to the sentence he was already serving in county prison.[14]

Bush was subjected to several very serious threats to his life. Robert Pickett was an accountant with the Internal Revenue Service who had been fired from his job in 1988 because of incompetence and poor work attendance. But Pickett believed he was dismissed because he reported a colleague who had been "violating regulations." He spent years trying to get reinstated to his job. On February 7, 2001, two weeks after the first inauguration of President Bush, Pickett, still simmering over the firing, visited the White House armed with a five-shot Taurus .38 caliber special revolver. Pickett fired some errant shots in the general direction of the executive mansion. A nearby police patrol car immediately pulled up, and an officer engaged Pickett. A standoff ensued, with Pickett alternately threatening to shoot himself and others. After ten minutes, Pickett was shot in the knee by a Secret Service agent and taken to the hospital. President Bush, who was exercising in the residence area of the White House at the time, was never in danger.[15]

Pickett was originally charged with discharging a firearm during a crime, which, if he had been found guilty, would have brought a ten-year mandatory sentence. But Pickett made a plea agreement and entered a guilty plea to a local firearms violation and an "Alford plea" (acknowledging there was enough evidence to convict him but not admitting he was entirely guilty) to assaulting a federal officer. In July 2001, Pickett was sentenced to three years at the Federal Medical Center in Rochester, followed by three years of probation. He was released on September 19, 2003.[16]

In 2002, the Secret Service arrested thirty-three-year-old New Hampshire resident Jeffrey Cloutier outside the White House after agents received an alert that Cloutier had been overheard threatening to kill Bush. Cloutier believed President Bush was doing a poor job and said he "was going to take care of him and take over." The Secret Service also heard that Cloutier had explosives.

The tip-off about Cloutier came from cab driver Frank Pauloski, an army veteran and retired New Jersey state trooper. Cloutier told Pauloski that he was going to see the president because he had "a chip implanted in his brain," was "the president's boss," "didn't like the way the operation went," and wanted to "talk to the president about it." Cloutier also told Pauloski that he had "mental telepathy and could tell what everyone was thinking." Pauloski said that when he dropped off Cloutier, he saw a rifle case wrapped in towels among the luggage.[17]

When Cloutier arrived in Washington on September 4, he rented a car and drove to the White House but was stopped by police and Secret Service agents. They found ten rifles and shotguns and six handguns in his car. Cloutier was jailed on felony charges of weapons possession.[18] In March 2003, Cloutier waived his insanity defense after prosecutors agreed on a reasonable disposition for his release. He pleaded guilty in District of Columbia superior court to carrying a pistol without a license, unlawful possession of a firearm, and unlawful possession of ammunition.[19]

One of the most bizarre threats to Bush's life came in 2004 from fifty-six-year-old Darrel David Alford. The Buffalo, New York, native told acquaintances that he wanted to equip one of his model airplanes with a bomb then detonate it over an arena or stadium where Bush was speaking. Darrel eventually pleaded guilty to making threats against the president.[20]

In 2005, President Bush was threatened by a deranged man who also sent threatening emails to people in Providence, Rhode Island. Beginning in March 2005, several Providence residents began to receive email threats from fifty-one-year-old Barry Clinton Eckstrom. Eckstrom, who was on antipsychotic medication, wrote that he was a serial killer and intended to murder, rape, and torture his victims. By April and May 2005, the threats began to include President Bush.

The FBI in Providence determined that the emails came from public libraries in Bethel Park, Mt. Lebanon, and Upper St. Clair. Working with the Secret Service, the FBI set up a sting operation at the Bethel Park Library. On May 14, an agent in the book stacks used binoculars to watch Eckstrom as another agent sat next to him as he was typing. The agent saw him type, "I hate and despise the scum President Bush! I am going to kill him in June on his father's birthday." Eckstrom was arrested and later pleaded guilty in a federal court to threatening the president. The judge ordered him to be held in the mental health unit of the Allegheny County Jail.[21]

No president has been targeted by Muslim fanatics more often than George W. Bush.

Bush may have been targeted for assassination by the terrorists who hijacked the fourth and final flight involved in the 9/11 attack. Flight 93 was allegedly heading for either the U.S. Capitol or the White House before passengers fought back against the hijackers and brought the plane down in a field near Shanksville, Pennsylvania.

Nearly two years after 9/11, the Secret Service investigated a plot by American citizen and Muslim fanatic Ahmed Omar Abu Ali, who obtained a "religious blessing" to assassinate President Bush. Ali was born in Houston, raised in Falls Church, Virginia, and was valedictorian of his class at the Islamic Saudi Academy high school in Alexandria, Virginia. He entered the University of Maryland in 1999 as an electrical engineering major but withdrew in the middle of the 2000 spring semester to study Islamic theology at the Islamic University of Medina in Saudi Arabia. He joined an al Qaeda cell there in 2001.

In June 2003, Ali was arrested by Saudi police in the wake of a bombing in Riyadh. He confessed to Saudi authorities that he had joined a terrorist cell in Medina led by senior al Qaeda members Ali al-Faqasi and Zubayr al-Rimi. He explained that he joined al Qaeda because he hated the United States for its support of Israel and admitted that he discussed numerous potential plots with his al Qaeda cell members, including plans to assassinate President Bush, conduct a 9/11-style attack using planes transiting through the United States, establish an al Qaeda cell inside the United States, and free Muslim prisoners held at Guantanamo Bay. He also admitted that he had received money from one or more of his coconspirators.

Ali told his Saudi interrogators that he dreamed up the plot to kill President Bush on his own but that it never got past the "idea stage ... I wanted to be the brain, the planner.... My idea was ... I would walk on the street as the President walked by, and I would get close enough to shoot him, or I would use a car bomb." Ali likened himself to Mohamed Atta, who led the terror cell that carried out the September 11, 2001, attacks.[22]

Ali was detained by the Saudi government for some twenty months before being transferred to U.S. custody. The U.S. government's indictment charged him with two counts of providing material support to terrorists, two counts of providing material support to a terrorist organization (al Qaeda), one count of contributing goods and services to al Qaeda, and one count of receiving services from al Qaeda. The indictment was later amended to add charges of conspiracy to assassinate the president, conspiracy to hijack aircraft, and conspiracy to destroy aircraft. During Ali's federal court appearances, more than one hundred of his supporters crowded the courtroom. They laughed when the charge was read aloud alleging that he conspired to assassinate Bush.

Abu Ali went on trial in November 2005. The government's evidence was focused on his detailed confession. His defense lawyers argued against its admissibility, claiming it was involuntary due to alleged torture he had suffered at the hands of the Saudis. They also said Ali should have been given certain constitutional protections because the interrogations were a joint venture between the FBI and Saudi authorities.

But on November 22, 2005, after deliberating for two and a half days, a jury returned a unanimous guilty verdict on all counts. It was believed that jurors had been convinced of Ali's guilt after viewing a videotaped confession showing him boasting about his plans. The thirteen-minute-long taped confession also showed Ali laughing to himself and yawning.

On March 29, 2006, Ali was sentenced to thirty years in prison. While prosecutors had pushed for a life sentence, the trial judge explained that the relatively light sentence was handed down because Abu Ali's actions "did not result in one single actual victim. That fact must be taken into account."[23]

On appeal, the U.S. Court of Appeals for the Fourth Circuit upheld Ali's conviction but overturned the sentence on the grounds that the prior court had deviated from federal sentencing guidelines, which call for life in prison. Accordingly, in 2009 Ali was resentenced to life in prison. A defiant Ali told Judge Gerald Bruce Lee, "I would like to remind you that you too will appear before the divine tribunal with me and everyone else. That day there will be no lawyers.... If you are comfortable with that, you can decree what you will."[24]

On November 28, 2006, three Jordanian Muslims were arrested the day before President Bush arrived in the Jordanian capital of Amman. The three were found with large plastic bottles filled with gasoline, meant to be used for bombs in an attack on the American and Danish embassies in Amman. (They were apparently unaware that Denmark has no embassy in Jordan.) Jordan's military court convicted them of plotting to assassinate Bush, and they received sentences of fifteen years in prison.[25]

The only incident in which a would-be assassin got close to actually killing Bush occurred in 2005, when the president visited Georgia, America's closest ally in the former Soviet Union. While Bush was giving a speech in Freedom Square in Tbilisi, on May 10, 2005, twenty-eight-year-old Vladimir Arutyunian threw a live, Soviet-made RGD-5 hand grenade toward the podium where Bush was standing. Georgian president Mikhail Saakashvili and their two wives and other officials were seated nearby. The grenade hit a girl, cushioning its impact. It landed just sixty-one feet from President Bush. A Georgian security officer quickly removed the live grenade. It did not explode because it had been wrapped in a red tartan handkerchief, which kept the firing pin from deploying quickly enough. Inside, two spoons were supposed to disengage causing a chemical reaction. The spoons got stuck. The FBI concluded that the grenade could have killed Bush if it had worked. Arutyunian later explained that he threw the grenade "towards the heads" so that "the shrapnel would fly behind the bulletproof glass." Bush and Saakashvili did not learn of the incident until after the rally.[26]

Arutyunian escaped into the dense crowd. But the FBI examined 3,000 photographs taken by a college professor during the event and found a facial portrait of a man who matched Arutyunian's physical description. The Georgian authorities distributed the photo to the media and posted it in public places. An informant identified Arutyunian.

Police, accompanied by an FBI agent, went to the would-be assassin's home, and as they approached he fired on them, killing a Georgian agent. After he was subdued, police found a cache of chemicals in the basement of Arutyunian's house, including twenty liters of sulfuric acid, several drawers full of mercury thermometers, a microscope, and enough dangerous substances to carry out several terrorist acts.[27]

The would-be assassin confessed and said he wanted to kill President Bush because he thought he was too soft on Muslims. At one hearing, Arutyunian sewed his lips together and demanded to meet human rights activists. He also said he would try again to kill Bush if he had the chance. Arutyunian was indicted by a U.S. federal grand jury for his assassination attempt on Bush. But Washington did not request extradition as he faced trial in Georgia on charges of the attempted murder of President Saakashvili and the murder of the Georgian agent. Arutyunian was found guilty and sentenced to life in prison without the possibility of parole.[28]

George W. Bush kept a relatively low profile after he left office. But he was still targeted by Muslim fanatics, including twenty-two-year-old Khalid Ali-M Aldawsari, a former Texas Tech University chemical engineering student. Aldawsari came to the United States in 2008 from Riyadh, Saudi Arabia, to study chemical engineering at Texas Tech and transferred in early 2011 to nearby South Plains College, where he studied business. Aldawsari kept a handwritten journal, in Arabic, in which he wrote that he had been planning a terror attack in the United States for years, even before he came to the country on a scholarship. "And now, after mastering the English language, learning how to build explosives and continuous planning to target the infidel Americans, it is time for Jihad," he wrote in his journal.[29] Aldawsari, who was heavily influenced by Osama bin Laden's speeches, also blamed Bush for the plight of Muslims worldwide.

On February 6, 2011, Aldawsari sent himself an email titled "Tyrant's House," in which he listed the former president's Dallas address.[30] The FBI discovered Aldawsari's plans after he made online purchases with a chemical company and a shipping company. The chemical company reported a suspicious $435 purchase to the FBI, while the shipping company notified Lubbock police and the FBI because it appeared that the order was not intended for commercial use. The chemical explosive Aldawsari was trying to make had about the same destructive power as TNT. FBI bomb experts said the amounts would have yielded almost fifteen pounds of explosive—about the same amount used per bomb in the London subway attacks that killed scores of people in July 2005.

When FBI agents secretly searched Aldawsari's apartment in Lubbock, Texas, in February 2011, they found almost everything needed to build a bomb, including chemicals, beakers, flasks, wiring, a hazmat suit, and clocks. Aldawsari had also ordered thirty liters of nitric acid and three gallons of concentrated sulfuric acid. Aldawsari's computer contained a video in which Ayman al-Zawahri, al Qaeda's leader, praised as martyrs two unnamed individuals killed by "American Crusaders." Two instructional videos on the computer showed how to prepare the explosive picric acid and how to use a cell phone as a remote detonator.[31]

At his trial, Aldawsari's attorneys used the insanity defense. But the jury found him guilty in less than two hours, and he was sentenced to life in prison in November 2012. Judge Donald E. Walter said the evidence against Aldawsari was "overwhelming."[32]

— — —

A new law enacted in the mid-1990s stipulated that any president elected or acceding to office after January 1997 would be protected by the Secret Service for no longer than ten years (outside exceptional circumstances) after his or her presidency. However, the cost-cutting laws were rescinded by Congress in 2013, and presidents and their spouses once again receive lifetime protection.

CHAPTER THIRTEEN

RENEGADE

There's no question his life is in danger. Tomorrow, Obama could be assassinated ... simply because the Secret Service was not doing what it used to do.
—Author Ronald Kessler, 2011

He would probably not last long, a black man in the position of president. They would kill him.
—Doris Lessing, novelist and Nobel laureate

Barack Obama became America's first black president in January 2009.[1] Obama's election was seen as representing a clear benchmark in America's efforts to move beyond race in politics.

His election also turned out to be a repudiation of President Clinton's "third way" centrism. Whereas Clinton promised "to end welfare as we know it," Obama unilaterally waived welfare work requirements. And while Clinton declared the era of big government over, Obama sought to expand the role of government in almost every aspect of American life, most prominently in healthcare through his signature legislative achievement, Obamacare.

Obama also pulled the Democratic Party and the country left by advancing a liberal agenda on everything from gay rights and abortion to environmental issues and government regulation of the economy.

Internationally, Obama broke liberal hearts (and numerous campaign pledges) by embracing many of his predecessor's counter-terrorism policies. His critics accused him of pandering to the Muslim world by apologizing for America's alleged mistreatment of Muslims. He was also accused of dismissing America's influence and reducing America's capacity as a world leader. In one of his only bipartisan successes, Obama gave the green light for the raid by navy SEALs that killed Osama bin Laden.

— — —

According to a 2009 congressional report, after 9/11 the ranks of officials who received Secret Service protection swelled to an "unprecedented" number. The list of protectees now includes not only presidents, vice presidents, their immediate families, and former presidents, but also presidential candidates, key cabinet secretaries and congressional leaders, and even their assistants. The congressional report noted that between October 1, 2008, and September 30, 2009, the Secret Service also protected 116 heads of state and 58 spouses. "The service's protection mission has increased and become more urgent, due to the increase in terrorist threats and expanded arsenal of weapons that terrorists could use in an assassination attempt or attacks on facilities," the report stated, adding that domestic threats against political VIPs had grown after Obama was elected.[2]

The size of the Secret Service rose from 6,700 employees in 2007 to 7,055 in 2010. Almost all of the new positions are dedicated to protecting government officials. During Obama's first term, the Secret Service protected thirty-two people—twenty-four full-time and eight part-time. It also coordinated security at high-profile events, such as meetings of world leaders and political party conventions.

The Service's overall budget request has grown by 20 percent since 2008 for so-called "protective intelligence activities" and efforts required to analyze and investigate threats. But a significant share of the agency's budget remains with the agency's divisions, which investigate financial and other crimes, including 142 national field offices and 22 international offices, which also assist in the search for missing and exploited children.

During Obama's candidacy, and throughout his first term in office, numerous politicians and celebrities— including his first secretary of state, Hillary Clinton, and his wife, Michelle—publicly commented that his life would be at risk from assassins. When Obama began to receive Secret Service protection as a presidential candidate in 2007, he was consulted in choosing a protectee code name, instructed only that it had to begin with the letter "R." He chose the rebellious Secret Service codename "Renegade." In keeping with the tradition of having all family members' code names start with the same letter, Michelle Obama became "Renaissance" and daughters Sasha and Malia, "Rosebud" and "Radiance," respectively.

Several Secret Service agents have spoken of President Obama's relationship with his detail. One agent told author Ronald Kessler that President Obama "treated [us] with respect" and "appreciated what [we] did." The source added that Obama invited agents to dinner twice, including a party for a relative, both at his home. Agents also spoke of Michelle Obama's friendliness and how she "insisted that agents call her by her first name ... Michelle is

friendly—she touches you."[3] But Obama's personal physician of
more than twenty years, Dr. David Scheiner, said Obama was "gra-
cious and polite" but "distant ... [he had] an academic detachment."[4] This "detachment" may account for Obama's reluctance or
inability to develop close relationships with his protectors in the
mold of President Reagan.

During Obama's first term, the Secret Service was severely criticized for the behavior of several agents on the president's protective
detail. In April 2012, eleven agents allegedly engaged prostitutes
while assigned to protect the president at the Sixth Summit of the
Americas in Cartagena, Colombia. Copies of President Obama's
schedule may also have been left out in the open when Colombian
women were in the rooms of Secret Service members. By April 2012,
nine employees involved had resigned or retired. After the incident
was publicized, the Secret Service implemented new rules for its
personnel, including prohibitions on visiting "non-reputable estab-
lishments" and consuming alcohol less than ten hours before starting
work. The new rules also restricted who was allowed in hotel rooms.

It was not the first time Secret Service agents had been involved
in scandals. A few weeks after the scandal broke, stories emerged of
Secret Service agents hiring strippers and prostitutes prior to Obama's
2011 visit to El Salvador.[5] In 2008, an off-duty agent was arrested
in Washington, D.C., for soliciting an undercover police officer posing as a prostitute. At the 2002 Winter Olympics in Salt Lake City,
three agents were caught partying in a hotel room with alcohol and
underage women.

— — —

Obama was assigned a Secret Service detail equivalent to a full
presidential team on May 3, 2007, a year and a half before the 2008

presidential election. It was an unprecedented level of protection for a candidate. But the Secret Service believed the early protection was necessary because of the significance of his campaign to be the first black president and the Service's anticipation that Obama's candidacy would spark a backlash. Contrary to the popular view at the time, Obama did not ask for protection. Illinois senator Dick Durbin asked for it, and he openly acknowledged that his request "had a lot to do with race." It was not because of any particular threat.

Taking Durbin's request into account, Homeland Security secretary Michael Chertoff authorized Obama's early protection based on the advice of a congressional advisory committee, the same congressional advisory committee that decided who was and who was not a "major" candidate. The committee is composed of the Speaker of the House, the House minority leader, the Senate majority and minority leaders, and one additional member selected by the other members of the committee.

By mid-October 2008, as it appeared that Obama would win the election, the Secret Service noticed a dramatic increase in the number of threats against his life. The day after Obama was elected, activity surged on hate sites across the internet, and several white supremacist groups saw a spike in membership requests.

Secret Service director Mark Sullivan told a House Appropriations subcommittee in 2009 that there had been an escalation of threats against Obama. "As the international, domestic and individual threat environment of the country was elevated during this period so too was the threat environment for Secret Service protected individuals, venues and infrastructure," Sullivan said. "Since these trends remain at high levels, the Secret Service will use designated funds … to hire and train additional staff to evaluate the increased volume of threat information received related to the new president, vice president and their families." He also said that the bulk of the threats were racial in nature.[6]

But Sullivan said the level of threats stabilized after Obama's first year in office and that Obama was not disproportionately threatened compared to previous presidents.

Obama treated the vitriol with equanimity. He said he never thought about assassination, "because I've got this pretty terrific crew of Secret Service guys that follow me everywhere I go but also because I have a deep religious faith and faith in people that carries me through the day."[7] Not that Obama failed to recognize the risks inherent in being America's first black president. But he knew how to keep it all in perspective. As he implored his supporters on the fortieth anniversary of Martin Luther King's assassination, "Stop worrying … I think anybody who decides to run for president recognizes that there are some risks involved just like there are risks in anything."[8] Obama also said he was "pretty familiar with the history" of the Martin Luther King and Robert F. Kennedy assassinations. "Obviously, it was an incredible national trauma," Obama said. "But neither Bobby Kennedy nor Martin Luther King had Secret Service protection."[9]

Barack Obama was targeted before he became president. Twenty-year-old weapons enthusiast Collin McKenzie-Gude planned to use homemade explosives to halt the 2008 presidential candidate's convoy, possibly on Interstate 270, and take him out with a high-powered rifle. He had come to despise Obama's views on gun control. Inside the second-floor bedroom of his parents' Bethesda, Maryland, home, McKenzie-Gude stored chemicals that are used to make homemade bombs, three semiautomatic rifles, two shotguns, and hundreds of rounds of ammunition, including armor-piercing rounds. When they searched his home in July 2008, authorities also found a fake CIA badge and a map of the Washington area with markings for a presidential motorcade route. McKenzie-Gude's friend told police about his plans to detonate the explosives, and he was arrested. McKenzie-Gude admitted at his trial that he and a friend had talked about trying to assassinate Obama by halting his convoy with roadside bombs. But prosecutors say they did not know whether he would have carried out the plot. The judge said it "seemed to be a serious plan." McKenzie-Gude told the judge, "The saddest part of the situation is that my own actions are responsible. I cannot tell you how sorry I am.... I wish only for the chance to be able to rebuild my life in a positive manner." He was sentenced to five years in prison.[10]

On July 15, 2008, a week after Hillary Clinton dropped out of the presidential race, Jerry Blanchard was indicted for threatening to kill Senator Obama during a breakfast at a Charlotte Waffle House. Two customers witnessed Blanchard say, "Obama and his wife are never going to make it to the White House. He needs to be taken out and I can do it in a heartbeat." He made similar threats against Obama later at the Crowne Plaza Hotel in Charlotte. Blanchard was overheard on his cell phone saying, "I'll get a sniper rifle and take care of it myself. Somebody's got to do it.... We both know Obama is the anti-Christ." Blanchard was arrested on August 1, 2008, and eventually fined $3,000 and sentenced to a prison term of one year and one day.[11]

Around the same time, FBI agents arrested three white supremacists for plotting to kill Obama using a high-powered rifle during his acceptance speech at the party's convention in Denver. The plot was only uncovered after police seized two high-velocity rifles, camouflage clothing, walkie-talkies, wigs, a bulletproof vest, and telescopic gun sights during a routine traffic stop. Federal authorities subsequently downplayed the men as drug addicts who did not have the means to carry out the plot. They also decided that the case did not meet the legal standard to charge the men with a federal offense. "There is a difference between a true threat and the reported racist rantings of drug abusers," U.S. Attorney Troy Eid said. "This involved a gang of meth-heads who were all impaired at the time."[12]

In October 2008, twenty-year-old Tennessean Daniel Cowart and eighteen-year-old Arkansan Paul Schlesselman hatched an ambitious and elaborate plot to kill eighty-eight people and decapitate fourteen African Americans before ending their killing spree with the assassination of Barack Obama. They planned to die in a blaze of glory as they drove toward Obama dressed in white tuxedos and firing out the windows of their car. Cowart's car was emblazoned with "Honk if you love Hitler," a large swastika, and the numbers 14 and 88 on the hood.

A friend of the white supremacist skinheads exposed their plans to the Secret Service, which arrested them in October 2008 at Cowart's grandparents' home in rural West Tennessee. Police seized a sawed-off shotgun, a high-powered rifle, a handgun, and several swords and knives. They were charged with conspiracy to steal firearms from a federally licensed firearms dealer, illegal possession of a sawed-off shotgun, and making a threat to a major presidential candidate. Schlesselman pleaded guilty to one count of conspiracy, one count of threatening to kill and inflict bodily harm upon a presidential candidate, and one count of possessing a firearm in furtherance of a crime of violence. Cowart pleaded guilty to eight charges, including threatening to kill and inflict bodily harm upon a presidential candidate. He also admitted to shooting out the window of a black church in Tennessee.[13]

— — —

The Secret Service appeared not to have been well prepared for Obama's inauguration, and there were glaring loopholes in the security. More than one hundred VIPs and major campaign donors were screened by metal detectors—but then walked along a public pavement before boarding "secure" buses without being screened again. It would have been relatively easy for an assassin to mingle with them in order to get close enough to shoot the new president.[14]

The night before his inauguration, Obama was warned that a group of Somali extremists were planning a major terrorist attack to take place during the ceremonies.[15] Juan Carlos Zarate, President Bush's deputy national security advisor for combating terrorism, said, "All the data points suggested there was a real threat evolving quickly that had an overseas component."[16] The threat, of course, came to naught.

By the time Obama was elected, the Secret Service kept files on some forty thousand U.S. citizens, including around four hundred deemed by the agency to pose a specific threat.[17] Additionally, according to the Southern Poverty Law Center, there had been a high incident rate of domestic terror crimes since the presidential campaign, "most of them related to anger over the election of Obama."[18]

The Secret Service has investigated numerous assassination "scares" throughout Obama's presidency. In July 2012, the agency interviewed a motorcycle police officer who was part of the president's motorcade. He had allegedly shown a fellow officer a cell phone photo of his gun and said he would use it to shoot Michelle

Obama. Secret Service spokesman Edwin Donovan said the officer was taken off his duties while the service investigated whether the remark was only a joke.[19] Later, the Secret Service said the officer would not be charged.

In 2013, forty-nine-year-old Glendon Scott Crawford and fifty-four-year-old Eric Feight planned to build an X-ray gun to target Muslims. But they also intended to kill President Obama with a lethal dose of radiation, "silently and from a distance," using their planned machine. They targeted the president because he "had allowed Muslims into the U.S."

Crawford traveled to North Carolina in October 2012 and asked for money for the weapon from a ranking member of the Ku Klux Klan. Crawford also approached Jewish organizations looking for funding and people to help him with technology that could be used to surreptitiously deliver damaging and even lethal doses of radiation against those he considered enemies of Israel. Both the KKK leader and the Jewish leaders tipped off the FBI, and the Crawford/Freight plot was infiltrated by two undercover FBI agents who supplied the would-be assassins with machine parts.

In a secret recording of a meeting between Crawford and the undercover agents, Crawford said, "I don't want money. You know what? After the last election the electoral process is dead." Crawford and Freight were arrested in June 2013 after Crawford tried to connect a remote activation device to an X-ray machine. But the machine had been rendered inoperable by agents. Prosecutor John Duncan said, "From our investigation, the device … would have been capable of emitting X-Ray radiation that would have caused death."[20]

The internet was a huge source of threats against Obama. For example, in late 2009, the Secret Service investigated a poll posted on Facebook asking whether Obama should be killed. The agency spoke with the child who posted it, and no charges were filed. "Case closed," said a spokesman. "I guess you could characterize it as a mistake." Facebook removed the poll after it was brought to its attention.[21] Dark Net is a cyber world where secrecy is guaranteed and anything goes. It enables anonymous communications between individuals and websites ensuring total privacy. The computer encryption most commonly used to enable secrecy is Tor, a system originally developed by the U.S. Naval Research Laboratory more than a decade ago. It works by sending messages around several computers before they reach their final destination. In 2013, a website on the Dark Net invited people to make donations toward a bounty on the head of President Obama. The fund for his assassination reached $20,000 by November.[22]

Twenty-one-year-old Nathan Wine admitted sending a threatening email to the U.S. Army Recruiting Command the day after Obama's election. "I will not rest until this tyrant of America is gunned down," he wrote, adding that he would "not mind going behind bars for being a trigger man on this tyrant" and that "The blood of Obama will run down the streets of D.C." The email was forwarded to the Secret Service and traced to Wine, who admitted to agents that he had sent the letter and that he planned to assassinate Obama. Wine pleaded guilty to threatening the president-elect and received a thirty-six-month prison sentence.[23]

In 2009, twenty-one-year-old Texan Timothy Ryan Gutierrez hacked into the websites of the U.S. Department of Defense and the FBI. "I wanted to see what was really going on," he said. "There are 500 acres of encryption data [to go through], but I found a slip through it. There's always a hole." Gutierrez said he "didn't think [the FBI] would actually find" the email message he left on its system.[24]

Earlier that year, Gutierrez had emailed the FBI's Washington office and announced, "I'm going to assassinate the new president of the United States of America. P.S., you have 48 hours to stop it from happening." A second email threatened to blow up the Mall of America in Minnesota. Gutierrez said he had also rigged forty pounds of explosives to seven cars outside the mall. "Good luck thank you and God bless, you know the rest time is wasting," he wrote. The vast Mall of America parking lot was swept for bombs.[25]

When Gutierrez, who had been staying with his brother in Cortez, Colorado, was tracked down, he was interviewed by FBI agents and two Cortez police officers. Although both threats were taken seriously, Gutierrez was not arrested at the time. A few weeks later, after investigators had compiled sufficient evidence against him, a warrant was issued for his arrest and he turned himself in.

Gutierrez said the threat against Obama was just a prank. "I'm not mad about him becoming president, but he's not doing what he said he was going to do," he said. "He's not doing anything for the lower class—just the middle and upper class. Medications are going up, not lowering and jobs are being lost. His actions are going to get him in trouble."[26]

In May 2009, Gutierrez pleaded guilty to "transmitting a communication," threatening to kill President Obama and blow up the Mall of America in Minneapolis. Gutierrez was sentenced to four years of probation, with the first ten months in home detention with electronic monitoring. The judge ordered him to live with his mother in Andrews, Texas, and also ordered him to stay off the internet except to look for work.[27]

On February 12, 2010, Secret Service agent Stephan M. Pazenzia received a telephone call from an FBI agent regarding an individual with a user name "Pain 1488," who had recently posted a poem titled "The Sniper" to a website named NaziSpace/NewSaxon.org. Originally posted in 2007, the chilling poem read, in part: "As the tyrant enters his cross hairs the breath he takes is deep, His focus is square on the target as he begins to release, A patriot for his people he knows this shot will cost his life, But for his race and their existence it is a small sacrifice, The bullet that he has chambered is one of the purest pride, And the inspiration on the casing reads 'die negro die,' He breathes out as he pulls the trigger releasing all his hate, And a smile appears upon his face as he seals that monkey's fate. The bullet screams toward its mark bringing with it death, And where there was once a face there is nothing left."

The FBI identified the user name as belonging to twenty-eight-year-old Johnny Logan Spencer. When the Secret Service found Spencer, he accepted full responsibility for writing the poem and admitted threatening the president.[28] In December 2010, Spencer pleaded guilty, telling the court that he was upset over his mother's death and had fallen in with a white supremacist group because it had helped him kick a drug habit. A U.S. district judge sentenced him to thirty-three months in prison.[29]

Obama was also threatened on numerous occasions by prison inmates and homeless people, the majority of whom suffered from mental illnesses. In February 2010, twenty-nine-year-old Christopher Coates was due to be released from Red Onion State Prison, in Virginia, after having spent his entire adult life in prison for repeatedly "demonstrating his propensity for violence." In 2009, Coates mailed a letter from the prison stating that he would kill President Obama and rape and kill his wife and children. Coates also stated that he would kill the prison warden. His letter contained numerous racial slurs and was smeared with his own blood. When interviewed by Secret Service agents and the Federal Bureau of Investigation, he admitted writing the letter.

Coates was charged with threatening the president. He pleaded guilty and was sentenced to the maximum possible sentence of ten years in prison for mailing threatening communications and "threatening the life of the President of the United States." After the sentencing, U.S. Attorney Timothy J. Heaphy said, "When a man with such a violent past threatens others, we must hold him accountable."[30]

Sixty-two-year-old Timothy Cloud was a transient who sent envelopes addressed to the Social Security Administration offices in New York, Kansas City, and Baltimore. Each contained a white powdery substance and an index card with the words "you stole my money" and "die." Police, fire, and hazardous material teams responded to emergency calls at each location. Employees had to be quarantined and affected areas decontaminated. The same day, a similar envelope was mailed to the White House with the words, "You are just another lying politision [sic]." He had also enclosed a newspaper photo of Obama with sniper crosshairs drawn over the president's face.

Cloud was arrested in San Francisco and charged with four counts of sending anthrax hoax letters, four counts of mailing threatening communications, one count of threatening the president, and one count of crossing state lines after failing to register as a sex offender.[31] He pleaded guilty in May 2010 and was sentenced to twenty years in prison.[32]

On December 30, 2009, New Orleans drug dealer John Turnpaugh threatened President Obama by calling a New Orleans Police

Department 911 operator and saying, "Yeah, hey, I'm going to kill President Barack Obama and his wife this month." The New Orleans Police Department and Secret Service agents investigated the call, located Turnpaugh, and advised him of his rights. Turnpaugh admitted his guilt. During their investigation, agents also discovered that Turnpaugh was selling marijuana and was illegally in possession of several firearms in furtherance of his drug trafficking. Turnpaugh was sentenced to serve thirty-six months in prison for the threat against President Obama and a consecutive sentence of sixty months on the gun and drugs charges.[33]

President Obama was the recipient of numerous threats by mass murderers and terrorists, both domestic and foreign. Norwegian Anders Behring Breivik plotted to assassinate Obama at the 2009 Nobel Peace Prize ceremony, where the president collected his Peace Prize. He had planned to drive a car packed with explosives onto the square next to Oslo City Hall and detonate it while the Nobel ceremony was taking place. He said the Obama attack would have been largely symbolic, as the security surrounding the visit would have prevented him from bringing the vehicle sufficiently close to the ceremony. But with hundreds of millions watching on television, Breivik believed it would have been a perfect way to promote his anti-Islamic message. He scrapped the plan because security would have been too tight to get anywhere close to the president.

Breivik went on to commit Norway's worst atrocity of modern times when he set off a bomb in the center of Oslo, which killed eight people, and then went on a shooting rampage on the island of Utoya, killing another sixty-nine, many of them teenage members of the Norwegian Labor party's youth wing attending a summer camp. The killings were designed to draw attention to the purported "Marxist-Islamic" takeover of Europe.[34]

In May 2011, Irish Muslim militant Terry "Khalid" Kelly was arrested for threatening to assassinate President Obama during the president's trip to Ireland for the G-8 Summit. Kelly was a former Catholic altar boy from inner-city Dublin who converted to Islam while imprisoned in Saudi Arabia in 2000 for selling illegal alcohol. On his return to Ireland, Kelly praised al Qaeda and Osama bin Laden on Irish TV. Kelly trained with the Taliban in northwest Pakistan and married a Pakistani woman. He named one of their two sons Osama, a name, he said, "to be proud of."

Kelly told Britain's *Sunday Mirror* newspaper that he expected al Qaeda to kill Obama during his visit to Ireland because the country's police force was poorly armed. He also said terrorists would likely pay up to $1.4 million to anyone who was prepared to kill Obama. Kelly said he would like to do it himself but was too well known. "Personally I would feel happy if Obama was killed," he said. "How could I not feel happy when a big enemy of Islam is gone?" He was arrested at his home in Dublin on suspicion of threatening to kill the president.[35]

The Islamic terrorist organization called "al Qaeda Aceh" planned several attacks on August 17, 2010, Indonesia's Independence Day. The plot included an attempted coup and the assassination of Obama during his visit to the country. But it was foiled when local police stumbled upon a terrorist training camp in the northern province of Aceh. Anti-terror police units conducted raids on terrorist hideouts based upon intelligence obtained from the interrogation of suspects arrested during the Aceh operation. The police arrested twenty suspected terrorists and seized a cache of firearms, ammunition, documents, and the plans for the Independence Day attack.[36]

In 2012, Obama was targeted by a domestic terror group of soldiers called F.E.A.R. ("Forever Enduring Always Read"), led by army private Isaac Aguigui, who described himself as "the nicest cold-blooded murderer you will ever meet." He funded the militia using $500,000 in insurance and benefit payments from the death of his pregnant wife in 2011. (Aguigui was not charged in his wife's death, but prosecutors claimed it was "highly suspicious.")

In 2012, the soldiers bought $87,000 worth of guns and bomb-making materials and plotted to take over Fort Stewart, in Georgia, bomb targets in Savannah and Washington State, as well as assassinate President Obama and overthrow the federal government. The conspiracy was exposed when the four men were charged with the murder of Michael Roark, who had been in on the plot but then fell out with the others, and his teenage girlfriend. At the time of this writing, the state and federal authorities were cooperating on whether to try the four soldiers on state or federal charges, or both.[37]

When navy SEALs raided Osama bin Laden's hideout in Pakistan in 2011, killing the al Qaeda leader, they found a cache of documents that provided insight into his future plans to assassinate American leaders. His prime target was President Obama. In an undated letter, bin Laden wrote, "We want to cut the tree at the root." He plotted to bring down Obama's plane as it would mean the accession of Joe Biden to the presidency. He wanted Biden as president because he was "utterly unprepared for the [presidency]." Accordingly, Biden was to "remain unharmed."

Bin Laden set up two units in Pakistan and Afghanistan to attack aircraft carrying Obama. Bin Laden hoped Pakistani terrorist Ilyas Kashmiri would carry out the attacks. "Please ask brother Ilyas to send me the steps he has taken into that work," bin Laden wrote to his top lieutenant, Atiyah Abd al-Rahman. A month after bin Laden's death, Kashmiri was killed in a U.S. drone attack.[38]

Perhaps the most dangerous threat to President Obama's life came from twenty-one-year-old Oscar Ramiro Ortega-Hernandez, who had criminal records in Idaho, Texas, and Utah for crimes involving drugs, underage drinking, domestic violence, resisting arrest, and assault on a police officer. In November 2011, Ortega-Hernandez drove to Washington, D.C., to spend time with the Occupy D.C. protesters across the street from the White House. He said God had given him a personal mission to attack the White House.

Ortega-Hernandez called himself a "modern-day Jesus" and considered Obama to be a devil. He was also convinced that the government was conspiring against him. He even suggested to an acquaintance that the president was planning to implant computer-tracking chips into children.

Shortly after 9:00 p.m. on November 11, 2011, Ortega-Hernandez slowed down as he passed the White House in his black Honda Accord and fired a Romanian Cugir assault-style semiautomatic rifle from the passenger window at the White House. At least one bullet struck the presidential residence. The shooting came from roughly 750 yards south of the White House, just outside the outer security perimeter. A bullet was found a few days later embedded in the bulletproof window of the second floor of the White House, where the president and his family had their living quarters. But there was no danger to President Obama as he was in San Diego on his way to an Asia-Pacific economic forum in Hawaii.

Secret Service agents responded, and one agent said he saw a car speed away west on Constitution Avenue. A few minutes after the shooting, Ortega-Hernandez abandoned his car about seven blocks away, leaving his rifle, ammunition, and nine spent shell casings inside. It didn't take long for agents to learn that the car belonged to Ortega-Hernandez.

Five days later the Secret Service, which had circulated photographs of the suspect around the country, was tipped off to Ortega-Hernandez's whereabouts by an employee at the Hampton Inn near Indiana, Pennsylvania. The employee recognized a photograph of him and called the Pittsburgh Secret Service field office. The field office alerted the Pennsylvania State Police, which dispatched troopers to the hotel and arrested the White House shooter.

When agents interviewed Ortega-Hernandez's relatives, they were told that the suspect had a "fixation" with the White House and had fantasies of killing the president. Friends suggested Ortega-Hernandez had been influenced by Alex Jones, an Austin-based talk show host who espoused numerous and ludicrous conspiracy theories. In the previous year, Ortega-Hernandez and others had watched an anti-government internet film called "The Obama Deception," which was written, directed, and produced by Jones.[39]

Psychiatrists determined that Ortega-Hernandez was mentally fit to stand trial, and a federal grand jury in the District of Columbia returned a seventeen-count indictment against him. In addition to the attempted assassination charge, he was charged with assaulting federal officers with a deadly weapon, injuring property of the United States, and related firearms charges.[40]

— — —

During his 2012 reelection campaign, Obama was confronted with a number of threats to his life, including a threat made on Twitter. In

September 2012, Donte Jamar Sims, a twenty-one-year-old Charlotte, North Carolina, man, threatened to kill President Obama in a series of tweets, one of which warned that "Ima hit president Obama with that Lee Harvey Oswald swag." In another posting he wrote, "Well Ima Assassinate president Obama this evening" and said he was as serious about his threats as "a Heart Attack." A Secret Service intelligence specialist soon discovered Sims's tweets, and he was arrested and charged with threatening the president's life. When Secret Service agents interviewed Sims, he admitted to posting the threats because "he hated President Obama." Sims also told the agents he was "high on marijuana when he made the threats" but "understood what he was doing and that it was wrong."[41]

Another threat was more serious. It involved a plan to assassinate Obama by Muslim terrorist Quazi Mohammad Rezwanul Ahsan Nafis. Nafis was a twenty-one-year-old Bangladeshi living in Queens, New York, who had ostensibly come to the United States to study. But he had been inspired by videos of sermons by hate preacher Anwar al-Awlaki, and his true purpose in moving to America was to "wage jihad." Between January 24 and October 3, 2012, Nafis reached out to fellow extremists in New York and answered a series of questions in which he hailed the Prophet Muhammad as "the greatest man ever" and predicted that the "future of Bangladesh" would be in a "Khalifa"—an Islamic caliphate under Sharia law. Nafis planned to detonate a car bomb in Manhattan and assassinate President Obama. Nafis used Facebook to contact men he thought were al Qaeda leaders to plot an assassination of Obama and the destruction of the New York Federal Reserve building. In fact, they turned out to be FBI agents, who thwarted his plans.[42]

— — —

Fears for President Obama's safety did not subside after his 2012 reelection. For the Secret Service, Obama's reelection meant four more difficult years of protecting the president against threats from bitter convicts, deranged mental patients, Muslim extremists, racists, and the ever-growing group of desperate people who consider assassination their only recourse against a president with whom they disagree.

NOTORIETY AND THE "COPYCAT EFFECT"

*If anything in this life is certain, if history
taught us anything, it's that you can kill anyone.*
—Michael Corleone in the movie *The Godfather Part II*

The Secret Service has a very difficult mission. It is nearly impossible for it and other law enforcement agencies to predict criminal behavior by previously law-abiding people, or to know when criminals or people with mental illnesses might suddenly become violent.

Singling out violent political fanatics is also problematic. Contrary to popular belief, most American assassins and would-be assassins are not motivated solely, or even primarily, by deep political convictions. Sirhan Sirhan, Robert F. Kennedy's assassin, for example, was certainly motivated by political fanaticism but also by a deep desire for fame and notoriety.

Despite the growing problem of terrorism and the potential threat that it poses to presidents, the overwhelming majority of the assassins, would-be assassins, and threateners examined in this book were engaged in acts prompted by their personal misfortune, mental health problems, or desire for fame, rather than by political motive. According to one unnamed researcher hired for a Secret Service study of would-be assassins, "It was very, very rare for the primary motive to be political, though there were a number of attackers who appeared to clothe their motives with some political rhetoric."[1] Professor James W. Clarke believes Francisco Duran, President Clinton's attacker, did not target Clinton because of his policies; rather Duran wanted to kill the "commander-in-chief ... a person who just happened to be Bill Clinton. Had he been re-elected in 1992 George Bush might have been that symbol.... It was President Clinton's position and prominence—not his politics—that determined Duran's course of action...."[2]

A 1999 Secret Service study found that American assassins embarked on assassination schemes for a variety of reasons, including: to bring attention to a personal or public problem, to avenge a perceived wrong, to end personal pain, to save the country or the world, to develop a special relationship with the target, or simply to make money. "None [of the assassins or would-be assassins] were models of emotional well-being," the report concluded. Many of the people studied for the report were experiencing or had experienced serious mental health issues: 44 percent had a history of depression, 43 percent a history of delusional ideas, and 21 percent heard voices. But, as Robert Fein, coauthor of the study, said, the way these people sought to address what they saw as their main problems—anonymity and failure—was not inherently crazy.[3]

The report also found that "notoriety" appeared to be an important motive for many would-be assassins. "These are lonely, alienated people who suddenly see an opportunity to become celebrities,"
Dr. Judd Marmor, president of the American Psychiatric Association,
said following the attacks on President Ford. "Publicity gives them
an ego massage."[4] Randy Borum, a professor at the University of
South Florida who has worked with the Secret Service, said, "If the
objective is notoriety or fame, [assassination is] the most efficient
instrumental mechanism by which to achieve that. I don't mean to
be flip about that, but a public official is likely to bring them a substantial amount of recognition instantly, without having to achieve
something."[5]

As John Wilkes Booth, the most famous presidential assassin of
all, put it when he shot Lincoln: "I must have fame, fame!... What
a glorious opportunity for a man to immortalize himself by killing
Abraham Lincoln."[6] Charles Guiteau became excited at the attention
he was about to receive when he assassinated President James Garfield. "I thought just what people would talk," he said, "and thought
what a tremendous excitement it would create and I kept thinking
about it all week."[7] Would-be FDR assassin Giuseppe Zangara went
quietly to the electric chair and only lost his composure when he
discovered there were no photographers present. Sirhan, who wanted
to be an Arab hero to the Palestinian people, said, "They can gas me,
but I am famous. I have achieved in one day what it took Robert
Kennedy all his life to do."[8] Arthur Bremer said at his trial that his
motive was to become a celebrity. Edward Falvey, who threatened
to kill President Carter, felt like a "movie star."

Nearly all assassins and would-be assassins researched for this
book were, to put it plainly, failures. "We got this psychological

profile that was supposed to help us spot a would-be assassin," former Secret Service agent Marty Venker once wrote. "It was distilled from the profiles of everybody from John Wilkes Booth to Sirhan Sirhan. History's most famous failures—you got to know their miserable lives by heart."[9]

Most were also motivated by real or imagined grievances and saw killing "the leader of the free world" as a way to catapult into the history books. Leon Czolgosz, a man who despaired of his lowly position in life and who assassinated President McKinley in 1901, had an alias, "Fred C. Nieman" (literally Fred "Nobody"). James Garfield's assassin, Charles Guiteau, "had failed at everything he ever tried," author Candice Millard wrote, "and he had tried nearly everything."[10] Both Kennedy assassins, Oswald and Sirhan, had been fired from jobs because of their disagreeable personalities. Would-be Nixon assassin Samuel Byck blamed political corruption, and Nixon in particular, for his marital and financial problems. Arthur Bremer, who first stalked Nixon before targeting Governor George Wallace, was a disgruntled busboy and janitor and a failure in his personal relationships. "Life has been only an enemy to me," he wrote in his diary. John Hinckley, another failure, lived in the shadow of his successful father. He failed to hold down a job and was an unsuccessful student. Australian opposition leader Arthur Caldwell's would-be assassin expressed it best when he said, "I realized that unless I did something out of the ordinary, I would remain a nobody."[11]

Gerald Ford's would-be assassins, Sara Jane Moore and Lynette "Squeaky" Fromme, were also failures in life. By 1975, Moore had suffered five broken marriages and borne four children, three of whom had been adopted by her parents. Lynette Fromme was a high school dropout who never worked a day in her life except to try to persuade the authorities to release her hero, Charles Manson, from prison.

Many presidential threateners also believed that they had exceptional qualities that society failed to recognize. Guiteau believed he was "a man of great distinction and promise."[12] Bremer believed he was "as important as the start of World War II" and that his diary "will be among the best read pages since the scrolls in those caves." Oswald imagined his future involved becoming a famous revolutionary and future prime minister of Cuba.

Many assassins and would-be assassins were "copycats," obsessed with assassins from the past. Some borrowed books from libraries or visited the scenes of famous assassinations. Giuseppe Zangara kept a newspaper clipping of the Lincoln assassination in his hotel room. Lee Harvey Oswald read books about the assassination of Louisiana governor Huey Long. Sirhan Sirhan read books about Oswald and European assassinations. John Hinckley not only visited Ford's Theatre, the scene of Lincoln's assassination, before he attempted to kill President Reagan, but also read extensively about Oswald, Sirhan, and Bremer and had a bibliography of published materials on the JFK assassination. Shortly before he attempted to shoot President Clinton, Francisco Martin Duran visited the Texas School Book Depository in Dallas, scene of the sniper killing of JFK, and checked into the Washington, D.C., hotel where Hinckley shot Reagan.

Copycat incidents have occurred after nearly every serious presidential threat or attack. And much has been written about the media's role in instigating copycat threats. The media's portrayal of assassinations and assassination attempts is a sensitive matter to the Secret Service and congressional leaders. The morning after Sara Jane Moore first made the nation's front pages and television screens for her attempt on President Ford's life, House of Representatives minority leader John Rhodes objected. "What possible good purpose can come from this intense coverage of terrorist activity?" he asked. "Individuals of questionable mental stability will surely begin to conclude that they too can obtain national publicity and an enlarged forum for their views on redwood trees and other irrelevancies simply by attempting to gun down the President." Senate minority leader Hugh Scott asked, "Do cover stories in national newsmagazines incite to violence?"[13]

But in a free and democratic society, few editors would accept the notion of self-censorship. And many argue that the consequences of preventing news organizations from reporting such incidents would be disastrous for democracy. As Norman E. Isaacs, editor in residence at the Columbia University School of Journalism put it, "There must be a sense of discretion, yet not to the point where we suppress news. The public wants every scrap of detail about someone deranged enough to take a pot shot at the President. We're going to cover it. There's no other way."[14]

ACKNOWLEDGMENTS

I wish to thank my literary agent, Barbara Casey, who has always worked hard on my behalf. I also thank Alex Novak at Regnery Publishing, who saw merit in the book at the outset, and my editor, Daniel Allott, who edited the manuscript brilliantly. When it comes to the exacting task of bringing a story to print, Regnery is the ablest of publishers in making the journey a smooth run.

There are too many authors to thank for making this book possible. But among the writers whose books became important to my research, I would like to acknowledge and thank author, journalist, and Secret Service expert Ronald Kessler; presidential assassins expert, Professor James W. Clarke; FBI profiler John Douglas; assassination experts Robert A. Fein and Bryan Vossekuil; former Secret Service agents Dennis V. N. McCarthy, Joseph Petro, Dan Emmett, Michael A. Endicott, and Marty Venker; and presidential threats experts J. Reid Meloy, Lorraine Sheridan, Jens Hoffman, and David A. Rothstein.

Two books were especially instructive with regard to the threats made against the lives of President Roosevelt and President Kennedy—former professor of criminal law Blaise Picchi's *The Five Weeks of Guiseppe Zangara* and former Secret Service agent Gerald Blaine's book, *The Kennedy Detail.*

NOTES

PREFACE

1. James Bamford, "The Secret Service Spills Its Secrets," *Washington Post*, August 23, 2009, http://articles.washingtonpost.com/2009-08-23/news/36801935_1_motto-kessler-claims-secret-service

CHAPTER 1: THE BOSS

1. "How FDR Narrowly Escaped Death," *Schenectady Gazette*, August 9, 1947, p. 5.
2. Dennis McCarthy, *Protecting the President* (New York: Dell, 1985), 141.
3. Michael F. Reilly, *Reilly of the White House* (New York: Simon & Schuster, 1947), 57.
4. "Reilly Tells All," *Evening Independent*, August 30, 1947, p. 10.
5. John and Claire Whitcomb, *Real Life at the White House: 200 Years of Daily Life at America's Most Famous Residence* (New York: Routledge, 2002), 312.

6.   Philip H. Melanson, *The Secret Service: The Hidden History of an Enigmatic Agency* (New York: Basic Books, 2005), 295.

7.   Robert Shogan, *The Double-Edged Sword: How Character Makes and Ruins Presidents, from Washington to Clinton* (Boulder, CO: Westview Press, 2000), 76.

8.   Whitcomb, *Real Life at the White House*, 300.

9.   "Monumental Debate Over FDR's Legacy," *St. Petersburg Times*, April 12, 1995, p. 16A.

10.   Jim Bishop, "Here Are Some Memories of a Dedicated American," *Rome News Tribune*, July 9, 1973, p. 4.

11.   U. E. Baughman, *Secret Service Chief* (New York: Harper and Brothers, 1961), 80.

12.   Reilly, *Reilly of the White House*, 15.

13.   "Credulity Unlimited," *New York Times*, November 22, 1934, p. 1.

14.   "Threat against Life of Roosevelt Probed," *Telegraph Herald*, May 23, 1938, p. 1.

15.   "Plot To Kidnap FDR Revealed," *Montreal Gazette*, November 30, 1959, p. 1.

16.   "Is It Really Wise to Expand the FBI's Investigative Techniques?," History News Network, article 54746.

17.   "Bomb Is Sent in Mail to Roosevelt, but Is Held before Delivery," *Palm Beach Post*, April 9, 1929, p. 1.

18.   "Palmer and Family Safe," *New York Times*, June 3, 1919, p. 1.

19.   "Porter Foils Plot of Bomb Sender on Life of Roosevelt," *Owosso Argus Press*, April 24, 1929, p. 1.

20.   Blaise Picchi, *The Five Weeks of Giuseppe Zangara* (Chicago: Academy Chicago, 1998), 20–29.

21.   Ibid., 150.

22.   Willard M. Oliver and Nancy Marion, *Killing the President: Assassinations, Attempts, and Rumored Attempts on U.S. Commanders-in-Chief* (Westport, CT: Praeger, 2010), 95.

23.   Picchi, *The Five Weeks of Gisueppe Zangara*, 191.

24.   Ibid., 183.

25.   Ibid., 198.

26.   Ibid., 200.

27.   Ibid.

28.   "Seek Man Who Sent Bomb to Roosevelt," *Lewiston Daily Sun*, February 23, 1933, 1.

29.   "Boy Admits Sending Bomb to Roosevelt," *San Jose Evening News*, June 20, 1933, 13.

30.   "Fear Plot on Train," *Lawrence Journal-World*, August 4, 1934, p. 1.

31.   "Crash of President's Train Investigated by Secret Service Agents," *Berkeley Daily Gazette*, April 9, 1935, p. 1.

32. "Admits Threat on FDR's Life after Losses," Youngstown Vindicator, January 12, 1936, p. 1.

33. Reilly, *Reilly of the White House*, 101.

34. Ibid., 103.

35. "Eccentric Rushes Presidential Auto," *Pittsburgh Press*, July 10, 1938, p. 12.

36. "Tommy-Gun Security at White House Nears End," *Reading Eagle*, September 11, 1946, p. 3.

37. Bishop, "Here Are Some Memories of a Dedicated American," *Rome News Tribune*, p. 4.

38. Whitcomb, *Real Life at the White House*, 312.

39. Douglas Larsen, "FBI Book Tells of Attempt to Assassinate FDR," *Newburgh News*, December 8, 1956, p. 6.

40. "Threats Land Man in Prison," *Pittsburgh Post-Gazette*, November 16, 1940, p. 2.

41. "Friend of Nazi Consul on Trial for Making Threats against President's Life," *St. Petersburg Times*, January 20, 1943, p. 18.

42. Frank J. Wilson and Beth Day, *Special Agent: 25 Years with the American Secret Service* (London: Frederick Muller Limited, 1966), 128.

43. Ibid., 129.

44. Ibid.

45. Ibid., 128.

46. Ibid., 132.

47. Ibid.

48. Ibid., 133.

49. "Strange Story Told of Plot to Assassinate Roosevelt," *St. Petersburg Times*, December 4, 1943, p. 1.

50. "Franklin D. Roosevelt Day by Day," FDR Presidential Library, http://www.fdrlibrary. marist.edu/daybyday/daylog/november-11th-1943/.

51. Duncan G. Groner, "Guardian of Presidents Reflects on 24 Years," *St. Petersburg Times*, November 12, 1968, p. 4B.

52. Wilson and Day, *Special Agent*, 221.

53. "Strange Story Told of Plot to Assassinate Roosevelt," *St. Petersburg Times*, December 4, 1943, p. 1.

54. "FDR Assassination Plot Is Revealed," *Reading Eagle*, December 3, 1943, p. 1.

55. "Franklin D. Roosevelt Day by Day," FDR Presidential Library, http://www.fdrlibrary. marist.edu/daybyday/daylog/november-14th-1943/.

56. James H. Winchester, "They Guard the President," *Boys' Life*, December 1962, p. 66.

57. Reilly, *Reilly of the White House*, 178.

58.	"FDR Reveals Soviets Got Wind of Nazi Plot to Kill Allied Big 3," *Ottawa Citizen*, December 18, 1943, p. 13.

59.	Charles Whiting, *Target Eisenhower: Military and Political Assassination in World War II* (Gloustershire, UK: Spellmount, 2005), 55.

60.	Gary Kern, "How 'Uncle Joe' Bugged FDR—The Lessons of History," Central Intelligence Agency, www.cia.gov/library/center-for-the-study-of- intelligence-article02.

61.	"Tehran-43: Wrecking the Plan to Kill Stalin, Roosevelt and Churchill," RIANOVOST, October 16, 2007, http://en.rian.ru/analysis/20071016/84122320.html.

62.	Ibid.

63.	Larsen, "FBI Book Tells of Attempts to Assassinate FDR," *Newburgh News*, p. 6.

CHAPTER 2: GENERAL

1.	Merriman Smith, *Merriman Smith's Book of Presidents: A White House Memoir* (New York: W. W. Norton, 1972), 32.

2.	Rufus W. Youngblood, *20 Years in the Secret Service: My Life with Five Presidents* (New York: Simon & Schuster, 1973), 33.

3.	U. E. Baughman, *Secret Service Chief* (New York: Harper and Brothers, 1961), 81.

4.	Ibid., 83.

5.	"Guard Senator Truman; Capitol Police Watch Galleries after Death Threat Is Received," *New York Times*, April 23, 1937, p. 24.

6.	"President Truman Irked by Secret Service," *Lewiston Daily Sun*, April 16, 1945, p. 1.

7.	Baughman, *Secret Service Chief*, 42.

8.	"Rowley Is Appointed Secret Service Chief," *Schenectady Gazette*, August 2, 1961, p. 2.

9.	"Stay Calm, Says Truman of Dangers," *Herald-Journal*, November 2, 1961, p. 14.

10.	John and Clair Whitcomb, *Real Life at the White House: 200 Years of Daily Life at America's Most Famous Residence* (New York: Routledge, 2002), 330.

11.	"Oral History Interview with Floyd M. Boring," Truman Library, September 21, 1988, http://www.trumanlibrary.org/oralhist/boring.html.

12.	Baughman, *Secret Service Chief*, 87.

13.	Ibid., 83–86.

14.	Ibid., 101.

15.	Holmes Alexander, "Donovan's Truman Didn't Panic," *Rome News Tribune*, November 25, 1977, p. 4.

16.	Fred Blumenthal, "A Stronger Secret Service: Better Protection for the President," *Palm Beach Post*, April 18, 1970, p. 48.

17.	Baughman, *Secret Service Chief*, 56.

18. "Secret Service Asks President to Quit Walks," *Prescott Evening Courier*, November 6, 1950.

19. "Secret Service Tells Threats against Truman," *Chicago Tribune*, January 25, 1950, p. 2.

20. "Secret Service Chief Says Threats against Truman Have Doubled," *Baltimore Sun*, February 5, 1952.

21. "Oral History Interview with Floyd M. Boring," Truman Library, Temple Hills Maryland, September 21, 1988, http://www.truman library.org/oralhist/boring.htm.

22. "Truman Sees Navy Win," *Reading Eagle*, December 3, 1950, p. 22.

23. "Woman Held on Threats to Truman," *Schenectady Gazette*, February 5, 1952, p. 7.

24. "Threat Notes to Truman Jail Student," *Toledo Blade*, April 28, 1951, p. 2.

25. "Man Sentenced for Truman Threat Seeks Deportation," *News Courier*, December 3, 1948, p. C1.

26. "Young Man Jailed for Threatening Truman," *Reading Eagle*, December 2, 1948, p. 3.

27. "Would-Be Killer of Truman Held," *Palm Beach Post*, August 4, 1946, p. 1.

28. "Accused of Threatening Eisenhower—Assassination Threats Mailed, Maniac Held," *Daytona Beach Morning Journal*, June 11, 1953, p. 1.

29. Margaret Truman, *Harry S. Truman* (New York: William Morrow, 1973), 489.

30. "Letter Bombs Nothing New," *Tuscaloosa News*, December 12, 1972, p. 3.

31. "Denies Attempt on Truman's Life," *Telegraph-Herald*, December 4, 1972, p. 2.

32. Whitcomb, *Real Life at the White House*, 329.

33. Collazo v. United States, United States Court of Appeals, District of Columbia Circuit—196 F. d 573, November, 19, 1951.

34. "The Presidency: Fanatics' Errand," *Time*, November 13, 1950, p. 10.

35. "Stay Calm, Says Truman of Dangers," *Herald-Journal*, November 2, 1961, p. 14.

36. Ibid.

37. "Oral History Interview with Floyd M. Boring," Truman Library, Temple Hills Maryland, September 21, 1988, http://www.truman library.org/oralhist/boring.htm.

38. Willard M. Oliver and Nancy E. Marion, *Killing the President: Assassinations, Attempts, and Rumored Attempts on U.S. Commanders-in-Chief* (Westport, CT: Praeger, 2010), 111.

39. "Stay Calm, Says Truman of Dangers," *Herald-Journal*, p. 14.

40. "Oscar Collazo," *Daily News*, March 21, 1999, p. 4.

41. Whitcomb, *Real Life at the White House*, 330.

42. "Secret Service Warns of Plots Against President," *Evening Independent*, December 15, 1950, p. 9.

43. "He's Bent on Truman's Death," *Saskatoon Star-Phoenix*, January 5, 1957, p. 11.

44.   Robert Phillips, "Truman Trips Recalled by Personal Aide," *Kansas City Star*, October 1, 1973, p. 1.

45.   "The Presidency: The World of Harry Truman," *Time*, January 8, 1973, p. 10.

46.   "Ex-President Truman Dies," *Palm Beach Daily News*, December 27, 1972, p. 1.

CHAPTER 3: SCORECARD

1.   "The Fifties and Ike: A Conversation with Stephen Ambrose," *Humanities* 18, no. 5 (September/October 1997), http://www.neh.gov/news/humanities/1997-09/ambrose.html.

2.   Evan Thomas, *Ike's Bluff: President Eisenhower's Secret Battle to Save the World* (New York: Little, Brown, 2012), 15.

3.   William D. Pederson and James David Barber, *The "Barbarian" Presidency* (New York: Peter Lang, 1989), 176.

4.   Merriman Smith, *Merriman Smith's Book of Presidents: A White House Memoir* (New York: W. W. Norton, 1972), 230.

5.   Philip H. Melanson, *The Secret Service: The Hidden History of an Enigmatic Agency* (New York: Basic Books, 2005), 295.

6.   Susan Eisenhower, *Mrs. Ike: Memories and Reflections on the Life of Mamie Eisenhower* (New York: Farrar, Straus and Giroux, 1996), 326.

7.   "Eisenhower Target for Fanatics Also—Secret Service Men Detected Puerto Rican Plot against President in November," *New York Times*, March 2, 1954, p. 1.

8.   Marquis Childs, "Washington Calling," *Daytona Beach Morning Journal*, November 19, 1952, p. 4.

9.   "Oral History Interview, Mrs. Mamie Doud Eisenhower," no. 3, Eisenhower Library, August 16, 1972, http://eisenhower.archives.gov/Research/Oral_Histories/oral_history_transcripts/Eisenhower_Mamie.pdf.

10.   U. E. Baughman, *Secret Service Chief* (New York: Harper and Brothers, 1961), p. 93.

11.   Dawn Langely Simmons and Anne Pinchot, *Jacqueline Kennedy: A Biography* (New York: Signet Books, 1966), 34.

12.   James Leyerzapf and Dennis Medina, "Oral History Interview with Barbara Eisenhower-Folz," Eisenhower Library, November 30, 2006, http://eisenhower.archives.gov/Research/Oral_Histories/oral_history_transcripts/Eisenhower-Foltz_Barbara_554.pdf.

13.   Gerald Blaine, *The Kennedy Detail* (New York: Gallery Books, 2010), 37.

14.   Ibid.

15. "National Affairs: The Dangers of Travel," *Time*, June 20, 1955, http://www.time.com/time/printout/0,8816,861574,00.html.

16. Merle Miller, *Ike the Solider: As They Knew Him* (New York: Random House Value, 1989), 562.

17. Rufus W. Youngblood, *20 Years in the Secret Service: My Life with Five Presidents* (New York: Simon & Schuster, 1973), 48.

18. "Life of Ike Threatened," *Gadsden Times*, November 24, 1963, p. 30.

19. "National Affairs: The Dangers of Travel," *Time*.

20. "The Sharpshooter Who Guards the President," *Popular Science*, July 1956, p. 67.

21. David Barnett, "Secret Service for President Has Tougher and Tougher Job," *Toledo Blade*, March 8, 1958, p. 9.

22. Baughman, *Secret Service Chief*, 182.

23. Charles Whiting, *Target Eisenhower: Military and Political Assassination in World War II* (Gloucestershire, UL: Spellmount, 2005), 98–110.

24. Ibid., 112.

25. Ibid., 114.

26. Timothy Naftali, "Blind Spot," *New York Times*, October 7, 2005, http://www.nytimes.com/2005/07/10/books/chapters/0710-1st-nafta.html?pagewanted=print.

27. Tony Paterson, "Revealed: Farce of Plot to Kidnap Eisenhower," *Daily Telegraph*, May 2, 2004, http://www.telegraph.co.uk/news/worldnews/europe/germany/1460846/Revealed-Farce-of-plot-to-kidnap-Eisenhower.html.

28. "Office Memorandum, To: Mr D.M. Ladd From: A. H. Belmont, Alleged Plot to Kill General Eisenhower," Federal Bureau of Investigation, December 1, 1951, http://vault.fbi.gov/dwight-david-ike-eisenhower/dwight-david-ike-eisenhower-part-01-of-06/view.

29. "From Earl Schoel, SAC, Denver to Director, FBI, President Dwight D. Eisenhower—Miscellaneous," Federal Bureau of Investigation, August 12, 1953, http://vault.fbi.gov/dwight-david-ike-eisenhower/dwight-david-ike-eisenhower-part-01-of-06/view.

30. "Each Six Hours Someone Threatens Eisenhower," *Daytona Beach Morning Journal*, September 26, 1954, p. 7.

31. "Politickin' With John Brown: A History of Secret Service Fails," Complex.com, December 3, 2009, http://www.complex.com/blogs/2009/12/03/politickin-with-john-brown-a-history-of-secret-service-fails/.

32. "State Man Held for Ike Threat," *Milwaukee Journal*, April 4, 1956, p. 2.

33. "National Affairs: The Dangers of Travel," *Time*.

34. "Woman Seized in Lunge at Ike," *Spoksman Review*, April 25, 1958, p. 1.

35. U. E. Baughman, "The Secret Service," *St. Petersburg Times*, October 4, 1959, p. 92.

36. "Kentuckian Facing Trial on Charge of Threatening Life of Chief Executive," *Times News*, March 31, 1956, p. 1; "Secret Service Worried about Man Who Threatens to Kill Ike," *Washington Observer*, March 18, 1959, p. 1.

37. Fred Blumenthal, "The New President and the Secret Service," *Parade*, January 19, 1969, p. 22.

38. "Secret Service Has Tougher and Tougher Job," *Toledo Blade*, March 8, 1958, p. 9.

39. Baughman, "The Secret Service," *St. Petersburg Times*, 92.

40. Ibid.

41. "Memorandum for the Record: Subject: Further Amplification of Deryabin's Report on the Planned Assassination of Eisenhower—Document No: 1195-1003A," CIA Historical Review Program, December 2, 1963, https://www.cia.gov/library/center-for-the-study-of-intelligence/csi-publications/csi-studies/index.html.

42. "Hit the Floor as Shots Flew," *Windsor Daily Star*, March 2, 1954, p. 2.

43. "Ike Assigned Extra Guards," *Pittsburgh Post-Gazette*, March 8, 1954, p. 1.

44. "Puerto Rican Plot to Kill Ike Bared," *Milwaukee Sentinel*, September 14, 1954, p. 1.

45. "They Shot at the Wrong Target," *Milwaukee Journal*, March 3, 1954, p. 22.

46. Drew Pearson, "Washington Merry-Go-Round," *Wilmington Sunday Star*, March 21, 1954, p. 16.

47. "Investigate Threat against the President—Secret Service Finds Report to Be False," *South-Eastern Missourian*, May 10, 1954, p. 1.

48. James Hagerty, *The Diary of James Hagerty: Eisenhower in Mid-Course, 1954–1955* (Bloomington: IN: Indiana University Press, 1983), 57.

49. "U.S. Jury Indicts Puerto Rican—Man Denies Threats to Kill President," *Reading Eagle*, March 3, 1954, p. 1.

50. "Ike Assigned Extra Guards," *Pittsburgh Post-Gazette*.

51. "Threat to Ike Nets Him 3 Years," *Milwaukee Sentinel*, April 29, 1954, p. 1.

52. "Life of Ike Threatened," *Gadsden Times*, November 24, 1963, p. 30.

53. George Rush, *Confessions of an Ex-Secret Agent: The Marty Venker Story* (New York: Donald I. Fine, 1988), 79.

54. Smith, *Merriman Smith's Book of Presidents*, 81.

55. Edward Clark, "Doesn't Drive an Auto but Can Move a Bull," Life, July 7, 1961, p. 71, http://books.google.co.uk/books?id=WFQEAAAAMBAJ&pg=PA71&dq=Doesn%27t+Drive+An+Auto+But+Can+Move+A+Bull%E2%80%9D+by+Edward+Clark,&hl=en&sa=X&ei=pE9qUsTYMYXZ0QW8lYDgCw&redir_esc=y#v=onepage&q=Doesn't%20Drive%20An%20Auto%20But%20Can%20Move%20A%20Bull%E2%80%9D%20by%20Edward%20Clark%2C&f=false.

CHAPTER 4: LANCER

1. "New Jackie Kennedy Tapes Offer White House Insight," BBC, September 14, 2011, http://www.bbc.co.uk/news/world-us-canada-14909983.

2. "Relax, No One Is Going to Shoot Me, Insisted JFK," Daily Mail, September 20, 2011, p. 10.

3. Jim Bishop, *The Day Kennedy Was Shot: An Hour-By-Hour Account of What Really Happened on November 22nd, 1963* (New York: Gramercy Books, 1968), 28.

4. White House, *Warren Commission Report*, November 29, 1963, p. 57.

5. William Manchester, *The Death of a President* (New York: Harper and Row, 1967), 149.

6. Ibid., 115.

7. Ronald Kessler, "Secret Service Describes JFK as Reckless," *Newsmax*, February 13, 2012.

8. Don Branning, "He Disregarded Security Steps," *Miami News*, November 24, 1963, p. 5D.

9. "Unpredictable Kennedys Present New Challenges to Secret Service Agents," *St. Petersburg Times*, March 15, 1961, p. 3A.

10. Emily Sohn, "JFK Requested Bodyguards to Back Off," Discovery, October 21, 2010, http://news.discovery.com/history/jfk-assassination-secret-service.html.

11. Gerald Blaine, *The Kennedy Detail* (New York: Gallery Books, 2010), 398.

12. John and Claire Whitcomb, *Real Life at the White House: 200 years of Daily Life at America's Most Famous Residence* (New York: Routledge, 2002), 362.

13. Seymour M. Hersh, *The Dark Side of Camelot* (New York: Little, Brown, 1997), 227.

14. Ibid., 229.

15. Whitcomb, *Real Life at the White House*, 362.

16. "Armed Men Seized at U.S. Rally—Near Sen. Kennedy," *Sydney Morning Herald*, November 6, 1960, http://news.google.com/newspapers?id=xfljAAAAIBAJ&sjid=v-UDAAAAIBAJ&pg=3798,1446673&dq=two+arrested+at+kennedy+rally+chicago&hl=en.

17. James H. Winchester, "They Guard the President," *Boys' Life*, December 1962, pp. 66–68.

18. Robin Erb, "Early Suicide Bomber," *Toledo Blade*, November 21, 2003, p. 10.

19. U. E. Baughman, *Secret Service Chief* (New York: Harper and Brothers, 1961), 11–12.

20. Frederick John, "Fate Foreshadowed—JFK Had Brush with Death in '60," *Deseret News*, November 19, 1989, http://archive.deseretnews.com/archive/print/74816/FATE-FORESHADOWED—JFK-HAD-BRUSH-WITH-DEATH-IN-60.html.

21. Erb, "Early Suicide Bomber," *Toledo Blade*.

22. Baughman, *Secret Service Chief*, 11.

23. Blaine, *The Kennedy Detail*, 51.

24. David A. Rothstein, "Presidential Assassination Syndrome," Archives of General Psychiatry, March 26, 1964, http://archpsyc.jamanetwork.com/article.aspx?articleid=488618.

25. "Untitled," *Nashville Banner*, January 25, 1992, p. A-1.

26. "Garda Received JFK Death Threats," BBC, December 29, 2006, http://news.bbc.co.uk/1/hi/world/europe/6216973.stm.

27. United States Court of Appeals Seventh Circuit, "United States of America, Plaintiff-Appellee, v. Abraham W. Bolden, Defendant-Appellant," no. 14907, HSCA Record 180-10070-10273, January 19, 1978, pp. 2–6. 355 F.2d 453, Dec. 29, 1965, Rehearing denied February 25, 1966, En Banc.

28. House Select Committee on Assassinations, "The Secret Service Was Deficient in the Performance of Its Duties," *Final Reports of the House Select Committee on Assassinations (HSCA Report)*, National Archives, 231–32.

29. Blaine, *The Kennedy Detail*, 357.

30. Ibid., 358.

31. Ibid., 62; Vincent Bugliosi, *Reclaiming History: The Assassination of President John F. Kennedy* (New York: W. W. Norton, 2007), endnotes 711–12.

32. Blaine, *The Kennedy Detail*, 68.

33. "Threats on Kennedy Made Here," *Tampa Tribune*, November 23, 1963, p. 1.

34. "Texas Student Described JFK Threat as a Joke," *Meriden Journal*, December 20, 1963, p. 19.

35. "McLarry Cleared of Kennedy Threat," *News Courier*, January 11, 1964, p. 1.

36. "JFK Reports and Documents," jfk-online.com, http://www.jfk-online.com/ready.html.

37. House Select Committee on Assassinations, "The Secret Service Was Deficient in the Performance of Its Duties," 227–37.

38. Ibid.

39. Kessler, "Secret Service Describes JFK as Reckless," *Newsmax.*

40. Sohn, "JFK Requested Bodyguards to Back Off," Discovery.

41. "I Completely Failed," *Daily Mail*, November 22, 2012, www.dailymail.co.uk/news/article-2236766/Clint-Hill-Jackie-Kennedys-bodyguard-reveals-decades-guilt-49th-anniversary-JFKs-assassination.html#ixzz2DbSURFkF.

CHAPTER 5: VOLUNTEER

1. Eisenhower Library, "Oral History Interview—Jack M. Woodward," National Archives, http://eisenhower.archives.gov/Research/Oral_Histories/oral_history_transcripts/Woodward_Jack_512.pd.f

2. Jack Anderson, "Hero in Assassination Quits Secret Service," *Spokane Daily Chronicle*, October 18, 1971, p. 4.

3. Fred Blumenthal, "The New President and the Secret Service," *Parade*, January 19, 1969, p. 24.

4. Harvey Sawler, *Saving Mrs. Kennedy: The Search for an American Hero* (Ontario: General Store, 2005), 59.

5. Gerald Blaine, *The Kennedy Detail* (New York: Gallery Books, 2010), 315.

6. Ibid.

7. Bill Gulley, *Breaking Cover* (New York: Simon & Schuster, 1980), 71.

8. Ibid., 74.

9. Dennis V. N. McCarthy, *Protecting the President* (New York: Dell, 1985), 165.

10. John and Claire Whitcomb, *Real Life at the White House: 200 Years of Daily Life at America's Most Famous Residence* (New York: Routledge, 2002), 371.

11. McCarthy, *Protecting the President*, 165.

12. Blaine, *The Kennedy Detail*, 318.

13. George Rush, *Confessions of an Ex-Secret Service Agent: The Marty Venker Story* (New York: Donald I. Fine, 1988), 64.

14. McCarthy, *Protecting the President*, 165.

15. "Secret Service Ruling Pits Privacy against Protection," *Press-Republican*, May 24, 1998, p. A7.

16. Blaine, *The Kennedy Detail*, 318.

17. McCarthy, *Protecting the President*, 24.

18. Rufus W. Youngblood, *20 Years in the Secret Service: My Life with Five Presidents* (New York: Simon & Schuster, 1973), 85.

19. Harvey Sawler, *Saving Mrs. Kennedy*, 79.

20. Blumenthal, "The New President and the Secret Service," *Parade*.

21. Blaine, *The Kennedy Detail*, 265.

22. Philip H. Melanson, *The Secret Service: The Hidden History of an Enigmatic Agency* (New York: Basic Books, 2005), 201.

23. Merriman Smith, *Merriman Smith's Book of Presidents: A White House Memoir* (New York: W. W. Norton, 1972), 230.

24. "The Secret Service: Living the Nightmare," *Time*, October 6, 1975.

25. "President Undismayed by Crowds," *Reading Eagle*, April 26, 1964, p. 1.

26. "Security Research Reveals Threats against Johnson," *Spokesman Review*, November 5, 1964, p. 18.

27. "Facts of Life," *Lawrence Journal World*, September 29, 1964, p. 4.

28. Hal Rothman, *LBJ's Texas White House* (College Station: Texas A&M University Press, 2001), 169.

29. Youngblood, *20 Years in the Secret Service*, 147.

30. "That Bullet Proof Vest," *St. Petersburg Times*, September 14, 1975, p. 2D.

31. "Security Research Reveals Threats against Johnson," *Spokesman Review*.

32. "Man Arrested after Threat to President," *News and Courier*, December 28, 1963, p. 2A.

33. "Despite Guards, It 'Could Have Happened,'" *Windsor Star*, December 9, 1963, p. 1.

34. "Cuban Held for Threat," *Reading Eagle*, December 9, 1963, p. 5.

35. Youngblood, *20 Years in the Secret Service*, 166.

36. "U.S. Agents Nab Ex-Marine on Johnson Threat Charges," *Deseret News*, April 24, 1964, p. 10A.

37. "Ex-Marine Who Threatened LBJ Gets 5-Year Sentence," *Bulletin*, December 18, 1964, p. 8.

38. "Is Jailed for Threat to LBJ," *Gettysburg Times*, January 19, 1965, p. 10.

39. "Man Said to Have Written Threatening Note to LBJ," *St. Petersburg Times*, July 11, 1965, p. 14A.

40. "Threat Results In 3 Year Term," *Spokane Daily Chronicle*, July 31, 1965, p. 7.

41. "Chattanooga Man Sentenced on Threat Charge," *Rome News Tribune*, April 15, 1966, p. 9.

42. "Jerseyan Is Given 5 Years in Threat to Kill Johnson," *New York Times*, May 12, 1966, p. 22.

43. Fred Blumenthal, "A Stronger Secret Service: Better Protection for the President," *Palm Beach Post*, April 18, 1970, p. 48.

44. "Threats of Violence Against Individuals," Justia.com, http://law.justia.com/constitution/us/amendment-01/43-threats-of-violence.html.

45. LAPD, *1969 Final Report*, California State Archives, http://www.sos.ca.gov/archives/collections/rfk/.

46. "LBJ Office Building Receives a Bomb Threat," *Bulletin*, April 2, 1970, p. 10.

47. Charles Claffey, "Johnson Lies in State at Capitol; Burial Is Today at Texas Ranch," Washington Post, January 25, 1973, p. A1.

CHAPTER 6: SEARCHLIGHT

1. Fred Blumenthal, "Better Protection for the President," *Palm Beach Post*, April 18, 1970, p. 48.
2. Rufus W. Youngblood, *20 Years in the Secret Service: My Life with Five Presidents* (New York: Simon & Schuster, 1973), 69.
3. "Warns Bodyguard of Tip on Assassination Plot," *Spokesman Review*, May 13, 1958, p. 1.
4. George Rush, *Confessions of an Ex-Secret Service Agent: The Marty Venker Story* (New York: Donald I. Fine, 1988), 185.
5. Eisenhower Library, "Interview with General Robert Cushman by Dr. Thomas Soapes," National Archives, March 4, 1977, http://www.eisenhower.archives.gov/research/oral_histories/c.html.
6. U. E. Baughman, *Secret Service Chief* (New York: Harper and Brothers, 1961), 247.
7. "Nixon Attack Well-Planned," *St. Petersburg Independent*, May 18, 1958, p. 6A.
8. Baughman, *Secret Service Chief*, 247.
9. "Agents Who Guarded Nixon Given Honors," *Sarasota Herald-Tribune*, July 7, 1958, p. 6.
10. "Nixon Was Repeatedly Exposed to Radiation," *Nashua Telegraph*, April 30, 1976, p. 8.
11. "Soviets Had Plot to Kill Nixon," *Free Lance Star*, March 17, 1975, p. 3.
12. Priscilla Johnson McMillan, *Marina and Lee* (New York: Collins, 1978), 295.
13. Blumenthal, "Better Protection for the President," *Palm Beach Post*.
14. Baughman, *Secret Service Chief*, 246.
15. Dennis V. N. McCarthy, *Protecting the President* (New York: Dell, 1985), 25.
16. Rush, *Confessions of an Ex-Secret Service Agent*, 185.
17. McCarthy, *Protecting the President*, 26.
18. Ibid., 25.
19. Bill Gulley, *Breaking Cover* (New York: Simon & Schuster, 1980), 238.
20. "The Secret Service: Living the Nightmare," *Time*, October 6, 1975.
21. Baughman, *Secret Service Chief*, 246.
22. Ibid., 244.
23. Youngblood, *20 Years in the Secret Service*, 68.
24. Rush, *Confessions of an Ex-Secret Service Agent*, 67.
25. Gulley, *Breaking Cover*, 167.
26. "Nixon Wants Fewer Security Men," *Lakeland Ledger*, August 23, 1973, p. 8A.
27. Rush, *Confessions of an Ex-Secret Service Agent*, 187.
28. Katie Paul, "Life with the Secret Service," *Newsweek*, November 13, 2008.

29. "Secret Service Shaken Up," *Daytona Beach Morning Journal*, February 13, 1973, p. 29.

30. John S. Lang, "Many White House Cases Detained by Secret Service," *Daytona Beach Morning Journal*, April 26, 1971, p. 6.

31. Ibid.

32. "Empty Threat against President Proves Dangerous," *St. Petersburg Times*, August 21, 1969, p. 8A.

33. "Two More Held for Threats," *Anchorage Daily News*, April 9, 1981, p. A6.

34. "Porter Found Guilty of Threatening Nixon," *Meridian Journal*, August 23, 1969, p. 5.

35. "Youth Arrested in Lindsay Plot," *Pittsburgh Press*, June 12, 1968, p. 27.

36. United States Court of Appeals, Tenth Circuit, "457 F.2d 1087: United States of America, Plaintiff-Appellee, v. Eugene M. Hart, Defendant-Appellant," Justia.com, April 7, 1972, http://law.justia.com/cases/federal/appellate-courts/F2/457/1087/308247/.

37. David Greenburg, *Nixon's Shadow: The History of an Image* (New York: W. W. Norton, 2003), 101.

38. "Scheme to Slay Nixon Probed in New Orleans," *Pittsburgh Post-Gazette*, August 21, 1973, p. 1; "Crime: The New Orleans Plots," *Time*, September 3, 1973, http://www.time.com/time/magazine/article/0,9171,910725-2,00.html.

39. "Black Panthers Have Record of Violence," *Beaver County Times*, January 8, 1970, p. A-6.

40. "Three Suspects Held," *Spokane Daily Chronicle*, November 11, 1968, p. 16.

41. Jack Anderson and Les Whitten, "Castro Wanted to Blow Up Nixon's Home," *Kingsman Daily Miner*, June 17, 1977, p. 4.

42. James F. Kirkham, Sheldon G. Levy, and William J. Crotty, *Assassination and Political Violence: A Staff Report to the National Commission on the Causes and Prevention of Violence* (New York: Bantam Books, 1970), 78–89.

43. "Assassination Plot Hinted in Shooting," *Calgary Herald*, June 25, 1971, p. 3.

44. Ibid.

45. "Diary Says Man Who Shot Wallace Also Intended to Assassinate Nixon," *Eugene Register-Guard*, May 29, 1980, p. 3A.

46. Frank A. Aukofer, "Jury Hears Bremer's Story of Plan to Kill President," *Milwaukee Journal*, August 3, 1972, p. 1.

47. "Arthur Bremer's Personal Diary Tells of Six Efforts to Kill President Nixon," *Bulletin*, August 3, 1972, p. 4.

48. "Trials: One Sick Assassin," *Time*, August 14, 1972, http://www.time.com/time/magazine/article/0,9171,906205-2,00.html#ixzz0X7VF48LH.

49. "Veteran Is Charged in Threat on Nixon," *St. Petersburg Times*, August 12, 1972, p. 1.

50. "Man Is Charged with Threats to Kill Nixon," *Reading Eagle*, August 29, 1972, p. 14.

51. Rush, *Confessions of an Ex-Secret Service Agent*, 85.

52. James W. Clarke, *Defining Danger: American Assassins and the New Domestic Terrorists* (Piscataway, NJ: Transaction, 2007), 128.

53. "Intentions of Byck Revealed," *Reading Eagle*, February 27, 1974, p. 36.

54. "New York Terrorist Pleads Guilty," *Telegraph-Herald*, February 6, 1995, p. 2.

CHAPTER 7: PASSKEY

1. Thomas M. DeFrank, *Write It When I'm Gone: Remarkable Off-the-Record Conversations with Gerald R. Ford* (New York: Berkley Books, 2007), 5.

2. Joseph Petro, *Standing Next to History: An Agent's Life inside the Secret Service* (New York: Thomas Dunne Books, 2005), 108.

3. Dennis V. N. McCarthy, *Protecting the President* (New York: Dell, 1985), 171.

4. George Rush, *Confessions of an Ex-Secret Service Agent: The Marty Venker Story* (New York: Donald I. Fine, 1988), 111.

5. Petro, *Standing Next to History*, 107.

6. Ibid., 108.

7. Ronald Kessler, *In the President's Secret Service: Behind the Scenes with Agents in the Line of Fire and the Presidents They Protect* (New York: Crown, 2011), 52.

8. "Report Ordered on Ford Car Crash," *Milwaukee Sentinel*, October 16, 1975, 2.

9. "Man Arrested for Alleged Threat to President's Life," *Toledo Blade*, October 9, 1975, p. 7.

10. "Bomb Drama at White House," *St. Joseph Gazette*, December 26, 1974, p. 1A.

11. "Protecting Chief Is a Tough Job," *Daily News*, January 23, 1975, p. 3.

12. Ibid.

13. "Other White House Attempts," *Milwaukee Journal*, February 8, 2001, p. 16A.

14. "Rams White House Fence," *Evening News*, December 2, 1976, p. 10A.

15. "Two Indicted in Coast Plot to Kill Ford," *Miami News*, October 21, 1975, p. 2A.

16. " … Then He Met Lynette Fromme," *Eugene Register-Guard*, September 6, 1975, p. 3A.

17. "Lynette 'Squeaky' Fromme Released from Prison," momlogic.com, August 14, 2009, http://www.momlogic.com/2009/08/lynette_squeaky_fromme_released_from_prison.php.

18. National Geographic Society, *Inside the U.S. Secret Service*, DVD, 2004.

19. "Lynette 'Squeaky' Fromme Released from Prison," momlogic.com.

20. "Woman Aims Gun at Ford," *Ellensburg Daily Record*, September 5, 1975, p. 1.

21. Ibid.

22. " … Then He Met Lynette Fromme," *Eugene Register-Guard*.

23. "'I Wanted Attention,' Squeaky Tells Jailer," *Deseret News*, September 8, 1975, p. 1.

24. "Lynette 'Squeaky' Fromme Released from Prison," momlogic.com.

25. National Geographic Society, *Inside the U.S. Secret Service*.

26. Geri Spieler, *Taking Aim at the President: The Remarkable Story of the Woman Who Shot at Gerald Ford* (New York: Palgrave Macmillan, 2009), 159.

27. Ibid., 163.

28. Ibid., 176.

29. "Gerald Ford's Would-Be Assassin Breaks Silence," *Independent*, May 28, 2009, http://www.independent.co.uk/news/world/americas/gerald-fords-wouldbe-assassin-breaks-silence-1692247.html.

30. Philip H. Melanson, *The Secret Service: The Hidden History of an Enigmatic Agency* (New York: Basic Books, 2005), 298.

31. Petro, *Standing Next to History*, 24.

32. Rush, *Confessions of an Ex-Secret Service Agent*, 116.

33. John and Claire Whitcomb, *Real Life at the White House: 200 Years of Daily Life at America's Most Famous Residence* (New York: Routledge, 2002), 412.

34. "Security: Protecting the President," *Time*, October 6, 1975.

35. "Threats to Ford Triple—Simon Blames Publicity for Rise in Danger," *Baltimore Sun*, October 1, 1975, p. A1.

36. "Man Accused of Threats on Ford and Rockefeller," *Palm Beach Post*, November 26, 1975, p. C6.

37. "Candidates Keep Secret Service 'Over-Extended,'" *Evening Independent*, November 21, 1975, p. 3A.

38. "Alphabet Killer Who Terrorized LA Stays behind Bars," *Los Angeles Times*, September 5, 2008, http://latimesblogs.latimes.com/lanow/2008/09/who-is-muharem.html.

39. "People v. Kurbegovic," Justia.com, http://law.justia.com/cases/california/calapp3d/138/731.html.

40. "Plot against Ford Revealed," *Ellensburg Daily Record*, December 9, 1983, p. 13.

41. Ibid.

42. Terry Pristen, "1st Parole Bid Denied for 'Alphabet Bomber,'" *Los Angeles Times*, August 26, 1987.

43. "Article Reveals Nerve Gas Threat against Ford," *Dispatch*, December 19, 1983.

44.   "People v. Kerbegovic," Justia.com.

CHAPTER 8: DEACON

1.   Stephen Hess, "Jimmy Carter: Why He Failed," Brookings Institute, January 21, 2000, http://www.brookings.edu/research/opinions/2000/01/21politics-hess.

2.   Jimmy Carter, *White House Diary* (New York: Picador, 2011), 14.

3.   Ronald Kessler, *Inside the White House* (London: Pocket Books, 1995), 88.

4.   Ibid., 97.

5.   George Rush, *Confessions of an Ex-Secret Service Agent: The Marty Venker Story* (New York: Donald I. Fine, 1988), 125.

6.   Ibid., 126.

7.   Ibid., 181.

8.   Ibid., 73.

9.   "Man Found Guilty of Threatening the President's Life," *St. Petersburg Times*, September 29, 1978, p. 3B.

10.   "Man Jailed for Threat Letter to Carter,"*Lakeland Ledger*, April 21, 1979, p. 5A.

11.   "Bank Robber in Federal Prison Admits Threatening Hillary Clinton," *Daily News*, January 4, 2004, p. 2A.

12.   "Probation Ruled in Carter Threat," *Sarasota Herald-Tribune*, May 31, 1978, p. 5C.

13.   "United States of America v. Fred Anthony Frederickson, Appellant," Justia.com, July 17, 1979, http://cases.justia.com/us-court-of-appeals/F2/601/1358/376991/.

14.   "United States of America v. Kenneth Harold Smith," Justia.com, February 12, 1982, http://cases.justia.com/us-court-of-appeals/F2/670/921/117985/.

15.   "Kansas Convict Found Guilty in Carter Death Threat," *Fort Scott Tribune*, April 10, 1981.

16.   "Man with Knife Holds Police at Bay on White House Lawn," *Sarasota Herald-Tribune*, October 4, 1978, p. 1.

17.   "Cultist Arrested for Threats," *Anchorage Daily News*, June 22, 1979, p. A4.

18.   "Nation: Skid Row Plot," *Time*, May 21, 1979, p. 24.

19.   "Drop Carter Plot Charges," *Telegraph Herald*, May 30, 1979, p. 1.

20.   "Investigation Dropped in Alleged Carter Assassination Plot," *Luddington Daily News*, May 24, 1979, p. 3.

21.   "Journey of Fear," *Evening Independent*, April 11, 1978, p. 3A.

22.   "Radicals Issue Threat," *Bangor Daily News*, March 17, 1977, p. 1.

23.   Jack Anderson and Les Whitten, "Religious Fanatic LeBaron Threatens President Carter," *Free Lance-Star*, July 13, 1977, p. 4.

24.   "The Nation: A Deadly Messenger of God," *Time*, August 29, 1977, http://www.time.com/time/magazine/article/0,9171,915334,00.html#ixzz2DhuTpwcu.

25.   "Agent's Killer Had History of Threatening Presidents," *Calgary Herald*, January 16, 1980, p. A24.

26.   Ibid.

27.   "Former White House Attacker Killed; Shoots Secret Service Agent," *Ellensburg Daily Record*, January 15, 1980, p. 14.

28.   "Secret Service Agent Is Slain, Attacker Killed," *Pittsburgh Post-Gazette*, January 15, 1980, p. 23.

29.   De Quentin Wilber, *Rawhide Down* (New York: Henry Holt, 2011), 70.

30.   Ibid., 251.

31.   "Doctor Claims Hinckley Driven by 'Inner World,'" *Toledo Blade*, May 14, 1982, p. 2.

32.   Rush, *Confessions of an Ex-Secret Service Agent*, 205.

33.   James W. Clarke, *On Being Mad or Merely Angry: John W. Hinckley Jr. and Other Dangerous People* (Princeton, NJ: Princeton University Press, 1990), 41.

34.   Rush, *Confessions of an Ex-Secret Service Agent*, 205.

35.   "Assassination Threats Mount," *Milwaukee Journal*, April 9, 1981, p. 1.

36.   "Public View Needed: Carter," *Rock Hill Herald*, April 1, 1981, p. 12.

37.   "Carter: I've Had Threats since Leaving the White House," *USA Today*, July 24, 2013, http://www.usatoday.com/story/theoval/2013/07/24/jimmy-carter-assassination-john-kennedy-larry-sabato/2583681/.

38.   Rush, *Confessions of an Ex-Secret Service Agent*, 181.

39.   Carter, *White House Diary*, 307.

CHAPTER 9: RAWHIDE

1.   John and Claire Whitcomb, *Real Life at the White House: 200 Years of Daily Life at America's Most Famous Residence* (New York: Routledge, 2002), 437.

2.   Joseph Petro, *Standing Next to History: An Agent's Life inside the Secret Service* (New York: Thomas Dunne Books, 2005), 53.

3.   Ronald Kessler, *In the President's Secret Service: Behind the Scenes with Agents in the Line of Fire and the Presidents They Protect* (New York: Crown, 2009), 89.

4.   Kessler, *Inside the White House* (London: Pocket Books, 1995), 89.

5.   Ibid., 109

6.   Ibid.

7.   Petro, *Standing Next to History*, 66.

8.   James W. Clarke, *On Being Mad or Merely Angry: John W. Hinckley Jr. and Other Dangerous People* (Princeton, NJ: Princeton University Press, 1990), 44.

9.   James S. Kunon, "Former Presidential Bodyguard Dennis McCarthy Tells of Life under Stress in the Line of Fire," *People* 23, no. 18 (October 28, 1985).

10.   Sue Anne Pressley, "When History, Destiny Converged," *Washington Post*, March 30, 2006, http://www.washingtonpost.com/wpdyn/content/article/2006/03/29/AR2006032902595.html.

11.   Kunon, "Former Presidential Bodyguard Dennis McCarthy Tells of Life under Stress in the Line of Fire," *People.*

12.   Michael Dorman, "Failures among a History of Success," *Newsday*, August 23, 1987, http://pqasb.pqarchiver.com/newsday/access/104531710.html.

13.   Philip H. Melanson, *The Secret Service: The Hidden History of an Enigmatic Agency* (New York: Basic Books, 2005), 126.

14.   Clarke, *On Being Mad or Merely Angry*, 12.

15.   Henri E. Cauvin, "President Offered in 1983 to Meet with Hinckley," *Washington Post*, June 12, 2004, p. A29, http://www.washingtonpost.com/wp-dyn/articles/A35524-2004Jun11.html.

16.   Michael Janofsky, "Man Who Shot Reagan Allowed to Visit Parents Unsupervised," *New York Times*, December 18, 2003, http://www.nytimes.com/2003/12/18/us/man-who-shot-reagan-allowed-to-visit-parents-unsupervised.html?pagewanted=all&src=pm.

17.   Dennis V. N. McCarthy, *Protecting the President* (New York: Dell, 1985), 67.

18.   Del Quentin Wilber, *Rawhide Down* (New York: Henry Holt, 2011), 65.

19.   John Leggett, "Buckley Resident Relives Years with Secret Service," *Enumclaw Courier Herald Reporter*, July 6, 2009, p. 8.

20.   "Threats on Increase to Kill President," *Reading Eagle*, April 9, 1981, p. 3.

21.   Alix Spiegel, "Fame Through Assassination: A Secret Service Study," NPR, January 14, 2011, http://www.npr.org/2011/01/14/132909487/fame-through-assassination-a-secret-service-study.

22.   George Rush, *Confessions of an Ex-Secret Service Agent: The Marty Venker Story* (New York: Donald I. Fine, 1988), 232.

23.   United States Court of Appeals, Sixth Circuit. 681 F.2d 462, "United States of America, Plaintiff-Appellee, v. James Anthony Vincent, Defendant-Appellant," Justia.com, http://cases.justia.com/us-court-of-appeals/F2/681/462/405068/.

24.   "Floridian Guilty of Making Threats," *Palm Beach Post*, January 13, 1982, p. A10.

25.   United States Court of Appeals, Second Circuit, 708 F.2d 77, "United States of America, Plaintiff-Appellee, v. Mary Frances Carrier, Defendant-Appellant," bulk.resource.org, https://bulk.resource.org/courts.gov/c/F2/708/708.F2d.77.82-1432.1182.html.

26.   "7 Held for Threats on Reagan," *Telegraph*, April 10, 1981, p. 4.

27.   "Reagan Thanks Agent, Talks to FBI," *Palm Beach Post*, April 8, 1981, p. 1.

28.   Rush, *Confessions of an Ex-Secret Service Agent*, 280.

29.   "Reagan Thanks Agent, Talks to FBI," *Palm Beach Post*.

30.   "Hinckley Spared, North Carolina Man Jailed—Four Other Men Threatened Presidents," *Times-News*, June 23, 1982, p. 9.

31.   "Two Pranksters Charged with Threatening Reagan," *Record-Journal*, March 15, 1985, p. 1.

32.   United States Court of Appeals, Sixth Circuit, 697 F.2d 152, "United States of America, Plaintiff-Appellant, v. Carlos Alberto Valle, Defendant-Appellee," bulk.resource. org, https://bulk.resource.org/courts.gov/c/F2/697/697.F2d.152.82-5262.html.

33.   Todd S. Purdum, "Suspect in Slaying Has Long Record," *New York Times*, July 26, 1986, http://query.nytimes.com/gst/fullpage.html?sec=health&res=9A0DE6DA113 EF935A15754C0A960948260.

34.   Tom Madden, "Hostage-Taker, in Bid to See Reagan, Charged," *Press-Republican*, October 24, 1983, p. 6.

35.   "Gate Crasher Suffers Alcoholism," *Pittsburgh Post-Gazette*, October 24, 1983, p. 2.

36.   "Federal Charges Dismissed in Golf Club Hostage Case," *Palm Beach Post*, October 26, 1983, p. A4.

37.   "Prison Changes Man Who Crashed Reagan Golf Game," *Albany Sunday Herald*, March 14, 1987, p. 1.

38.   Petro, *Standing Next to History*, 73.

39.   James Rowley, "Shotgun-Wielding Man Wounded by Guards outside White House," *Free Lance Star*, March 16, 1984, p. 2.

40.   "Armed Man Shot near White House," *Pittsburgh Press*, March 16, 1984, p. 1.

41.   Rowley, "Shotgun-Wielding Man Wounded by Guards outside White House," *Free Lance Star*.

42.   "State Man Guilty of Assault," *Observer-Reporter*, September 11, 1984, p. A5.

43.   United States Court of Appeals, Eighth Circuit, 868 F.2d 1000, "United States of America, Appellee, v. James Neavill, Appellant," Justia.com, http://cases.justia.com/ us-court-of-appeals/F2/868/1000/17105/.

44.   "Man Convicted for Bomb," *Dispatch*, October 27, 1982, p. 1.

45.   Kessler, *In the President's Secret Service*, 91.

46.   "Man Pleads Guilty to Threats on Reagan," *Los Angeles Times*, May 20, 1987, http:// pqasb.pqarchiver.com/latimes/doc/292610886.html?FMT=ABS&FMTS=ABS:FT& type=current&date=May%2020,%201987&author=&pub=Los%20Angeles%20

Times%20(pre-1997%20Fulltext)&edition=&startpage=&desc=Man%20Pleads%20 Guilty%20to%20Threats%20on%20Reagan.

47.   Peter Baker, "Starr vs. Secret Service: Two Definitions of Duty," *Washington Post*, May 15, 1998, p. A1.

48.   "Man Guilty of Threatening Reagan," *Telegraph*, March 7, 1991, p. 22.

49.   "Conviction Upheld in Reagan Incident," *New York Times*, September 6, 1992, p. 2, http://www.nytimes.com/1992/09/06/us/conviction-upheld-in-reagan-incident.html.

50.   "Lennon's Killer—Hollywood Hit List!," *National Enquirer*, October 4, 2012, p. 31.

51.   Johanna Neuman, "Former President Reagan Dies at 93," *Los Angeles Times*, June 6, 2004, http://www.latimes.com/news/obituaries/la-reagan,0,7255115,full.story.

52.   Ibid.

CHAPTER 10: TIMBERWOLF

1.   National Geographic Society, *Inside the U.S. Secret Service*, DVD, 2004.

2.   Ronald Kessler, *In The President's Secret Service: Behind the Scenes with Agents in the Line of Fire and the Presidents They Protect* (New York: Crown, 2009), 133.

3.   Ibid.

4.   Kessler, *Inside the White House* (London: Pocket Books, 1995), 131.

5.   Kessler, *In the President's Secret Service*, 133.

6.   John and Claire Whitcomb, *Real Life at the White House: 200 Years of Daily Life at America's Most Famous Residence* (New York: Routledge, 2002), 447.

7.   Kessler, *In the President's Secret Service*, 135.

8.   "President Taking a Risk by Attending Drugs Summit," *Dispatch*, February 13, 1990, p. 9.

9.   "Florida Man Arrested for Threatening Bush," *Ocala Star-Banner*, January 15, 1989, p. 2B.

10.   Kessler, *In the President's Secret Service*, 142.

11.   "Bush Threatened," *Milwaukee Journal*, April 19, 1990, p. 5A.

12.   "Jury Acquits Man in Threat against Bush," *Reading Eagle*, May 18, 1990, p. 10.

13.   "Pittsburgh Man Sentenced for Threatening President," *Observer-Reporter*, August 30, 1991, p. D3.

14.   "Man Sentenced in Threat to Bush, Quayle," *Tuscaloosa News*, November 12, 1989, p. 8A.

15.   "Man Found Guilty of Threatening President," *Los Angeles Times*, September 2, 1990, http://articles.latimes.com/1990-09-02/news/mn-2079_1_president-threatening-man.

16. "Michael Jackson," Federal Bureau of Investigation, File No: 9A-LA-142276, http://vault.fbi.gov/Michael%20Jackson/Michael%20Jackson%209%20File%20Part%201%20of%201/view.

17. Ibid.

18. United States Court of Appeals, Second Circuit, 14 F.3d 766, "United States of America v. Leroy Johnson, Jr.," Justia.com, http://cases.justia.com/us-court-of-appeals/F3/14/766/612841/.

19. "Man Admits Threatening Bush," *Lewiston Morning Tribune*, February 24, 1991, p. 2A.

20. "Former Soldier Sentenced for Threat to Kill Bush," *Los Angeles Times*, December 15, 1991, http://articles.latimes.com/1991-12-15/news/mn-1013_1_terrorist-threats.

21. "Terrorism—President Target of Plots," *South-East Missourian*, July 16, 1991, p. 5A.

22. Nadine Gurr and Benjamin Cole, *The New Face of Terrorism: Threats from Weapons of Mass Destruction* (New York: I. B. Tauris, 2000), 285.

23. "Man Given 22 Months for Bush Threat," *Kentucky New Era*, May 17, 1989, p. 8A.

24. "Man Held in Possible Plot against Bush Security," *Los Angeles Times*, October 23, 1991, p. 3.

25. "Bush—Threat Suspect Guilty of Illegally Owning Guns," *Bulletin*, February 14, 1992, p. D6.

26. United States Court of Appeals, Ninth Circuit, 26 F.3d 1469, "United States of America v. Roger Leroy Hines," Justia.com, http://cases.justia.com/us-court-of-appeals/F3/26/1469/619449/.

27. Ibid.

28. "Ex-Felon Pleads Guilty to Plot against Bush," *Bulletin*, June 2, 1992, p. D3.

29. "Legal Secretary Arrested Accused of Stalking Bush," *Spokesman Review*, September 23, 1992, p. A4.

30. Ibid.

31. "Woman Who Stalked Bush Sentenced," *Free Lance Star*, January 9, 1993, p. A5.

32. "Secret Service Weighs Assassination Threat," *Hour*, September 14, 1989, p. 14.

33. "President Taking a Risk by Attending Drugs Summit," *Dispatch*.

34. "Colombia Denies Drug Cartel Plot to Murder Bush," *Lodi News-Sentinel*, January 25, 1990, p. 14.

35. "Bush Targeted in Missile Plots," *Daily Gazette*, May 10, 1990, p. A12.

36. Stewart M. Powell, "Ending Iraqi Threat Is Personal for Bush; Assassination Attempt on President's Father Pointed to as Proof of Saddam's Evil Intentions," *Times Union*, November 10, 2002, http://www.timesunion.com/ASPStories/story.asp?StoryID=70750#ixzz0a8ZpMIRP.

37. Michael Isikoff, "Saddam's Files," *Newsweek*, March 23, 2008, http://magazine-directory.com/Newsweek.htm.

38. Michael Conlon, "Bush Says Plot to Kill Him Was Genuine," *Pittsburgh Post-Gazette*, May 24, 1993, p. A4.

39. Kessler, *In the President's Secret Service*, 80.

40. Greta Van Susteren, "President Bush 41 Describes Losing '92 Presidential Election to Bill Clinton," Gretawire, http://gretawire.foxnewsinsider.com/2012/06/12/president-bush-41-describes-losing-92-presidential-election-to-bill-clinton/.

CHAPTER 11: EAGLE

1. National Geographic Society, *Inside the U.S. Secret Service*, DVD, 2004.

2. John and Claire Whitcomb, *Real Life at the White House: 200 Years of Daily Life at America's Most Famous Residence* (New York: Routledge, 2002), 461.

3. David Seidman, *Secret Service Agents: Life Protecting the President* (New York: Rosen, 2002), 50.

4. Gary Aldrich, *Unlimited Access: An FBI Agent inside the Clinton White House* (Washington, D.C.: Regnery, 1996), 53.

5. Ronald Kessler, *In the President's Secret Service: Behind the Scenes with Agents in the Line of Fire and the Presidents They Protect* (New York: Crown, 2009), 147.

6. Aldrich, *Unlimited Access*, 53.

7. Whitcomb, *Real Life at the White House*, 461.

8. Aldrich, *Unlimited Access*, 139, 203.

9. Ibid., 203.

10. Ibid., 90.

11. "Agents: Keeping Tabs," *Press Republican*, July 16, 1998, p. B7.

12. National Geographic, *Inside the U.S. Secret Service*.

13. Ibid.

14. Aldrich, *Unlimited Access*, 138.

15. James F. Pfiffner, *The Modern Presidency* (Stamford, CT: Wadsworth, 2008), 378.

16. Michael Duffy, "Flight of the Intruder," *Time*, June 24, 2001.

17. "Homeless Man Shot near the White House Dies," *New York Times*, December 22, 1994, http://select.nytimes.com/gst/abstract.html?res=F20C11FC3A5C0C718EDDAB0994DC494D81&pagewanted=print.

18. "Modjeski Held in Custody Pending Trial," *Buffalo News*, June 2, 1995, http://nl.newsbank.com/nl-search/we/Archives?p_product=BN&p_theme=bn&p_action=search&p_maxdocs=200&p_topdoc=1&p_text_direct-0=0EAF

9893D722750D&p_field_direct-0=document_id&p_perpage=10&p_sort=YMD_
date:D&s_trackval=GooglePM.

19. U.S. government info, "A Threat from the Pulpit," About.com, http://usgovinfo.about.
com/library/weekly/aa040398.htm.

20. "Alleged Threat to Clinton Brings Order for Exam," *Daily Gazette*, February 27, 1993,
p. D16.

21. "Man Admits He Threatened Clinton," *Eugene Register-Guard*, June 12, 1993, p. 3A.

22. "Man Accused of Threatening President," *Eugene Register-Guard*, July 20, 1994, p.
3A.

23. "German Man Convicted of Threatening Clinton," CNN, January 23, 1998, http://
edition.cnn.com/ALLPOLITICS/1998/01/23/reuters/threat/.

24. "Man Guilty of Threat to Clinton," *Eugene Register-Guard*, January 24, 1998, p. 2.

25. "Plot to Use Cactus Thorn to Assassinate Clinton," *New Strait Times*, July 16, 1998,
p. 18.

26. Mark Pitcavage, "Afraid of Bugs—Assessing Our Attitudes towards Biological and
Chemical Terrorism," *Militia Watchdog*, http://www.adl.org/mwd/anthrax.asp.

27. "Indiana Fugitive Arrested," *Times Union*, January 26, 1995, p. 7A.

28. Ibid.

29. "Man Pleads Guilty to Threatening Clinton," *Herald Journal*, January 6, 1996, p. A4.

30. "Man Pleads Guilty to Threat on Clinton," *Reading Eagle*, April 16, 1999, p. A3.

31. Bob Drogin, "U.S. Details Threats Linked to Clinton Trip," *Los Angeles Times*, March
23, 2000, http://articles.latimes.com/2000/mar/23.

32. Tom Leonard, "Osama Bin Laden Came within Minutes of Killing Bill Clinton," *Daily
Telegraph*, December 22, 2009, http://www.telegraph.co.uk/news/worldnews/asia/
philippines/6867331/Osama-bin-Laden-came-within-minutes-of-killing-Bill-
Clinton.html.

33. Bob Drogin, "U.S. Details Threats Linked to Clinton Trip," *Los Angeles Times*.

34. Dan Emmett, *Within Arm's Length* (N.p.: iUniverse, 2012), 152.

35. "Limousine Driver's Threats Weren't Idle, Prosecutor Says," *Vindicator*, May 27, 1994,
p. A7.

36. "Man Remains Jailed for Reported Threats against President," *Sarasota Herald-Tribune*,
February 21, 1994, p. 6B.

37. Ibid.

38. James W. Clarke, *Defining Danger: American Assassins and the New Domestic Terrorists* (Piscataway, NJ: Transaction, 2007), 228.

39.   United States Court of Appeals for the District of Columbia Circuit, no. 95-3096, "United States of America v. Francisco Martin Duran," Justia.com, http://cases.justia. com/us-court-of-appeals/F3/96/1495/504003/.

40.   Eric Scmitt, "Rifle Suspect Was a Veteran Discharged Dishonorably," *New York Times*, October 30, 1994, http://www.nytimes.com/1994/10/30/us/rifle-suspect-was-a-veteran-discharged-dishonorably.html?pagewanted=print.

41.   "Jumping the Gunman," *People* 42, no. 20, http://www.people.com/people/archive/ article/0,,20104360,00.html.

42.   Ibid.

43.   Toni Locy, "Man Charged with Clinton Assassination Attempt," *Washington Post*, November 18, 1994, p. 1.

44.   "Chuck Baker: 'Armed Revolution' Ideas Prompt Duran Attack on White House," Virtual School, May 5, 1995, http://www.virtualschool.edu/mon/SocialConstruction/ Sedition.html.

45.   Robert L. Jackson, "White House Gunman Gets Prison Term," *Los Angeles Times*, June 30, 1995, http://articles.latimes.com/1995-06-30/news/mn-18914_1_white-house.

46.   National Geographic, *Inside the U.S. Secret Service*.

CHAPTER 12: TRAILBLAZER

1.   Ronald Kessler, *In the President's Secret Service: Behind the Scenes with Agents in the Line of Fire and the Presidents They Protect* (New York: Crown, 2009), 185.

2.   Ibid., 184.

3.   Ibid., 185.

4.   "Guilty Plea to Presidential Threat," *Spokesman Review*, January 8, 2005, p. B2.

5.   "Mentally Ill Florida Man Charged with Threatening to Shoot President Bush," Fox News, August 26, 2007, http://www.foxnews.com/story/0,2933,294639,00.html# ixzz269NrydPy.

6.   "Polls and Threatening the President," CYB3RCRIM3, October 5, 2009, http:// cyb3rcrim3.blogspot.co.uk/2009/10/polls-and-threatening-president.html.

7.   "Officer Threatens President to Get Back at Ex-Girlfriend," *Vindicator*, January 19, 2002, p. B4.

8.   "National Briefing, Angry Letter Is Ruled Free Speech," *New York Times*, April 9, 2005, http://query.nytimes.com/gst/fullpage.html?res=9E06E7D8143EF93AA35757C0A 9639C8B63&pagewanted=print.

9.   "Purdue Student Found Guilty of Threatening to Kill President Bush," SouthBendTribune. com, June 29, 2007, http://articles.southbendtribune.com/2007-06-29/news/26801317_1_ messages-threats-purdue-university.

10. "Guttenberg Man Who Threatened President Bush Found Not Guilty Due to Insanity," NewJersey.com, June 9, 2011, http://www.nj.com/jjournal-news/index. ssf/2011/06/guttenberg_man_who_threatened.html.

11. United States Court of Appeals, Seventh Circuit, 387 F.3d 643, "United States of America v. Charles E. Fuller," http://cases.justia.com/us-court-of-appeals/ F3/387/643/532560/.

12. Ibid.

13. "Man Found Guilty for Bush Threats," *Bismarck Tribune*, October 17, 2007, http:// bismarcktribune.com/news/state-and-regional/article_0229db1a-df84-5207-a1f4-224af104c2de.html; "Fargo Man Gets 19 Months for Threatening President Bush," *Bismarck Tribune*, January 3, 2008, http://bismarcktribune.com/news/state-and-regional/article_36a82a65-186b-5664-b378-2a3bf58fd83c.html.

14. Mary Flood, "Spring Man Sentenced for Threatening President Bush," *Houston Chronicle*, November 12, 2008, http://www.chron.com/neighborhood/spring-news/article/Spring-man-gets-30-months-for-threatening-1792091.php.

15. David E. Sanger, "Officer Shoots Armed Man near White House Fence," *New York Times*, Feburary 8, 2001, http://www.nytimes.com/2001/02/08/us/officer-shoots-armed-man-near-white-house-fence.html?pagewanted=all.

16. "White House Shooter Sentenced," CNN, July 31, 2001, http://articles.cnn.com/2001-07-31/justice/whitehouse.shooting_1_alford-plea-shooting-incident-indiana-man?_ s=PM:LAW.

17. Francie Grace, "Arrested with Car Full of Guns," CBS News, February 11, 2009, http:// www.cbsnews.com/2100-201_162-520867.html.

18. "Man with Guns Is Arrested in Washington," *New York Times*, September 5, 2002, p. 4.

19. Michelle Firmbach, "N.H. Man Put on Probation," Seacoastonline.com, March 11, 2003, http://www.seacoastonline.com/apps/pbcs.dll/article?AID=/20030311/NEWS/303119994.

20. "Buffalo Man Pleads Guilty to Threatening Bush," *South-East Missourian*, January 10, 2005, p. 3A.

21. "Man Pleads Guilty to Threatening President Bush," *Pittsburgh Post-Gazette*, October 21, 2005, p. B3.

22. Jerry Markon, "Al Qaeda Suspect Tells of Bush Plot," *Washington Post*, September 20, 2005, http://www.washingtonpost.com/wpdyn/content/article/2005/09/19/AR2005091901513_pf.html.

23. Sridhar Krishnaswami, "Arab-American Convicted of Plotting to Assassinate Bush," OutlookIndia.com, November 23, 2005, http://news.outlookindia.com/item.aspx?336992.

24. Matthew Barakat, "American Al-Qaeda Sentenced to Life for Bush Plot," Associated Press, July 27, 2009.

25. "Jordan Assassination Plot, 3 Men Sentenced for Bush Assassination Plot," *USA Today*, May 14, 2008, http://www.usatoday.com/news/world/2008-05-14-jordan-bush-plot_N.htm.

26. "Life for Grenade Toss at Bush Rally," CBS News, February 11, 2009, http://www.cbsnews.com/stories/2006/01/11/world/main1202544.shtml.

27. "The Case of the Failed Hand Grenade Attack," Federal Bureau of Investigation, January 11, 2006, http://www.fbi.gov/news/stories/2006/january/grenade_attack011106.

28. Tom Parfitt, "Bush's Would-Be Assassin Begins Life Term," *Guardian*, January 12, 2006, http://www.guardian.co.uk/world/2006/jan/12/usa.georgia.

29. Debbie Schlussel, "Khalid Aldawsari: Another Saudi Student Bush Welcomed Tries to Kill Bush, Americans," DebbieSchlussel.com, February 24, 2011, http://www.debbieschlussel.com/33432/hey-another-saudi-student-visa-holder-work-aldawsari-tried-to-obtain-wmd-to-kill-americans-bush/.

30. FBI, Office of Public Affairs, "Texas Resident Arrested on Charge of Attempted Use of Weapon of Mass Destruction Suspect Allegedly Purchased Bomb Materials and Researched U.S. Targets," U.S. Department of Justice, Feburary 24, 2011.

31. United States District Court, Northern District of Texas, "United States of America v. Khalid Ali M Aldawsari," Criminal Complaint Case Number 5-11-MJ-017, November 23, 2011.

32. "Saudi Man Aldawsari Sentenced to Life in Prison in Failed U.S. Bomb Plot," *Washington Post*, November 13, 2012, http://www.washingtonpost.com/national/saudi-man-convicted-in-failed-us-bomb-plot-to-be-sentenced-faces-life-in-prison/2012/11/13/eeab2a34-2d69-11e2-b631-2aad9d9c73ac_story.html.

CHAPTER 13: RENEGADE

1. ObamaCSI.com, "Predictors of an Obama Assassination," https://sites.google.com/site/csiobama/.

2. Brian Bender, "Secret Service Strained as Leaders Face More Threats," *Boston Globe*, October 18, 2009, http://www.boston.com/news/nation/washington/articles/2009/10/18/secret_service_under_strain_as_leaders_face_more_threats/.

3. Ronald Kessler, *In the President's Secret Service: Behind the Scenes with Agents in the Line of Fire and the Presidents They Protect* (New York: Crown, 2009), 223.

4. Ed Klein, *The Amateur* (Washington, D.C.: Regnery, 2011), 17.

5. Norah O'Donnell and Jillian Hughes, "New Code of Conduct Issued for Secret Service Agents," CBS News, April 27, 2012, http://www.cbsnews.com/8301-250_162-57423390/new-code-of-conduct-issued-for-secret-service-agents/.

6. "Perfect Storm of Hate," *Philadelphia Tribune*, September 6, 2009, p. 1.

7. Kessler, *In the President's Secret Service*, 224.

8. Alex Spillius, "Barack Obama Is the Most Heavily Guarded U.S. Presidential Candidate Ever," *Daily Telegraph*, October 28, 2008, http://www.telegraph.co.uk/news/worldnews/northamerica/usa/barackobama/3275443/Barack-Obama-is-the-most-heavily-guarded-US-presidential-canditate-ever.html.

9. Caitriona Palmer, "Operation 'Renegade'—Why Barack Obama Is the Most Closely Guarded U.S. Politician after the President," *Independent*, May 24, 2008, http://www.independent.ie/world-news/americas/operation-renegade-1385864.html?service=Print.

10. Dan Morse, "Bethesda Man Linked to Obama Death Plot Sentenced to 5 Years," *Washington Post*, January 20, 2010, http://www.washingtonpost.com/wp-dyn/content/article/2010/01/19/AR2010011904460.html.

11. "Jerry Michael Blanchard Sentenced to Prison for Threatening to Shoot, Kill Obama Last Year," Huffington Post, June 8, 2009, http://www.huffingtonpost.com/2009/06/08/jerry-michael-blanchard-s_n_212907.html.

12. David Gardner, "White Supremacists Cleared of Gun Plot to Assassinate Barack Obama," *Daily Mail*, August 28, 2008, http://www.dailymail.co.uk/news/article-1049169/White-supremacists-cleared-gun-plot-assassinate-Barack-Obama.html#.

13. U.S. Department of Justice, "Arkansas Man Pleads Guilty to Conspiring to Commit Murders of African-Americans," Federal Bureau of Investigation, January 14, 2010, http://memphis.fbi.gov/dojpressrel/pressrel10/me011410.htm.

14. Kessler, *In the President's Secret Service*, 228.

15. Glynnis MacNicol, "NYT Reveals Obama Was Warned of 'Major Terrorist Plot' to Attack Inauguration," Mediaite.com, January 4, 2010, http://www.mediaite.com/online/game-changer-nyt-reveals-obama-warned-of-major-terrorist-plot-to-attack-inauguration/.

16.   Peter Baker, "Obama's War over Terror," *New York Times*, January 17, 2010, http://
        www.nytimes.com/2010/01/17/magazine/17Terror-t.html?pagewanted=all&_r=0.

17.   Katie Paul, "Life with the Secret Service," *Daily Beast*, November 12, 2008, http://
        www.thedailybeast.com/newsweek/2008/11/12/life-with-the-secret-service.html.

18.   Brian Bender, "Secret Service Strained as Leaders Face More Threats," *Boston Globe*,
        October 18, 2009, http://www.boston.com/news/nation/washington/articles/
        2009/10/18/secret_service_under_strain_as_leaders_face_more_threats/.

19.   "Obama Guard 'Gun Threat to Michelle,'" Daily Mail, July 14, 2012, p. 59.

20.   "KKK Fanatic Planned to Assassinate Obama with a Giant X-Ray Gun," Daily Mail,
        June 21, 2013, p. 390.

21.   Rachel Slajda, "Facebook Poll: 'Should Obama Be Killed?,'" TPM Livewire, Septem-
        ber 28, 2009, http://tpmlivewire.talkingpointsmemo.com/2009/09/facebook-poll-
        should-obama-be-killed.php.

22.   Steve Boggan, "Special Investigation," *Daily Mail*, November 23, 2013, p. 50.

23.   "USA v. Nathan Wine," Justia.com, January 14, 2011, http://law.justia.com/cases/
        federal/appellate-courts/ca11/10-10526/201010526-2011-01-14.html.

24.   "Timothy Ryan Gutierrez, Accused of Threatening President Obama, Surrenders to
        FBI," *New York Daily News*, January 30, 2009, http://articles.nydailynews.com/2009-
        01-30/news/17914667_1_fbi-system-indictment-e-mailed.

25.   United States District Court for the District Of Colorado, 18 U.S.C. § 875(c) 18 U.S.C.
        § 844(e), "United States of America v Timothy Ryan Gutierrez," www.justice.gov.

26.   United States Attorney's Office—District of Colorado, "Cortez Man Pleads Guilty to
        Making Threats against President and Mall of America," Justice.gov, May 5, 2009,
        http://www.justice.gov/usao/co/press_releases/archive/2009/May09/5_5_09.html.

27.   Ibid.

28.   Dylan Lovan, "Johnny Logan Spencer Sentenced to Nearly 3 Years in Prison for Threat-
        ening Obama in Poem," Huffington Post, June 12, 2010, http://www.huffingtonpost.
        com/2010/12/06/johnny-logan-spencer-obama-threat_n_792894.html.

29.   Ibid.

30.   United States Attorney's Office, Western District of Virginia, "Red Onion Inmate
        Receives 10-Year Sentence for Threatening President and Warden" and "Christopher
        Coates Mailed Threatening Letter to President Obama," Federal Bureau of Investiga-
        tion, February 19, 2010, http://richmond.fbi.gov/dojpressrel/pressrel10/ri021910.
        htm.

31.   United States Attorney's Office, Eastern District of California, "Anthrax-Hoax Letters
        Sent to White House and Social Security Administration Offices," April 29, 2010.

32.   Cathy Locke, "Man Gets 20 Years in Prison for Anthrax Hoax, Threat to Obama," *Sacramento Bee*, August 23, 2010, http://blogs.sacbee.com/mt/mt-search.cgi?Includ eBlogs=36&search=Timothy+Cloud+&keywords=Timothy+Cloud+&aff=5.

33.   "NO Man Who Threatened President Gets 96 Months Imprisonment," ABC, May 11, 2010, http://www.abc26.com/news/local/wgno-news-president-threat-jail-story,0,4009710.story.

34.   "Anders Behring Breivik 'Planned to Bomb Barack Obama at Nobel Peace Prize Ceremony,'" *Telegraph*, April 1, 2012, http://www.telegraph.co.uk/news/worldnews/europe/norway/9179146/Anders-Behring-Breivik-planned-to-bomb-Barack-Obama-at-Nobel-Peace-Prize-ceremony.html#.

35.   "Is Anywhere Safe? Ireland Arrests 'Taliban Terry' over Threats to Kill Obama," *Daily Mail*, May 13, 2011, http://www.dailymail.co.uk/news/article-1386748/Irish-al-Qaeda-supporter-Taliban-Terry-arrested-suspicion-threatening-kill-Obama-visits-Ireland.html.

36.   Phil Boehmke, "Obama Assassination Plot Uncovered in Indonesia," *American Thinker*, March 27, 2012, http://www.americanthinker.com/blog/2010/05/obama_assassination_plot_uncov.html.

37.   "Army Charges Four Soldiers with Murder," *New York Daily News*, March 29, 2012, http://articles.nydailynews.com/2012-03-29/news/31251918_1_soldiers-premeditated-murder-military-charges.

38.   David Gardner, "Assassinate the President," *Daily Mail*, May 4, 2012, p. 6.

39.   William Yardley, "White House Shooting Suspect Had Only Recently Begun Behaving Strangely, Friends and Family Say," Statesman.com, November 20, 2011, http://www.statesman.com/news/nation/white-house-shooting-suspect-had-only-recently-begun-1984132.html.

40.   "Oscar Ramiro Ortega-Hernandez Indicted for Attempting to Assassinate the President of the United States," Federal Bureau of Investigation, January 17, 2012, http://www.fbi.gov/washingtondc/press-releases/2012/oscar-ramiro-ortega-hernandez-indicted-for-attempting-to-assassinate-the-president-of-the-united-states.

41.   "Secret Service Arrests Charlotte Man for Twitter Death Threats against Barack Obama," *Smoking Gun*, September 6, 2012, http://www.thesmokinggun.com/buster/obama-twitter-death-threats-486712 .

42.   Mark Hughes, Dean Nelson, Muktadir Rashid, and David Bergman, "Federal Reserve Terror Suspect Had Discussed Plot to Kill Barack Obama," *Telegraph*, October 18, 2012, http://www.telegraph.co.uk/news/worldnews/northamerica/usa/9618856/Federal-Reserve-terror-suspect-had-discussed-plot-to-kill-Barack-Obama.html.

EPILOGUE: NOTORIETY AND THE "COPYCAT EFFECT"

1.   Scott Hensley, "Author Sees Parallel in Gifford's Shooting and JFK Assassination," NPR, November 14, 2011, http://www.npr.org/blogs/health/2011/01/14/132937650/author-sees-parallel-in-giffords-shooting-and-jfk-assassination.

2.   James W. Clarke, *Defining Danger: American Assassins and the New Domestic Terrorists* (Piscataway, NJ: Transaction, 2007), 229.

3.   Robert A. Fein and Bryan Vossekuil, "Assassination in the United States: An Operational Study of Recent Assassins, Attackers, and Near Lethal Approachers," *Journal of Forensic Sciences* 44, no. 2 (March 1999): 324.

4.   "The Press: Her Picture on the Cover," *Time*, October 6, 1975, http://www.time.com/time/magazine/article/0,9171,913550,00.html.

5.   Alix Spiegel, "Fame through Assassination: A Secret Service Study," NPR, January 14, 2011, http://www.npr.org/2011/01/14/132909487/fame-through-assassination-a-secret-service-study.

6.   "Those Dangerous Loners," *Time*, April 13, 1981, http://www.time.com/time/magazine/article/0,9171,954701,00.html.

7.   Candice Millard, *Destiny of the Republic: A Tale of Madness, Medicine and the Murder of a President* (New York: Anchor, 2012), 135.

8.   Albert Ellis and John Gullo, *Murder and Assassination* (New York: Lyle Stuart, 1971), 221.

9.   George Rush, *Confessions of an Ex-Secret Service Agent: The Marty Venker Story* (New York: Donald I. Fine, 1988), 36.

10.   Millard, *Destiny of the Republic*, 1.

11.   Ellis and Gullo, *Murder and Assassination*, 221.

12.   Millard, *Destiny of the Republic*, 1.

13.   "The Press: Her Picture on the Cover," *Time*.

14.   Ibid.

BIBLIOGRAPHY

GOVERNMENT REPORTS

1969 Final Report. Los Angeles Police Department Records of the Robert F. Kennedy Assassination Investigation. California State Archives. 10 volumes, microfilm, http://www.sos.ca.gov/archives/collections/rfk/.

Assassination Records Review Board. Secret Service agents' interviews, January 3, 1978, HSCA, 180-10071-10165, Agency File No: 007996, January 11, 1996, http://www.fas.org/sgp/advisory/arrb98/part08.htm.

FEDERAL BUREAU OF INVESTIGATION RECORDS (WWW.FBI.GOV)

American Nazi Party: http://vault.fbi.gov/American%20Nazi%20 Party%20.

Black Mafia: http://vault.fbi.gov/black-mafia family/Black%20Mafia%20
Family%20Part%206%20of%208%20/view.

Black Panther Party: http://vault.fbi.gov/Black%20Panther%20Party%20.

Charles Manson: http://vault.fbi.gov/Charles%20Manson.

CIA Historical Review Program: https://www.cia.gov/library/.

Edward M. Kennedy: http://vault.fbi.gov/Senator%20Edward%20
Kennedy.

Eisenhower: http://vault.fbi.gov/dwight-david-ike-eisenhower.

Franklin Roosevelt Assassination Attempt: http://digital.library.miami.edu/
gov/FDRAssn.html.

Johnson: http://vault.fbi.gov/lyndon-b.-johnson, http://vault.fbi.gov/
lyndon-b.-johnson/lyndon-b.-johnson-part-01-of-01/view; http://vault.
fbi.gov/lyndon-b.-johnson-1/lyndon-b.-johnson-part-02-of-02/view;
http://vault.fbi.gov/Lady%20Bird%20Johnson.

Reagan: http://vault.fbi.gov/president-ronald-reagan-assassination-
attempt.

Robert F. Kennedy: http://vault.fbi.gov/Robert%20F%20Kennedy%20
%28Assassination%29%20.

Threats against Members of Congress, 2000–2010: http://vault.fbi.gov/
threats-against-members-of-congress.

Truman: http://vault.fbi.gov/harry-s.-truman/Harry%20S.%20
Truman%20Part%2001%20of%2003/view.

Kaiser, Frederick M. *Direct Assaults against Presidents, Presidents-Elect,
and Candidates.* Congressional Research Service, Library of Congress,
June 7, 2008.

———. *Report for Congress—Direct Assaults against Presidents,
Presidents-Elect, and Candidates.* Congressional Research Service,
Library of Congress, Order Code RS20821. April 5, 2006.

Reese, Shawn. *Report for Congress—The U.S. Secret Service: An Examination and Analysis of Its Evolving Missions.* Congressional Research
Service. December 16, 2009.

FBI. "The Vault." Federal Bureau of Investigation. http://vault.fbi.gov/.

Fein, R. A., and B. Vossekuil. *Preventing Assassination: Exceptional Case
Study Project (ECSP).* National Institute of Justice US Department of
Justice NIJ publication (NCJ 167224). National Criminal Justice Refer-
ence Service, 1997.

House Select Committee on Assassinations Final Report. "The Secret Service Was Deficient in the Performance of Its Duties." *Final Report of
the House Select Committee on Assassinations (HSCA Report)* 227–37,
http://www.archives.gov/research/jfk/select-committee-report/part-1d.
html.

Hudson, Rex A. *The Sociology and Psychology of Terrorism: Who
Becomes a Terrorist and Why? A Report Prepared under an Inter-
agency Agreement by the Federal Research Division.* Library of Congress. September 1999, www.loc.gov/rr/frd/.

Kirkham, James F., Levy, Sheldon G., and William J. Crotty. *Assassination
and Political Violence: A Staff Report to the Commission on the Causes
and Prevention of Violence.* New York: Bantam/Matrix Books, 1970.

*Public Report of the Vice President's Task Force on Combating Terrorism,
Part 2 U.S. Policy and Response to Terrorists, Part 3 Task Force Conclusions and Recommendations.* Center for Research on Population
and Security. February 1986, www.population-security.org.

*The Report of the U.S. President's Commission on the Assassination of
President John F. Kennedy.* Appendix 7: "A Brief History of Presidential
Protection." Washington, D.C.: U.S. Government Printing Office, 1964,
505.

U.S. SECRET SERVICE

The Secret Service prepared two short histories of its law enforcement role, each of which includes a helpful description of the agency's presidential protective function:

U.S. Secret Service. *Excerpts from the History of the United States Secret Service, 1865–1975.* Ann Arbor: University of Michigan Library, 1978.

U.S. Secret Service. *Moments in History, 1865–1990.* Washington, D.C.: U.S. Government Printing Office, 1990.

SEE ALSO:

U.S. Secret Service. *Fiscal Year 2009 Annual Report.* U.S. Department of Homeland Security. http://www.secretservice.gov/USSS_FY2009AR.pdf.

Fein, Robert A., and Bryan Vossekuil. *Protective Intelligence and Threat Assessment Investigations: A Guide For State and Local Law Enforcement Officials.* U.S. Department of Justice, National Institute of Justice, July 1998. http://www.ojp.usdoj.gov/nij; http://www.ojp.usdoj.gov.

Fein, Robert A., Bryan Vossekuil, and Gwen A. Holden. *Threat Assessment: An Approach to Prevent Targeted Violence.* U.S. Department of Justice, National Institute of Justice, July 1995. http://www.ojp.usdoj.gov/nij.

Treasury Department. *Public Report of the White House Security Review.* Foundation of American Scientists. http://www.fas.org/irp/agency/ustreas/usss/t1pubrpt.html

U.S. Senate Intelligence Committee, Foreign and Military Intelligence. *Final Report, U.S. Congress: The Select Committee to Study Governmental Operations with Respect to Intelligence Activities, Foreign and Military Intelligence Book 1.* Report no. 94-755, 94th Cong., 2d Sess. Washington, D.C.: U.S. Government Printing Office, 1976.

PRESIDENTIAL LIBRARIES

Barack Obama Presidential Library and Museum, http://barackobama presidentiallibrary.com/.

Dwight D. Eisenhower Presidential Library and Museum, http://www. eisenhower.archives.gov/.

Franklin D. Roosevelt Presidential Library and Museum, http://www. fdrlibrary.marist.edu/.

George Bush Presidential Library and Museum, http://bushlibrary.tamu. edu/index.php.

George W. Bush Presidential Library and Museum, http://www. georgewbushlibrary.smu.edu/.

Gerald R. Ford Presidential Library and Museum http://www. fordlibrarymuseum.gov/.

Harry S. Truman Library and Museum, http://www.trumanlibrary.org/.

Jimmy Carter Library and Museum http://www.jimmycarterlibrary.gov/.

John F. Kennedy Presidential Library and Museum, http://www.jfklibrary. org/.

LBJ Presidential Library, http://www.lbjlibrary.org/.

Nixon Presidential Library and Museum http://www.nixonlibrary.gov/.

Ronald Reagan Presidential Foundation and Library, http://www. reaganfoundation.org/.

William J. Clinton Presidential Library and Museum, http://www. clintonlibrary.gov/.

SEE ALSO:

The American Presidency Project, http://www.presidency.ucsb.edu/ws/.

BOOKS

Aldrich, Gary. *Unlimited Access*: *An FBI Agent inside the Clinton White House*. Washington, D.C.: Regnery, 1996.

Ambrose, Stephen. *Eisenhower: The President*. New York: Simon & Schuster, 1984.

Andrew, Christopher. *For the President's Eyes Only: Secret Intelligence* in *the American Presidency from Washington to Bush*. New York: HarperCollins, 1995.

Ayton, Mel. *The JFK Assassination: Dispelling the Myths*. West Sussex, England: Woodfield, 2002.

———. *Questions of Controversy: The Kennedy Brothers*. Sunderland, UK: University of Sunderland Press/BEP, 2001.

Baughman, U. E. *Secret Service Chief*. New York: Harper and Brothers, 1961.

Bell, J. Bowyer. *Assassin: Theory and Practice of Political Violence*. Piscataway, NJ: Transaction, 2005.

Bishop, Jim. *The Day Kennedy Was Shot: An Hour-By-Hour Account of What Really Happened on November 22nd, 1963*. New York: Gramercy Books, 1968.

Blaine, Gerald. *The Kennedy Detail*. New York: Gallery Books, 2010.

Blee, Kathleen M. *No Middle Ground: Women and Radical Protest*. New York: New York University Press, 1998.

Bogart, Leo. *Commercial Culture: The Media System and the Public Interest*. St. Louis: Transaction, 1995.

Boon, J., and L. Sheridan, eds. *Stalking and Psychosexual Obsession*. Hoboken: John Wiley and Sons, 2002.

Bowen, Walter S., and Harry Edward Neal. *The United States Secret Service*. Toronto: Popular Library, 1961.

Bugliosi, Vincent. *Reclaiming History: The Assassination of President John F. Kennedy*. New York: W. W. Norton, 2007.

Carter, Jimmy. *White House Diary*. New York: Picador, 2011.

Clarke, James W. *American Assassins: The Darker Side of Politics*. Princeton: Princeton University Press, 1982.

———. *Defining Danger: American Assassins and the New Domestic Terrorists*. Piscataway, NJ: Transaction, 2007.

———. *On Being Mad or Merely Angry: John W. Hinckley Jr. and Other Dangerous People*. Princeton: Princeton University Press, 1990.

Coleman, Loren. *The Copycat Effect: How the Media and Popular Culture Trigger the Mayhem in Tomorrow's Headlines*. New York: Paraview Pocket Books, 2004.

Crotty, William J. *Assassinations and the Political Order*. New York: Harper and Row, 1971.

DeFrank, Thomas M. *Write It When I'm Gone: Remarkable Off-the-Record Conversations with Gerald R. Ford*. New York: Berkley Books, 2007.

Denton, Sally. *The Plots against the President: FDR, a Nation in Crisis and the Rise of the American Right*. New York: Bloomsbury, 2012.

Donovan, Robert J. *The Assassins of American Presidents*. London: Elek Books, 1956.

Douglas, John, and Mark Olshaker. *The Anatomy of Motive*. London: Pocket Books, 1999.

———. *The Cases That Haunt Us*. London: Pocket Books, 2000.

———. *Mindhunter: Inside the FBI Elite Serial Crime Unit*. London: Arrow Books, 1997.

Doyle, William. *Inside the Oval Office: The White House Tapes from FDR to Clinton*. Montgomery County, OH: London House, 1999.

Eisenhower, Susan. *Mrs. Ike: Memories and Reflections on the Life of Mamie Eisenhower*. New York: Farrar, Straus and Giroux, 1996.

Elliott, Paul. *Assassin! The Bloody History of Political Murder*. London: Cassell Illustrated, 1999.

Ellis, Albert, and John Gullo. *Murder and Assassination*. New York: Lyle Stuart, 1971.

Emmett, Dan. *Within Arm's Length*. N.p.: iUniverse, 2012.

Endicott, Michael A. *Walking with Presidents: Stories from Inside the Perimeter Book*. N.p.: BookSurge, 2009.

Evans, Rowland, and Robert Novak. *Lyndon B. Johnson: The Exercise of Power*. New York: The New American Library, 1966.

Gibbs, Nancy, and Michael Duffy. *The Presidents Club: Inside the World's Most Exclusive Fraternity*. New York: Simon & Schuster, 2012.

Goldberg, Robert Alan. *Enemies Within: The Culture of Conspiracy in Modern America*. New Haven, CT: Yale University Press, 2001.

Goode, Stephen. *Assassination!*. London: Franklin Watts, 1979.

Greenberg, David. *Nixon's Shadow: The History of an Image*. New York: W. W. Norton, 2003.

Gulley, Bill. *Breaking Cover*. New York: Simon & Schuster, 1980.

Gurr, Nadine, and Benjamin Cole. *The New Face of Terrorism: Threats from Weapons of Mass Destruction*. New York: I. B. Tauris, 2000.

Hagerty, James. *The Diary Of James Hagerty: Eisenhower in Mid-Course, 1954–1955*. Bloomington, IN: Indiana University Press, 1983.

Hamilton, Nigel. *American Caesars: Lives of the U.S. Presidents, from Franklin D. Roosevelt to George W. Bush*. London: The Bodley Head, 2010.

Hare, Robert D. *Without Conscience: The Disturbing World of the Psychopaths among Us*. New York: The Guilford Press, 1993.

Hayward, Steven F. *The Politically Incorrect Guide to the Presidents: From Wilson to Obama*. Washington, D.C.: Regnery, 2012.

Hazelwood, Roy, and Stephen G. Michaud. *Dark Dreams: A Legendary FBI Profiler Examines Homicide and the Criminal Mind*. New York: St. Martins, 2001.

Healey, Thomas S. *The Two Deaths of George Wallace*. Montgomery, AL: Black Belt Press, 1996.

Hersh, Seymour M. *The Dark Side Of Camelot*. New York: Little, Brown, 1997.

Hewitt, Christopher. *Understanding Terrorism in America: From the Klan to Al Qaeda*. New York: Routledge, 2003.

Holden, Henry. *To Be a Secret Service Agent*. London: Motorbooks International, 2006.

Hurwood, Bernhardt J. *Society and the Assassin: A Background Book on Political Murder*. London: Parents Magazine Press, 1970.

Hyams, Edward. *Killing No Murder: A Study of Assassination as a Political Means*. London: GB Nelson, 1969.

Jeffrey-Jones, Rhodri. *The FBI: A History*. New Haven, CT: Yale University Press, 2007.

Joynt, Robert J., and James F. O'Toole. *Presidential Disability: Papers and Discussions on Inability and Disability among U.S. Presidents*. Rochester: University of Rochester Press, 2001.

June, Dale L. *Introduction to Executive Protection*. Boca Raton, FL: CRC Press, 1998.

Kaiser, Robert Blair. *RFK Must Die*. New York: E. P. Dutton, 1970.

Kessler, Ronald. *In the President's Secret Service: Behind the Scenes with Agents in the Line of Fire and the Presidents They Protect*. New York: Crown, 2009.

———. *Inside the White House*. London: Pocket Books, 1995.

———. *The Secrets of the FBI*. New York: Crown, 2011.

Kittrie, Nicholas N. *Rebels with a Cause: The Minds and Morality of Political Offenders*. Boulder, CO: Westview Press, 2000.

Klein, Ed. *The Amateur*. Washington, D.C.: Regnery, 2011.

Krassner, Paul. *One Hand Jerking: Reports from an Investigative Satirist.* New York: Seven Stories Press, 2005.

Lance, Peter. *1,000 Years for Revenge: International Terrorism and the FBI.* New York: Regan Books, 2003.

Latell, Brian. *Castro's Secrets: The CIA and Cuba's Intelligence Machine.* Hampshire, UK: Palgrave Macmillan, 2012.

Manchester, William. *The Death of a President.* New York: Harper and Row, 1967.

Marrs, Jim. *Crossfire.* New York: Carroll & Graf, 1993.

Matusky, Gregory and John P. Hayes. *The U.S. Secret Service.* New York: Chelsea House Publishers, 1988.

McCarthy, Dennis V. N. *Protecting the President.* New York: Dell, 1985.

McKinley, James. *Assassination in America.* New York: Harper and Row, 1977.

McMillan, Priscilla Johnson. *Marina and Lee.* New York: Collins, 1978.

Melanson, Philip H. *The Secret Service: The Hidden History of an Enigmatic Agency.* New York: Basic Books, 2005.

Meloy, J. Reid, Lorraine Sheridan, and Jens Hoffman. *Stalking, Threatening, and Attacking Public Figures: A Psychological and Behavioral Analysis.* New York: Oxford University Press, 2008.

Millard, Candice. *Destiny of the Republic: A Tale of Madness, Medicine and the Murder of a President.* New York: Anchor, 2012.

Miller, Merle. *Ike the Soldier: As They Knew Him.* New York: Random House Value, 1989.

National Geographic Society. *Inside the U.S. Secret Service.* DVD. 2004.

Newton, Jim. *Eisenhower: The White House Years.* New York: Doubleday, 2011.

Oliver, Willard M., and Nancy E. Marion. *Killing the President: Assassinations, Attempts, and Rumored Attempts on U.S. Commanders-in-Chief.* Westport, CT: Praeger, 2010.

O'Toole, James F. *Presidential Disability.* Rochester: University of Rochester Press, 2001.

Parrish, Michael. *For the People: Inside the Los Angeles County District Attorney's Office, 1850–2000.* Los Angeles: Angel City Press, 2001.

Patterson, Bradley Hawkes. *The White House Staff: Inside the West Wing and Beyond.* Washington, D.C.: Brookings Institution, 2001.

Pederson, William D., and James David Barber. *The "Barbarian" Presidency.* New York: Peter Lang, 1989.

Petro, Joseph. *Standing Next to History: An Agent's Life inside the Secret Service.* New York: Thomas Dunne Books, 2005.

Pfiffner, James F. *The Modern Presidency.* Stamford, CT: Wadsworth, 2008.

Picchi, Blaise. *The Five Weeks of Giuseppe Zangara.* Chicago: Academy Chicago, 1998.

Pipes, Daniel. *Conspiracy: How the Paranoid Style Flourishes and Where It Comes From.* New York: The Free Press, 1997.

Piszkiewicz, Dennis. *Terrorism's War with America: A History.* Westport, CT: Greenwood Publishing Group, 2008.

Reich, Walter, ed. Foreword by Walter Laqueur. *Origins of Terrorism.* Washington, D.C.: Woodrow Wilson Center Press, 1998.

Reilly, Michael F. *Reilly of the White House.* New York: Simon & Schuster, 1947.

Ressler, Robert K., and Tom Shactman. *Whoever Fights Monsters.* London: Pocket Books, 1993.

Rhodes, Richard. *Why They Kill: The Discoveries of a Maverick Criminologist.* New York: Vintage Books, 1999.

Rothman, Hal. *LBJ's Texas White House*. College Station: Texas A&M University Press, 2001.

Rush, George. *Confessions of an Ex-Secret Service Agent: The Marty Venker Story*. New York: Donald I. Fine, 1988.

Russo, Gus. *The Outfit: The Role of Chicago's Underworld in the Shaping of Modern America*. New York: Bloomsbury, 2001.

Sabato, Larry J. *The Kennedy Half Century: The Presidency, Assassination, and Lasting Legacy of John F. Kennedy*. New York: Bloomsbury, 2013.

Sawler, Harvey. *Saving Mrs. Kennedy: The Search for an American Hero*. Ontario: General Store, 2005.

Schafer, Stephen. *The Political Criminal: The Problem of Morality and Crime*. New York: The Free Press, 1974.

Schroeder, Alan. *Celebrity-in-Chief: How Show Business Took Over the White House*. Boulder, CO: Westview Press, 2004.

Seidman, David. *Secret Service Agents: Life Protecting the President*. New York: Rosen, 2002.

Seigenthaler, John. *A Search for Justice*. Nashville: Aurora, 1971.

Shogan, Robert. *The Double-Edged Sword: How Character Makes and Ruins Presidents, from Washington to Clinton*. Boulder, CO: Westview Press, 2000.

Simmons, Dawn Langley, and Anne Pinchot. *Jacqueline Kennedy: A Biography*. New York: Signet Books, 1966.

Smith, Merriman. *Merriman Smith's Book of Presidents: A White House Memoir*. New York: W. W. Norton, 1972.

Spieler, Geri. *Taking Aim at the President: The Remarkable Story of the Woman Who Shot at Gerald Ford*. New York: Palgrave Macmillan, 2009.

Starling, Edmund W. *Starling of the White House*. New York: Simon & Schuster, 1946.

Steers, Edward. *Blood on the Moon: The Assassination of Abraham Lincoln*. Lexington, KY: The University Press of Kentucky, 2005.

Stockton, Bayard. *Flawed Patriot: The Rise and Fall of CIA Legend Bill Harvey*. Washington, D.C.: Potomac Books, 2006.

Summers, Anthony. *Conspiracy*. New York: Sphere, 1998.

Thomas, Evan. *Ike's Bluff: President Eisenhower's Secret Battle to Save the World*. New York: Little, Brown, 2012.

Time-Life Books. *True Crime: Assassination*. Fairfax, VA : Time-Life Books, 1994.

Truman, Margaret. *Harry S. Truman*. New York: William Morrow, 1973.

Updegrove, Mark K. *Second Acts: Presidential Lives and Legacies after the White House*. Guilford, CT: The Lyons Press, 2006.

Vorpagel, Russell. *Profiles in Murder: An FBI Legend Dissects Killers and Their Crimes*. New York: Dell, 1998.

Vowell, Sarah. *Assassination Vacation*. New York: Simon & Schuster, 2005.

Whitcomb, John and Claire. *Real Life at the White House: 200 Years of Daily Life at America's Most Famous Residence*. New York: Routledge, 2002.

Whiting, Charles. *Target Eisenhower: Military and Political Assassination in World War II*. Gloucestershire, UK: Spellmount, 2005.

Wilber, Del Quentin. *Rawhide Down*. New York: Henry Holt, 2011.

Wilson, Frank J., and Beth Day. *Special Agent: 25 Years with the American Secret Service*. London: Frederick Muller Limited, 1966.

Youngblood, Rufus W. *20 Years in the Secret Service: My Life with Five Presidents*. New York: Simon & Schuster, 1973.

JOURNALS

Abrams, Herbert L. "The Contemporary Presidency: Presidential Safety, Prosecutorial Zeal and Judicial Blunders: The Protective Function Privilege." *Presidential Studies Quarterly* (June 2001). http://www.jstor.org/discover/10.2307/27552191?uid=3738032&uid=2129&uid=2&uid=70&uid=4&sid=21101522830827.

Blumenthal, Fred. "Luci, Pat and the Secret Service." *Parade* (April 10, 1966). http://news.google.com/newspapers?nid=888&dat=19660410&id=ffhRAAAAIBAJ&sjid=_XMDAAAAIBAJ&pg=3481,6630539.

Borum, Randy, et al. "Threat Assessment : Defining an Approach for Evaluating Risk of Targeted Violence." *Behavioral Sciences and the Law* 17, no. 3 (1999): 323–37.

Cain, S. "The Psychodynamics of the Presidential Assassin and an Examination of the Theme/Graphic Variables of His Threatening Correspondence." *Forensic Sciences International* 19, no. 1 (January–February 1982). http://www.ncbi.nlm.nih.gov/pubmed/7054060.

Fein, Robert, and Bryan Vossekuil. "Assassination in the United States: An Operational Study of Recent Assassins, Attackers, and Near Lethal Approachers." *Journal of Forensic Sciences* 44, no. 2 (March 1999): 321. www.secretservice.govwww.secretservice.gov/ntac/ntac_jfs.pdf.

"The Fifties and Ike: A Conversation with Stephen Ambrose." *Humanities* 18, no. 5 (September/October 1997). http://www.neh.gov/news/humanities/1997-09/ambrose.html.

Frey, Bruno S. "Overprotected Politicians." *Center for Research in Economics, Management and the Arts*. Working paper no. 2007-7. www.crema-research.ch/papers/2007-07.pdf.

Hoffman, Bruce, and Peter Chalk, with Timothy E. Liston and David W. Brannan. "Security in the Nation's Capital and the Closure of Pennsylvania Avenue: An Assessment." *RAND Public Safety and Justice* (2002), http://www.rand.org/pubs/monograph_reports/MR1293-1.html.

Hoffman, Jay L. "Psychotic Visitors to Government Offices in the National Capital." *American Journal of Psychiatry* 99 (1943): 571–75. http://ajp.psychiatryonline.org/article.aspx?articleid=142391.

Institute of Medicine (U.S.) Division of Mental Health and Behavioral Medicine. "Behavioral Science and the Secret Service." *National Academy Press* (September 1981). http://books.google.co.uk/books/about/Behavioral_science_and_the_Secret_Servic.html?id=fCYrAAAAYAAJ&redir_esc=y.

Jones, Benjamin F., and Benjamin A. Olken. "Hit or Miss? The Effect of Assassinations on Institutions and War." *National Bureau of Economic Research*. Working paper no. 13102 (May 2007). http://www.nber.org/papers/w13102.

Mayman, Daniel M., and Melvin Guyer. "Not Guilty by Reason of Insanity Defense." *Journal of the American Academy of Psychiatry and Law* 36, no. 1, http://www.jaapl.org/content/36/1/143.full.

Megargee, Edwin I. "A Psychometric Study of Incarcerated Presidential Threateners." Florida State University's *Criminal Justice and Behavior* 13, no. 3 (September 1986): 243–60. http://cjb.sagepub.com/content/13/3/243.abstract.

Meloy, J. Reid. "The Psychology of Stalking." *Scribd*. http://www.scribd.com/doc/76962424/The-Psychology-of-Stalking.

Meloy, J. Reid, and Cynthia Boyd. "Female Stalkers and Their Victims." *American Journal of Psychiatry and the Law* 31, no. 2 (2003). www.jaapl.org/content/31/2/211.full.pdf.

———. "Stalking and Violence." Excerpt within Boon, J., and L. Sheridan, eds. *Stalking and Psychosexual Obsession: Psychological Perspectives for Prevention, Polcing, and Treatment*. West Sussex, UK: John Wiley & Sons, 2002. www.popcenter.org/problems/stalking/PDFs/Meloy_2002.pdf.

———. "Threatening Communications and Behavior: Perspectives on the Pursuit of Public Figures—Approaching and Attacking Public Figures: A Contemporary Analysis of Communications and Behavior." *National*

Academies Press (2011). http://www.nap.edu/openbook.php?record_id=13091&page=75.

Munsey, Christopher. "Secrets behind the Service." *Monitor on Psychology* 39, no. 8 (September 2008): 26. http://www.apa.org/monitor/2008/09/secrets.aspx.

Phillips, Robert T. M. "Assessing Presidential Stalkers and Assassins." *Journal of the American Academy of Psychiatry and the Law* 34 (2006): 154–64. http://www.ncbi.nlm.nih.gov/pubmed/16844794.

"Political Assassination: Regicide's Risk—Killing a Leader Doesn't Always Work." *Economist*, May 17, 2007. http://www.economist.com/node/9205876.

Pontius, Anneliese A. "Threats to Assassinate the King-President while Propitiating Mother." *Journal of Analytic Psychology* 19, no. 1 (1974): 38–53.

Rothstein, David A. "Presidential Assassination Syndrome." *Archives of General Psychiatry* 11, no. 3 (September 1964). http://archpsyc.jamanetwork.com/article.aspx?articleid=488618.

Sebastian, Joseph A., and James L. Foy. "Psychotic Visitors to the White House." *American Journal of Psychiatry* 122 (December 1, 1965): 679–86. http://ajp.psychiatryonline.org/article.aspx?articleid=150147.

"The Sharpshooter Who Guards the President." *Popular Science* (July 1956).

Shore, David, et al. "White House Cases: Psychiatric Patients and the Secret Service." *American Journal of Psychiatry* 142, no. 3 (March 1985). www.pn.psychiatryonline.org/data/Journals/AJP/3381/308.pdf.

Sparr, Landy F. "Personality Disorders and Criminal Law: An International Perspective." *American Journal of Psychiatry and the Law* 37, no. 2 (2009): 168–81. http://www.jaapl.org/content/37/2/168.abstract.

Spitzberga, Brian H. and William R. Cupach. "What Mad Pursuit? Obsessive Relational Intrusion and Stalking Related Phenomena." *Aggression and Violent Behavior*, no. 8 (2003): 345–75. www.josotl.indiana.edu/article/download/1894/1879.

Winchester, James H. "They Guard the President." *Boys' Life* (December 1962).

Zitek, Brook. "Assessment and Management of Patients Who Make Threats against the President in the Psychiatric Emergency Service." *Psychiatric Services* 56, no. 8 (August 2005): 1017. http://ps. psychiatryonline.org/article.aspx?articleID=90391.

INTERNET WEBSITES

Alan Colmes Presents Liberaland: http://www.alan.com.

Albion Monitor: www.albionmonitor.com.

Alternet.org: http://www.alternet.org.

American Conservative: http://www.theamericanconservative.com.

American Thinker: http://www.americanthinker.com.

Anti-Defamation League: http://www.adl.org.

Associated Press: www.ap.com.

BBC News: http://www.bbc.co.uk.

CBS News: http://www.cbsnews.com.

CIA: www.cia.gov/library/center-for-the-study-of- intelligence-article02.

CNN: www.cnn.com.

CYB3RCRIM3: http://cyb3rcrim3.blogspot.co.uk.

Daily Beast: http://www.thedailybeast.com.

Daily Mail: http://www.dailymail.co.uk.

Dance with Shadows.com: www.dancewithshadows.com/politics.

Debbie Schlussel.com: http://www.debbieschlussel.com.

Discovery Channel, Discovery News http://news.discovery.com/history/ jfk-assassination-secret-service.html.

Fox News: http://www.foxnews.com.

Globe and Mail online: http://www.theglobeandmail.com.

Gretawire: www.gretawire.foxnewsinsider.com.

History News Network: http://hnn.us.

Huffington Post: www.hufingtonpost.com.

Justia—U.S. Law: http://law.justia.com/.

Kennedy Assassination by John McAdams: http://mcadams.posc.mu.edu/home.htm.

Kennedy Detail: http://www.kennedydetail.com/about.asp.

Mediaite.com: http://www.mediaite.com.

Militia Watchdog: http://www.adl.org.

National Public Radio: www.npr.org.

NJ.com: http://www.nj.com/jjournal-news.

New Yorker: www.newyorker.com.

NowPublic.com: http://www.nowpublic.com.

ObamaCSI.com https://sites.google.com.

OutlookIndia.com: http://news.outlookindia.com.

People: http://www.people.com.

People's Daily, China: http://english.peopledaily.com.

Politickin' with John Brown: http://www.complex.com/blogs/2009/12/03/politickin-with-john-brown-a-history-of-secret-service-fails/.

Popular Mechanics: http://www.popularmechanics.com.

Reuters: http://www.reuters.com.

RIANOVOST: http://en.rian.ru/analysis/20071016/84122320.html 16/10/2007.

Seacoastonline.com: http://www.seacoastonline.com.

Smoking Gun: http://www.thesmokinggun.com/.

SouthBendTribune.com: http://articles.southbendtribune.com.

Statesman.com: http://www.statesman.com.

Suite 101: http://suite101.com/article/american-assassins—demographics-from-the-20th-century-onward-a233022.

Times Union: www.TimesUnion.com.

TPM Livewire: http://tpmlivewire.talkingpointsmemo.com.

Trey Dunn: www.trinity.edu/jdunn/whitehouseattacks.htm.

TucsonCitizen.com: http://tucsoncitizen.com.

Virtual School: http://www.virtualschool.edu.

WGNO/ABC: http://www.abc26.com.

WSPA.com: http://www2.wspa.com.

INDEX